'An elegantly written and enthralling account of an action-packed but tragically short life that has all the ingredients of a modern-day picaresque. This is a brilliantly researched act of biographical reclamation; with this masterful biography, John Lodwick's life has been perfectly commemorated.'

COLM TÓIBÍN

ALSO BY GEOFFREY ELLIOTT

I Spy
'One of the five best spy stories' *The Wall Street Journal*

From Siberia, with Love
'A magnificent, subtle evocation of Russia, romance
and revolution' Simon Sebag Montefiore

Secret Classrooms (with Harry Shukman)
'A highly entertaining read' *The Spectator*

Kitty Harris: The Spy With Seventeen Names (with Igor Damaskin)
'The book's strength is as a history of Soviet operations and a refreshing antidote to the fleshpot vamps of espionage fiction' *The Times*

The Mystery of Overend and Gurney
'This entertaining account of the greatest upset of the Victorian city' *The Spectator*

The Shooting Star
'This sparkling biography… is required reading both for
Resistance and social historians' *The Spectator*

Gentleman Spymaster
'Provides unusual insight into both double agent operations and the life
of one of the best at the task' *Studies in Intelligence*, Washington DC

Dangerous Games: The Tangled Lives of Two Women at War
'A wonderful book that has dexterity and sensitivity in the way it sews together the
lives of two exceptional people who find themselves inhabiting extraordinary times'
Robert Service, Emeritus Professor of Russian History, Oxford University

A
Forgotten
Man

The Life and Death of
John Lodwick

GEOFFREY ELLIOTT

I.B. TAURIS
LONDON · NEW YORK

Published in 2017 by
I.B.Tauris & Co. Ltd
London • New York
www.ibtauris.com

ISBN: 978 1 78453 840 8
eISBN: 978 1 78672 199 0
ePDF: 978 1 78673 199 9

A full CIP record for this book is available from the British Library
A full CIP record is available from the Library of Congress

Library of Congress Catalog Card Number: available

Typeset by Tetragon, London
Printed and bound in Great Britain by T.J. International, Padstow, Cornwall

MIX
Paper from
responsible sources
FSC
www.fsc.org   FSC® C013056

To the extended Lodwick family in gratitude

CONTENTS

LIST OF ILLUSTRATIONS — ix

ACKNOWLEDGEMENTS — xi

INTRODUCTION — 1

1   *The Blood of India* — 13

2   *Captain Courageous* — 23

3   *Schooldays with Grandpapa* — 31

4   *Carry on, Sailor* — 43

5   *Dublin's Fair City* — 51

6   *Faces in the Rain* — 59

7   *'A Marriage has been Arranged'* — 63

8   *The Leg and the Legionnaire* — 71

9   *One Step Forward, Two Steps Back* — 83

10   *Orange Blossoms* — 91

11   *Beating the Bookmaker* — 99

12   *Highlands and Islands* — 117

13   *Killing Them Loudly* — 125

14   *Jailhouse Blues* — 131

15   *Guerrilla War* — 137

16   *South of the Border* — 147

17   *Riviera Glimpses* — 155

18   *On the Road Again* — 175

19   *Reader and Writer* — 181

20	*Publish and Be Damned*	193
21	*Scorecard*	199
22	*Death in the Morning*	209
23	*After the Ball*	219
	NOTES	225
	BIBLIOGRAPHY	235
	JOHN LODWICK'S BOOKS	241
	INDEX	243

LIST OF ILLUSTRATIONS

1. The young John Lodwick. (Family collection)
2. John Lodwick relaxed. (Family collection)
3. The Lodwick Memorial in India. (Getty)
4. The tools of Captain Lodwick's trade. (Public domain)
5. War as Captain Lodwick would have seen it. (Public domain)
6. The SS *Persia*. (Imperial War Museum)
7. German U-boat, the same type which sank SS *Persia*. (Wikipedia)
8. 'The Cradle of Neptune' – Royal Naval College Dartmouth. (Public domain)
9. Hermann Görtz – German agent in Éire. (Public domain)
10. Iseult Gonne, the face of poetry. (Public domain)
11. W.B. Yeats – Irish poet of genius. (Wikipedia)
12. Francis Stuart, maverick genius. (Online)
13. Eoin O'Duffy, Irish Blueshirt Leader, with a few right-minded friends. (Getty)
14. Jammet's restaurant, Dublin, where the Irish literary elite met to compete. (Public domain)
15. Eamon de Valera. (Wikipedia)
16. Getting ready for the London Surrealist Exhibition. (Getty)
17. Sheila as the 'Phantom of Love' in Trafalgar Square. (Public domain)
18. Sheila by Man Ray. (Public domain)
19. Sheila's bilingual memorial. (Public domain)
20. Selwyn Jepson, SOE talent spotter, author and friend of Lodwick. (Public domain)

21. Evelyn Waugh in martial mode. (Public domain)

22. George Jellicoe. (Wikipedia)

23. First Special Boat Service, 'K' Patrol. (Imperial War Museum HU 71414.)

24. Chetniks with Wehrmacht prisoners. (Public domain)

25. Walter Starkie, genial polymath. (Public domain)

26. A young W.S. Merwin. (Public domain)

27. Georges Pelorson, later Belmont. (Author's collection)

28. W. Somerset Maugham, an admirer of Lodwick's work. (Public domain)

29. A hidden aspect of Franco's Spain – budding bullfighters practise in the backstreets. (Public domain)

30. Old and new in Franco's Spain. (Public domain)

31. Josep Janés with Spanish composer Federico Mompou. (Public domain)

32. Peter de Polnay and Dodo. (Public domain)

33. Rebecca West, author and sharp editorial reader for Heinemann. (Public domain)

34. Gregory Ratoff, the archetypical image of a movie director. (Getty)

35. Building the tower, an event Lodwick never got to see. (Public domain)

36. *Calsotadas*, a coincidental link back to Grandpapa's asparagus trench. (Public domain)

ACKNOWLEDGEMENTS

Though the author has to fall on his sword for any errors and omissions, it is important to recognise that debts – without responsibility – are owed to many. My especial debt is to Malachy Lodwick, who went to great lengths – literally – to provide so many of the personal documents which are at the heart of this study, and many private memories; his brother Rodrigo, who has safeguarded many of John Lodwick's papers for years; and to Miqui, Nieves and Vanessa. The Lodwicks are an extended family, each with different memories of John Lodwick and of different mothers at different times and in different places. Though I have tried, I doubt I have fully reflected every aspect of the man they knew, or thought they knew, but hope the composite picture which emerges is of a man of talent and character.

To Judith Ashton, David Bell at the Imperial War Museum, the British Library Sound Archives, Lieutenant Colonel Antoine Boulant and his archival colleagues at the Ministère de la Défense, Vincennes, David Brighty CVO for help and guidance in so many ways, not least in sharing with me his father's letter from John Lodwick, Zan Cammack and Betsy Doherty at Southern Illinois University, Zed Cama, Professor Alice Caplan, Kevin Kiely, who probably knows more about Stuart than Stuart himself did, the unrelated Declan Kiely at the Morgan Library and Museum, who unearthed the Hemingway quote, Christine Leighton of Cheltenham College, the London Library for access to miles of shelves and its electronic newspaper archives, the online archives of the *Irish Times*, Bob O'Hara, without whose encyclopedic knowledge of the National Archives so many writers would be lost, and his colleague Phil Tomaselli, Didy Grahame CBE, James D. Jenkins at Valancourt Books, the Headmaster and staff of Bickley Park School, Maria Jesus Gonzalez Hernandez, Professor Malcolm Gaskill at the University of East Anglia, steeped in the history of witchcraft, John Lewis at the *Bookseller* who explained the mystique of publishers' sales charts, Professor Paul Preston, Richard Davies and the late Chris Sheppard of the Brotherton Library, Leeds, Andrew Lycett, Richard

Rooze of 'El British', the Service Historique de la Défense, Pau, Curtis Small, Jr of the University of Delaware Special Collections Department, Rachel Bairstow of the British Dental Association, Señor Don Rafael Borràs Betriu, Kirstin Foster at Curtis Brown, Nicky Dunne and Venetia Vyvyan at Heywood Hill, the *nec plus ultra* of bookselling, and especially Joanna Godfrey at I.B.Tauris, who piloted this from a jumbled manuscript and authorial introspection to a 'real' book.

To list all the files in the National Archives from which this book has benefited, and for access to which I am deeply appreciative, makes for unneeded complications. For instance, many of the MI5 comments are on Lodwick's Personal File HS 9/933/7, which has references to Sheila Legge, Heimann and Hinton, while the SBS file is in the WO series, a security review of the contentious Berlin broadcasts is in the KV2 series 230, and a post-mortem on the security problems in World War II Éire is in the POLF53 series. In addition there are the files of Heimann and Hinton themselves. But some of Lodwick's personal papers have important additional World War II 'finds'; there are brief mentions of Sheila in the consular records and weaving all this together with cross-references would try any reader's patience. The Imperial War Museum in London has a significant collection of sound recordings, photographs and other material relating to the Special Boat Service and several films have dramatised some of its more noteworthy sorties. Other than those cited below, a useful list of books on its adventures in the Aegean can be accessed via www.worldnavalships.com/forums. Likewise, other than the main reference works cited here, books, films and research materials on SOE, including the Imperial War Museum collections, are too numerous to cite here. (It is not really an acknowledgement but from time to time when checking names I have looked at the Gestapo 'Black Book' or *Sonderfahndungsliste GB*, the list of the many prominent politicians, exiles, intellectuals, business heads, leading lights in the Jewish community, alleged members of the intelligence services, as well as book and newspaper publishers and trades unions whom the Nazis planned to round up or raid had they invaded Britain. Apart from paranoia about Freemasonry, including a claim that the Boy Scout Movement was 'closely connected' with it, it makes chilling reading. Among the hundreds of greater and lesser lights singled out, along with Sigmund Freud and Paul Robeson, 'the Negro singer', are C.P. Snow and Rebecca West, while both Methuen and Heinemann are listed as publishers of at least one anti-Nazi book and de Gaulle is succinctly sandwiched between J.L.

Garvin, the Editor of the *Observer*, and a Polish Bishop as 'former French General, London…' Little did they know.

The last shall be first – without Fay Elliott's patience and encouragement in putting up with the muddles, distractions and tests of her patience involved in this exercise the book would never have seen the light of day.

INTRODUCTION

> No todos podemos ser frailes, y muchos son los caminos por donde
> lleva Dios a los suyos al cielo; religión *es* la caballería.
>
> We can't all be friars, and God has many roads along which to lead
> his own to Heaven. Knight-errantry *is* religion.
>
> MIGUEL CERVANTES, *DON QUIXOTE*, 1605

Someone asked me, out of the blue, why I thought John Lodwick was 'important'. It's a fair question. Taking the word as most people understand it he probably wasn't. He didn't leave a political or corporate legacy – no Lodwick triumphs in the House of Commons or on the field of battle, no multi-tentacled Lodwick Holdings PLC, no artfully accumulated fortune, carefully doled out to fashionable charities in an unspoken bargain for social prominence or even titles. As we shall see, compared to some of his contemporaries, much of his literary legacy has faded. He was essentially a self-made man, not one of 'the great and the good' or the literary glitterati. He knew a lot of interesting people, especially in Ireland and France, but he wasn't always easy to get on with – far from it, as those who crossed him and even his long-suffering publishers knew to their cost.

So why should you want to know more about him? The answer is simple: because he was such an interesting character, cut from a very different cloth. His story includes a family background in the Indian Raj, a father who died in a World War I U-boat attack before Lodwick was born, a difficult early life with his genial ogre of a grandfather, and several marriages. Some of these were far from simple, and one was brushed under the carpet, while another brought him together for some happy years with a 'Surrealist Phantom'. He had a brilliant record in World War II, but one that in its way was just as complicated, fighting first with the Foreign Legion, then at the 'rough trade' end of Britain's clandestine forces, shuffling through several jails in manacles with his head shaved to the bone.

More importantly for his reputation, he was also a writer, who lived much of his life in exile, and whose many novels, often incorporating scantily veiled allusions to real experiences and real people, were the cobblestones with which his bumpy life journey was paved. But while they are an important part of the story, not least because they provided his often precarious livelihood, they are just one of his life's kaleidoscopic images.

He died on 16 March 1959, in the morphine-muted aftermath of an early-morning car crash on a Spanish hillside, a couple of weeks after his 43rd birthday. Far too young a death for anyone, let alone an author with much written but so much still left to do. Before the crash he had finished only the first 80 pages of what was clearly intended as a definitive autobiography. If – if only – he had reached even the biblical standard of threescore years and ten, how much more would he have had to tell us? This book aims to fill in the gaps and provide the answers; or some of them, at least.

Why exhume him after all these years from the cluttered literary graveyard to which commentators seem to have consigned him? The answer again is that our focus is Lodwick the man, rather than Lodwick the writer: Lodwick the lover, Lodwick the friend, Lodwick the hero, Lodwick the parent.

Like so much else nowadays, this project was sparked by the internet. A trawl for e-books to read on the enchanting train ride from Vienna to Zurich brought up by chance the name of an author I vaguely remembered: a reissue of one of Lodwick's grimmer tales, *Brother Death*, seen by one reviewer when it first appeared as 'tough and hideous all through – but in its way admirable'. Downloading it to read as the mountains and meadows rolled by sparked a memory of my fascination with *The Asparagus Trench*, too brief by far to be called his autobiography; it was just a preliminary sketch which his publishers no doubt picked up as an interesting trifle and memento after he died. I remembered I had read it many years ago, in an age when libraries were an integral part of every neighbourhood, and still had shelves of books with real pages between hard covers. What had become of him? He hadn't been elected to the literary pantheon to which Waugh, Greene and other contemporaries had been elevated, but he had been an entertaining novelist, and memory tugged at a patch of World War II history in which he had figured bravely. What was he all about?

Finding out wasn't easy. Piecing together Lodwick's story was a challenge rather like a fiendish jigsaw puzzle with no picture on the box. Although that recent reprint of *Brother Death* which started the hunt provided a new 'blip', like the sighting of debris from a missing aircraft, he had long since all but vanished from the literary radar screen despite a prodigious output – including 18 novels, an account of his World War II experiences, and the co-authored and controversial biography of an international oil tycoon. In 1990 the novelist and critic Anthony Burgess[1] mused in a history of Lodwick's principal publishers, 'Who now remembers John Lodwick? None of the Heinemann editors I have lately spoken to have even heard of him.' Burgess was one who had remembered; his judgement on Lodwick's work will be revealed later on, as will a fuller account of what that Heinemann history tells us about the company's relationship with Lodwick.[2]

In 1993, D.J. Taylor, himself an admired author and a thoughtful commentator who has watched over the English literary scene for many years, thought that Lodwick's 'doomy romanticism sat queerly alongside the comic realism of [Keith] Waterhouse and [Kingsley] Amis and his reputation did not survive the 1960s'. And when Taylor resurveyed the landscape of letters in 2016, Lodwick went unmentioned.[3]

Commentators and reviewers may have been harsh. They may have been right. And Lodwick is hardly the only writer whose star sparkled for a few years only to be blanked out by brighter, more fashionable astronomical discoveries. But what if he had lived…?

In any case, as this book seeks to underline, Lodwick as a man, a soldier, a friend of the unfriended, and as a parent, adds up to much more than his books, and his story should not be allowed to shrivel untold.

The vital dimension was provided by the memories and different perspectives – different in time and in place – of several members of his several families, backed by curling, stained and fading letters which have lain bundled away for many years. Cheltenham School and Dartmouth Naval College reports, newspaper files in London, Dublin and Spain, and especially an Irish marriage register were important pieces in the puzzle. So too were the once 'Top Secret' archives of Britain's World War II Special Operations Executive (SOE), Special Boat Service (SBS) and the Security Service, better known as MI5, as well as an unexpected bonus: his slim but intriguing French Foreign Legion dossier.

What emerges from it all is not just another biography of a long-forgotten author – though he was a hard-working master of his art – but rather the complex image of a genuine war hero, simultaneously tough and touchy; a better family man than many more mundane souls, especially in the face of death and domestic turbulence; and a restless exile who was never quite sure whether he belonged in Ireland, England, France, Spain, or even the Imperial India he knew as a child.

Lodwick was a rebel from childhood on. But had he been looking for a portmanteau term to describe himself (an unlikely thought), rather than the familiar 'rebel without a cause', he might have preferred, not least because it was French, the title of Huysmans' novel *À rebours*, usually translated as *Against the Grain*. Whatever teachers, parents, commanding officers, consular officers, publishers, critics suggested – and quite often his wives too – he reflexively went the other way. Complex, widely read, and even more widely attuned to the world of danger and human frailty, his personality brings to mind an improbable parallel from a much earlier era, the patrician British politician Arthur Balfour,[4] who once remarked that he rather liked praise, and did not particularly mind abuse, 'but I have moments of uneasiness when being explained'. We might debate whether Lodwick fully shared Balfour's professed disregard of abuse and criticism, since his reactions, sometimes gleeful and sometimes irritable, showed that he had a thin skin, but the quote captures much of the essence of the man. Those carefully hoarded letters and papers were surely kept against the day he would mine them to write his own full autobiography and explain himself, to himself and to others. It is one of the saddest elements of this story that the day never came.

Lodwick himself wrote in 1958 that 'usually I do not like to see letters of mine in the hands of their recipients, even if they have not been imprudent or aggressive in tone', as they often were. 'The combination of my somewhat Neolithic script with an always bizarre choice of writing paper provides a result which like certain wines neither travels nor ages with elegance.' As he told readers of that autobiographical fragment: 'A certain tendency towards belligerence, a lack of tact in private relations, has always been noticeable in the family and remains so to this day', an admission borne out by some of his more pugnacious letters.

The bulk of the correspondence we have been privileged to see, and the many first-hand background comments, have been provided by members of his family. To insert 'Private Papers' after every reference to these sources would pepper the text with even more distracting brackets and footnotes. Likewise a reference for every single citation from an SOE or MI5 file would interrupt rather than enlighten. The same holds true for many of the characters who crossed Lodwick's winding path. Where they might be thought relatively obscure, a few brief details have been added but for figures of prominence – Arthur Balfour, for example – there seems little need for such extra distractions. Because this is a book much more about the man than about his novels, we will not attempt potted summaries of each, though we shall use a cross-section of critics' comments to see how the literary world judged them. In any case, since fragments of his real life and domestic upsets, some of them painfully jagged, can be glimpsed not too deeply buried in his novels, notably *Brother Death* and *Somewhere a Voice is Calling*, trying to disentangle each and every one would serve little purpose. As a young man he also wrote short stories, newspaper articles and several plays. These, though briefly performed, have long since dropped out of sight through a Dublin stage trapdoor. He also had interesting times with a James Bond film script.

One lesson for all who write about the lives of others is the danger of rushing to judgement, in this case not just about Lodwick but about his various marriages and his many friends. As to marriage, a family tree drawn up by his mother Kitty shows three wives, four children and several grandchildren. It is not the full story. Once one knows the clues, some of the family side can be traced as threads in his novels, from correspondence, from memories and other research; but this is Lodwick's life, and the lives of his family are their own domain, ground on which we shall do our best not to trespass. As to his many fascinating friends, two – Francis Stuart and Georges Belmont, born Georges Pelorson – had controversial histories, largely centred around what they did or did not do in World War II. Many academics and commentators have concluded that, despite their considerable talents, the two men deserved the often heavy criticism levelled at their behaviour. Yet reading the letters the pair exchanged with Lodwick – the genuine long-term friendliness, the personal intimacies – adds a more human dimension to men often written off as having wilfully followed the wrong lodestar as they navigated their lives; men whom others more fretful of their reputation than Lodwick might have sought to avoid. It does not refute the allegations, but they go unmentioned; not so much out of tact, perhaps, since tact was not a strong suit with any of them, more likely because they thought them irrelevant.

Others who have something to tell us or who peek around the edges of the stage scenery include viscerally suspicious SOE and MI5 officers, the ascetic American poet W.S. Merwin, Somerset Maugham, who was way above Lodwick's league as an author, but who still showed him kindness, and Rebecca West, ambivalent about the man but an admirer of his style: he 'folds a sentence round a fact or a thought as the girl in the shop ties a scarf round your neck and you can't do it at home in the same way, not ever'. By contrast there were the drink-bedevilled Irish playwright Brendan Behan, a war-jaded and possibly spiteful Evelyn Waugh, the stereotypical Hollywood producer Gregory Ratoff, and Lodwick's astute and long-suffering publisher Alexander Frere. The list goes on – he knew the polymath Irishman Walter Starkie, the gallant George Jellicoe ('The Belted Earl'), Georges Kopp, who had been George Orwell's commander in the Spanish Civil War, and who fought alongside Lodwick in the Foreign Legion, and the Catalan poet and publisher Josep Janés. Even the late George Melly, flamboyant blues singer, author and art connoisseur, has a tangential memory to share with us about the 1930s 'Surrealist Phantom' Sheila Legge, a dominant figure in Lodwick's love life.

Capturing mental images of Lodwick (photos are rare) isn't easy either. It is like one of those 35mm slide shows of his time, now replaced by modern technology. Click, and we see him first as a mischievous schoolboy, small and nimble enough to make him a natural pick as a darting scrum half in rugby games, then as a gangling Dartmouth cadet in shorts, a blancoed lanyard round his neck. Click again, through a sequence of shots of the tweedy literary neophyte in Dublin, glass in hand, a troubling secret in his head, scrambling and flattering for a foothold on the fringes of literary life, then the ruthless, bearded Foreign Legionnaire, in action and on the run in the early days of World War II. With another click we see him later in the war as the overconfident 'thug' dropped into the French dark by SOE – perhaps considered inappropriate today, although not wholly inaccurate, 'thug' is a term that crops up several times in SOE 'job descriptions' in its formative years – followed by tough times as a gun-toting Aegean warrior and a German prisoner in some unpleasant jails, and edgy days with Yugoslav resistance fighters. As peace came, the slides would show us a crotchety, financially harassed writer at his desk in Spain, a glass of red wine close at hand, and the father taking his eldest daughter to her first Communion. One last click gives us the final image of a smashed car on a Spanish roadside. The photograph on Plate 2 gives a sense of the grown man, and that is the best core image, though each of his families and many of his friends would have seen a different man, a different husband and a different father.

As an adult he was five feet seven inches tall, thickset. In 1940 a form-filling French Army clerk described his full head of wavy hair as 'blond', no doubt after many months in the Provençal sun and messing about dangerously in boats. It later mellowed back to brown, its growth stimulated by having his head shaved to the skull several times as part of the entry ritual in French, Spanish and German jails, a ritual intended as much to crush the personality as to rid the scalp of lice. His life ended before it could turn grey. He once wrote that though he was not 'genetically comely' he took pride in the cleft chin inherited from his grandmother and 'the long, truculent, sensual nose of the Lodwicks'.

Lodwick's rebel streak, a 'tough guy' personality that was undoubtedly real, was put to savage use in his wartime service and then mixed liberally into the recipes of his novels. Along with his spell in Dublin and his 'Jack the Lad' life in the South of France they are one side of the coin. There too is his latent violence, seen by one acute observer as 'like the fin of a shark' and by one of his wives as 'always there, like Etna or something'. Flip the coin, perhaps a Spanish doubloon in his case, and we find a writer praised by many. Writing long before PVC pipework became commonplace, Lodwick told the readers of his wartime memoirs:

> I write from love, as all novelists must – from disappointed love sometimes, but still love, whose other name is Tolerance [*sic*]. That's why novelists, like plumbers in another profession which is concerned with divination, are so often right, though they cannot, like plumbers, prove their thesis with the knock of iron on lead.

He had fought, and fought bravely, for the French and then the British in World War II. He could be cruel and he could be kind, and, in the face of sad and occasionally turbulent domestic circumstances, was a good father. 'Autodidact' may suggest a new 'teach yourself to drive' app, but its real translation as someone who is self-taught describes a voyage of discovery, calling for focus and a voracious intellectual appetite, leading to success without the need to spend tweedy time at ivy-coated colleges. Looking at what, by today's demanding standards, would seem a rather rudimentary educational record, Lodwick matches the definition well. He was widely read as well as having a way with words, multilingual, with an eye for art, a deep understanding of Spain and its history, and an intellectual curiosity. He was in good company: a random sample from the many others who found little value in schoolbooks might include Borges, George Bernard Shaw, Hemingway and William Blake; and not forgetting Winston Churchill.

But faced with the inevitable gaps, how do we evaluate the information we have? The world's spymasters try hard not to act on hunch or gossip or under political pressure; not always successfully, as recent events have made embarrassingly clear. But they do their best to fit the material flowing in from their station officers, their official and unofficial human sources and their electronic vacuum cleaners into a matrix which rates both the source and the reliability of its information. An A1 rating means there are no doubts about the source's authenticity, trustworthiness or competency; it comes with a history of complete reliability, and the secret information being provided is logical, consistent with other relevant data, and independently confirmed.

At the other end of the scale, a rating of F6 is a polite way of expressing the analysts' view that there is insufficient information to evaluate the source, which may or may not be reliable, nor can the validity of the information be gauged. In plainer language, it may well be no more than barroom gossip or a creative leap based on a newspaper report, proffered by a tout in the hope of getting money, a visa or help with some personal problem. Ratings apart, assessment is made even harder when we take into account the dictum of an urbane British veteran of the clandestine Cold War that 'even when you have all the facts, you may still not know the truth'; counsel as valid for biographers as it is for spies. Writing here about a long-dead subject with long-dead friends sets the hurdle of 'independent confirmation' even higher, but on balance our end result is somewhere in the A zone, even though at times, reaching for the aspirin bottle like those frustrated jigsaw puzzlers, we find ourselves sheltering behind qualifiers such as 'probably'.

When his friend and fellow author Selwyn Jepson was fitting – or fitting up – Lodwick with a false identity for his first (and last) mission for SOE, Jepson purred that the bogus persona they had invented was 'picaresque, very slightly improbable, as indeed you do appear yourself, if you will forgive me for saying so'. One dictionary defines 'picaresque' – a word which crops up several times in comments about Lodwick – as 'a style of fiction dealing with the adventures of a rough and dishonest but appealing hero'.[5] A more nuanced definition, and perhaps more apt for Lodwick, is of 'an alienated outsider who constructs his own self and his world'.[6]

In the aftermath of his SOE mission, a harsh assessment by one of Jepson's superiors, a stony-faced British spymaster, rated his 'moral integrity as 'minus 0'. It was no doubt compounded by the organisation's rapidly crystallising negative view of Lodwick's cavalier attitude towards authority and security – 'against the grain', they might have said. The secret world being what it was – and is – this did not lead to Lodwick being cast into professional outer darkness. Instead it brought about his abrupt transfer via the Commandos to the SBS, encountering Evelyn Waugh on the way.

Lady Caroline Lamb is said to have described the poet Byron as 'mad, bad and dangerous to know', a snap judgement which did not stop her from launching into a stormy love affair with him. Lodwick was neither mad nor bad. 'Dangerous to know' would also be going too far, though he could be vituperatively bad-tempered and described one of his characters, almost certainly a self-portrait, as 'a man, perhaps not devoid of natural kindness, but with whom it would be far from safe to trifle. The instinct of self-preservation is too evident.'

And in another fictionalised image of his World War II role he saw himself as 'one of the "hit and run" men… the *condottieri*, the licensed brigands of their age'. He killed when he had to, and saw men 'put to the knife', but those were the realities, the price, of war. Though he had no need to embroider his real bravery, either he did from time to time to make a good story better or those to whom he was telling the stories misremembered or added their own embellishments in the retelling. As to Lodwick the writer, this is not an attempt at literary criticism, though it is sometimes hard to separate the man from his books. Many distinguished reviewers have judged his work over the years, and rather than try our hand at an inevitably amateur re-appraisal, where relevant we will share their comments. (Like all criticism, it was sometimes positive, sometimes not, often mixed.) In any case, only fools would now rush in where Anthony Powell, Anthony Burgess, Angus Wilson, C.P. Snow and, more recently, Chris Petit did not fear to tread.

Lodwick did not 'put himself about' on the London literary scene, so few of its opinion formers knew him well, if at all. Even more important is that, whatever his reputation, the reviewers did not have any insight into the real stories in his Whitehall files, then still secret, nor access to other material, notably a weathered marble plaque in Banyuls-sur-Mer and the ragged remnants of family memories and papers – letters, postcards and telegrams; plane and bullfight tickets – which highlight how he lived his life, and how the real and the fictional merged.

It is a sad fact that Lodwick's premature end did not just leave potential novels unwritten. His own version of his life story, which he left us in *The Asparagus Trench: An Autobiographical Beginning* with only the first 80 or so pages completed, might have explained some of the puzzles we shall encounter. Or then again, it might not. Whether they describe a humdrum life, or one punctuated with insider accounts of great events and the names of once prominent people, all life stories have gaps in the retelling. Memories fade like dreams at which the drowsy sleeper clutches as dawn frames the curtains. Or, as time passes, they are embellished in the retelling to wide-eyed grandchildren. In the blurred mirror of hindsight things we may have said or done, or left undone, may seem too painful, embarrassing, best forgotten, wiped by the Delete button. And as we all know to our cost, 'Delete' doesn't always do the trick.

Had Lodwick lived longer, had he finished his autobiography, we would have known more, but even then not necessarily the whole truth as distinct from the truth as he saw it and how he wanted others to remember it. In the end though, as to Lodwick the man, readers must judge for themselves, though with another caution, one which is a given for all biographies, especially of subjects who, like Lodwick, have lived through spells of extreme stress and hardship. Even if, again like Lodwick, they have written their own accounts, there is something in human nature, if just the urge to make a 'good read' out of a bad experience, or what the English would call the 'stiff upper lip', which prompts them to make light of the sheer terror of the moment; of long periods of being hunted, on the run from a watchful and pitiless enemy, or behind barbed wire and jailhouse bars, the stench made more oppressive by the threat of brutality or death.

Those fortunate enough not to have suffered in this way can imagine, but cannot begin to describe. Neither can they pretend to stand in their subject's shoes, to know why they did what they did; or didn't. It would be fair to say that, as in Lodwick's case, the reality was and is always worse than the written word. A family photograph of Lodwick peeking with a mischievous grin from behind a tree trunk reinforces our sense that he would have preferred chunks of his life to remain in the shadows.

The various strands of Lodwick's story and his complicated persona make it hard for the narrator to find the right voice. Is it the cool detachment of the would-be professional biographer? Should we copy Anton Walbrook, purring suavely as he connects the interrelated Viennese stories of love and lust in Max Ophuls' film *La Ronde*? That took a *mitteleuropäisch* style and bearing, not to mention a cloak and top hat, which sadly we don't have. Anyway, Walbrook's central role in the film was to respond to the audience's desire 'to know everything', which is impossible to fulfil here. Can we temper that with the voice of someone who knows something about SOE and who through personal experience can guess at some facets of Lodwick's temperament, what World War II did to him, and his marital fits and starts? Possibly. As it unfolded Lodwick's story did indeed strike some personal chords, though these are best left to the end. So the voice wavers, a blend of tones, none of them judgemental although, apart from *La Ronde*'s sexual over- and undertones, the comparison between the film and our story is not that fanciful a framework. One character leads to another; their tracks and memories, sorrows, successes and surprises intersect.

All that said, we now lift off the unhelpfully blank lid of the puzzle box and begin to put the pieces together as the Roundabout turns.

1

The Blood of India

Stereotypes can mislead. It is too easy to typecast John Lodwick, born on 2 March 1916, as a 'Child of the Raj' or an 'army brat', even though his father was a soldier, one of a long line of military men with an Indian background and an even earlier Huguenot and Essex yeoman backstory. He was born in England but spent some infant years in the dusty heat in which generations of his father's family had served. His mother's too. They were among the hundreds of thousands of loyal military men and civil servants, supported by long-suffering, wilting wives, through whom that huge, mysterious subcontinent was administered over the centuries; paternal-istically, sometimes cruelly, often profitably but by and large efficiently. It was an expatriate's life; the British who served there were not expected to settle in India, or to have much to do with its people. The white community lived in segregated cantonments, where the only Indians allowed in were servants or delivery wallahs. The sad half-castes whom neither community wanted to accept had their own segregated areas, and the teeming towns and villages where the real Indians lived were passed through at speed and with eyes averted. There were clear demarcation lines of protocol and hierarchy, as rigidly patrolled as the grounds of the Viceroy's vast palace, although the social 'patrols' were more likely to be snobbish senior memsahibs than bored British soldiers. The wives were often listless and lonely but clung on to, indeed were encouraged to cling on to, the thought of the Mother Country as their real home. It was a warp compounded by the routine separation of young children from their families, sent 'home' to a climate which, however chill and foggy, was thought better for their health than the heat and disease of the subcontinent. Chilblains were preferable to cholera, and Anglo-Saxon moral discipline was, they felt, better than the lassitude, Eastern superstitions and even the accents to which they were exposed in India. There was an element of dutiful sacrifice too. As one mother wrote: 'Our separations are expiation enough for holding the country.' Their positions of authority, their terms of service, their own servile squads of Indian servants, the Viceroy's caparisoned elephants, the whole exaggerated, white-gloved flummery of Empire underscored to them and the millions over whom they ruled that this vast subcontinent was controlled from a square mile or so of imposing Parliament buildings and grandiose offices in the capital city of a small island in the North Sea. They were in India to do London's bidding.

But though India murmured in Lodwick's background, many other factors, not least the poignancy of his birth and the rebellious streak baked into his DNA, shaped what he was: a man who fitted no stereotypes.

The Lodwicks were not among the 'nabobs' who in centuries gone by had extracted vastly more wealth from India than a few ivory carvings and lovingly polished Benares brassware. When John was born, they were positioned contentedly in the stratum of the English 'pecking order' reserved for long-standing Service families of senior rank, loyal links in what Rudyard Kipling called 'the chain gangs of the East, from sire to son'.[1] They were 'comfortable' and the name carried respect. Others lower in the Raj hierarchy were less fortunate, their retirement bringing them down with a bump from a large bungalow with a shady verandah and servants to indulge every need or caprice to a pensioner's coin-counting life in a suburban semi-detached or a cramped flat in Earls Court. John Lodwick was to experience just such a contrast as a schoolboy, though perhaps because it struck deep, like Dublin, it is another part of his life of which he tells us little.

The Lodwicks could trace their origins back well beyond India to the Huguenot weavers driven out of Flanders by waves of sixteenth- and seventeenth-century religious persecution. By contrast Lodwick's mother was a Roman Catholic, and though he does not seem to have been especially devout, and could write scornfully about hypocritical priests and the oppressive power of the Church in Spain, in some of his writing – for instance in *Brother Death* – he showed more than a passing familiarity with Catholic rituals and saints. Elsewhere, one of his fictional heroes, a thinly disguised Lodwick, is asked by a Spanish secret policeman: 'Are you a Catholic?'

'I was born a Catholic,' he replies.

'Then you will die a Catholic.'

He did.

But we should look first at memorials rather than graves. Mahabaleshwar, in the Indian state of Maharashtra, blanketed by one of the evergreen forests which are an unexpected feature of the Indian subcontinent and nicknamed 'The Land of Strawberries', is nowadays a major tourist attraction. Centuries ago it was the summer capital of Bombay (now Mumbai) province, when the officers, families and a supporting cast of nannies, maids, grooms and batmen fled the torrid heat along the coast. On the summer day these words are written, the sweaty humidity is said to make the Mumbai temperature 'feel like' 38 degrees Celsius, or a notch over 100 on the Fahrenheit scale; but up in the hills it is the rainy season, and the Mahabaleshwar temperature is a less oppressive 20 degrees C or 68 F. There, probably out of breath, since we are some 1,200 metres above sea level, the modern visitor can find one of the first tangible traces of the Lodwicks, a 25-foot column topped by a small urn, on a promontory which still bears the family name.

One side of the plaque on the column's base tells us in neatly chiselled letters (how many stifling days must it have taken to carve them?):

In memory of
General Peter Lodwick,
Second son of John Lodwick, Esq., S. Shoebury, Essex,
who entered the Hon. E.I. Co.'s service in 1799
and died at Bagnères de Bigorre, France,
August 28th, 1873, aged 90.
SENIOR OFFICER OF H. M.'S. FORCES IN INDIA

The other tells us:

In 1803–04, he saw service as subaltern in connection with the operation of the Army under Sir Arthur Wellesley. He was Brigade Major of Captain Ford's Subsidiary Force at the Battle of Kirkee, November 5th 1817, when 2800 British Troops defeated the Peshva's Army, and was present at the taking of Purandhar and other hill forts. He commanded a Regiment at Kittur in 1824; he subsequently became Town Major of Bombay; and closed his career in India as Resident of Satara.

The first European who set foot on these hills, he made known the salubrity of the climate, and led to the establishment of the Mahabaleshwar Sanatorium, thus conferring an inestimable benefit on the Bombay Presidency.

The Point, now by order of Government designated Lodwick Point in honour of his name, he reached alone in 1827, after hours of toil through the dense forest. Here, therefore, as the most appropriate spot this monument has, with the permission of Government, been erected by his only son, R.W. Lodwick, of Her Majesty's Bombay Civil Service. Accountant General of Madras in 1874.

The reference to 'Sir Arthur Wellesley', as he then was, loops us giddily back in time to the Dublin-born leader who would later achieve fame and glory as the Duke of Wellington. The Battle of Kirkee, now spelled Khadki, saw a numerically far smaller British force rout the Maratha army, a defeat which toppled the Peshva's almost bankrupt little empire. The abbreviation 'Hon. E.I.' refers to the Honourable East India Company, first chartered in 1600, which for centuries, until the British government took it over, controlled India's trade and, to all practical purposes, India itself. From 1796 to 1805 Wellington's brother Richard was in effect India's viceroy on the Company's behalf. 'R.W. Lodwick' is the curried curmudgeon we shall come to know, and whom John Lodwick as a child knew well, as Grandpapa.

John Lodwick was born in Cheltenham Spa, on the edge of the Cotswolds, about 100 miles west of London in a spacious, but not grand, memorabilia–encrusted home. The 'most complete Regency town in England', built on the discovery of its fashionable mineral springs in 1716, developed into the social and educational centre of gravity for many Raj families – at one point it was nicknamed, rather less kindly, 'The Calcutta of the Cotswolds'.[2] For our purposes we simply see it as the Lodwicks did, its almost Continental 'Promenade' patrolled by moustachioed ex-officers. Some still had the briskness of military men; a few were doddering into old age; most were grumbling about their gout or their internal plumbing in between boasting about their Service years.

But despite the quiet ticking of the marble clocks on their marble mantelpieces and the fading photographs of family, school and regiment arrayed in parade-ground order, the disturbing news delivered daily by *The Times* reminded them that the certainties and values of Empire to which they clung had in fact been crumbling for years and would soon be upended by the tragedies and the social and political upheavals of World War I and its aftermath. Comfort there may have been, but Lodwick was also born into family grief. Family first. We will try to keep things simple by referring to John Lodwick's father, John Thornton Lodwick, as 'Captain Lodwick' and, going back one more generation, to R.W. Lodwick as 'Grandpapa Lodwick'.

It is a perverse twist of his craft and career that it was only in his last book, *The Asparagus Trench*, the first of his works I had read all those years ago, that John Lodwick began to paint a picture of his childhood and his irascible octogenarian Grandpapa. It is subheaded, most likely by his publishers grabbing one all-too-brief last bite of the cherry, 'An Autobiographical Beginning'. Arguably some of his best writing, even almost Proustian in its evocations of the past, it was intended as the prelude to a much fuller retrospective narrative. But, as so often in this story, fate intervened and other than family folk memory and school records it is all we have on his childhood years. The best recommendation for the book, if rather succinct, came from an anonymous reviewer in *The Times*, who told its readers: 'No comment is apt, except – read these 80 pages.'

In a review for the *Observer*, Jeremy Brooks, himself a fine writer, thought that had Lodwick lived to write the full story 'there can be little doubt that it would have been one of the most distinguished autobiographies to have been published for many years'. But the fragment stood alone, 'perfect in form, tantalisingly allusive, full of youth's irrecoverable imaginative vitality'.[3]

As we move on, we should not lose sight of that Indian plaque, since another engraved slab of marble in a sunny spot halfway across the world has a sad story of its own to tell us as Lodwick's life unfolds.

Grandpapa Lodwick was born in 1831. The family's Indian ties went even further back than the General commemorated on the memorial; an earlier Lodwick is said to have given evidence for Warren Hastings, a former Governor of Bengal, when the latter was impeached, tried in London for corruption and acquitted in 1795. Corruption and unbounded greed were charges often levelled at the East India Company in the eighteenth century; not unjustifiably, and not unlike the onslaughts on twenty-first-century bankers, to whom the East India Company could have taught a lesson or two in venality. One satire of the day pretends to describe a session of the Company's Court attended by Sir Janus Blubber, Shylock Buffaloe, Caliban Clodpate, Skeleton Scarecrow, Jaundice Braywell and Sir Judas

Venom. They had gathered to defend the depredations of Clive of India, tagged in the pamphlet as 'Lord Vulture', a precursor to the 'Great Vampire Squid' jibe hurled more recently at a prestigious Wall Street firm.

Against this background it is hardly surprising that Grandpapa was sent to the school now known simply as 'Haileybury' but which was then still building on its grand foundation as 'The Honourable East India College'. In 1942 it became 'Haileybury and Imperial Service College'.

In Grandpapa's day, Haileybury – he was remembering it as it had been in 1846 – lived up to its formal title and was much more a college than a school, with boys entering from 17, some even after a presumably less than successful short spell at Oxford or Cambridge. They had their own rooms, and were attended by servants known as 'gips', and, though exposed to the core elements of the then standard British public school curriculum – rote learning, a heavy emphasis on sports, team spirit, bowel movements and cold baths – they also had lessons in Sanskrit, Persian, Gujarati and Telugu, the language spoken by millions of Dravidians, and in Indian and Asian history. None of this came cheap, though the hefty fees were heavily subsidised by the Company. Books and stationery were 'extras' and parents also had to supply their sons with 'a table spoon, a tea-spoon, knife and silver fork, six towels, tea equipage and a looking glass' as well as at least two pairs of sheets, two pillow cases and two 'breakfast cloths'. Their teachers were designated as 'Professors' and in addition to languages they tried their best to give the young men a grounding, according to the report of the Chairman's speech at a mid-Victorian Prize-Giving, in 'the principles of morals, law, logic and jurisprudence'. He also made clear that as well as instilling principles, Haileybury's aim was to produce men 'capable of coping with the subtlety of the Hindoo [sic] intellect', men who could understand 'the phases of the Oriental vices of deceit, dissimulation and treachery'.

The College was supported by the Company, out of self-interest as much as altruism, since it and the Colonial government which eventually superseded it needed a pipeline of men to run their vast domain: clever men – but not too clever – who followed orders but were able to use common sense and take the initiative when their Empire's rulers, so far away, were reachable in the early days only by ships under sail, and later by a fragile telegraph network. They were being moulded to become administrators, tax collectors, budget controllers, magistrates, managers of railways and signals systems and 'political advisors', patiently explaining the interests and wishes of Whitehall and Delhi to often obdurate rajahs, who disliked being told what to do by their Imperial masters but disliked even more the thought that they might be deposed and lose their hereditary power and often immense wealth.

It was an increasingly troubled century for the Raj, with incessant internal strife and the complex dynamics of the 'Great Game' against Russia, so it was inevitable that some young men would find 'administration' melding with intelligence, signals interception and matters military. A hint of this is found in the 1888 publication by Stuart Godfrey of the Bombay Staff Corps of a literal translation of Pushkin's *The Captain's Daughter* 'for those trying to learn Russian'.

Grandpapa retired in 1877, a year after Queen Victoria had been proclaimed Empress of India, bringing to a successful climax another Lodwick career in the Raj. Quite how much military rather than administrative service he saw is unclear and his title may have been an extrapolation from his post as Accountant General. Haileybury rules dictated that men were expected to spend 35 years in the Service after leaving the College, but the burdens of the climate, and the local difficulties which so often flared up, would have made this hard to apply across the board. But neither the climate nor the work had sapped his vitality. He lived to be 99, had two wives and fathered nine children, the last sired when he was well over 70. John Lodwick wrote later that it could not have been a happy home. Those of the children who had not died left as soon as they could, mostly for Canada, to escape what he remembered as his Grandpapa's 'splenetic peevishness' and 'wicked disposition'. In *The Asparagus Trench* Lodwick writes, one senses approvingly, of Grandpapa's 'unflagging pursuit' of maids, and his Leporello-like list of women with 'a plus or minus sign' against each name. Grandpapa prudently locked it away but, as Lodwick remembers with relish, 'it did not take me long to obtain a duplicate key.' Grandpapa had dissipated much of his capital on ill-fated investments in mines and railways in South America, a continent about which his lack of first-hand knowledge intensified, if anything, his claim to be an expert in its geography and politics. He also lost a good deal of money in a Cornish tin mine which turned out to be on the verge of running out of ore, and a partnership with his father-in-law to fence in 200 acres of Dartmoor where rabbits would be bred for the local and London markets. The rabbits multiplied energetically as nature intended, but most then burrowed free, a leporine *Great Escape*. Were the joke not so laboured, the scheme might well merit the adjective 'hare-brained' until we find from a new history of the British railways that the trade in wild rabbits from North Devon was substantial, with the 'rabbit special' carrying up to twenty tons of furry carcasses up to London every night.[4] In *The Asparagus Trench*, Lodwick identifies Grandpapa's hard-riding 'squire-parson' father-in-law as the Reverend Thornton, the middle name given to Lodwick's father, the Captain, and used by Lodwick himself for many of his fictional anti-heroes.

The Reverend William Henry Thornton (1830–1916) was just as remarkable as Grandpapa or John himself. A character who would not have been out of place in Trollope's *Hunting Sketches*, he is remembered as 'of charming personality and air', and a man from solid religious stock. He was also strikingly handsome, to judge from a contemporary photograph, and thought nothing of a fifty-mile ride or a thirty-mile walk across the moors. He combined hunting with his parish duties, was leader for 25 years of the Clerical Association, a group devoted to study of the Greek Testament, and made prolific contributions to a host of literary, historical and scientific journals. He was also an author, whose memoirs attracted the enthusiastic attention of the *Daily Telegraph* when they were re-published in 1991.[5] One episode which, like *The Asparagus Trench*, leaves us hungry to know more is Grandpapa's proposal of marriage to Thornton's daughter Florence in 1878, when she was a mere slip of 17 and her suitor, in Thornton's careful words, was 'considerably older'. He was actually 47. In keeping with what seems to have been expected of a paterfamilias of the times – Trollope has a version of the theme in *The Duke's Children* – Thornton whisked Florence away to Italy for three months, to look before she leaped. Grandpapa meanwhile gave his word that he would not follow or even write to her to 'press his intentions'. But when he heard that Florence had fallen seriously ill, an infection he chose to blame on her father's lack of care, Grandpapa fired off a volley of 'impassioned letters', no doubt in fine Lodwick style, claiming he was now free from his undertaking. Misdirected as they were to another holidaying Thornton family, in a confusing coincidence worthy of a Gilbert and Sullivan operetta, their effect was understandably muted. The couple eventually married, so we can assume tempers cooled, though to judge from Lodwick's much later comment that it was not 'a happy home' and that his grandmother was 'a beautiful recluse surrounded by much masculine ugliness', we may not be able to go so far as to say that 'they lived happily ever after'. But then, who does?

Grandpapa was also an author, who relished squabbling with the Reverend Thornton about their relative sales and their printers' bills, though his two-volume semi-autobiographical novel *John Bolt* makes much heavier reading than his grandson's books.[6] But although it was written in Victorian times, in Victorian style, it is easy to see aspects of John Lodwick in Grandpapa's eye and ear for places, people, love, social gradations and, above all, excitement. John had read the novel and transmuted Grandpapa into the ghost of Lord Drawbridge, the noble, Haileybury-schooled senior servant of the Raj, when he wrote *The Butterfly Net*. On the other hand there is no evidence that he had read Grandpapa's *Humorous Sketches of the World We Live In*, 40 pages of his lithographed caricatures published by the Education Society Press in Bombay in 1856, describing 'the absurdities of Indian life in a good-humoured manner' (though Grandpapa circumspectly added that 'no real people are intentionally caricatured'). Nor did John apparently come across an even rarer work, a pamphlet privately printed by Peter Lodwick in 1840 complaining in measured but clearly aggrieved terms to the 'Honourable Court of Directors of the East India Company' about his 'supersession' as Resident at Sattara after its Rajah had been deposed; it was an affair which rattled around the columns of *The Times* and the leather-upholstered lounges of London clubs for a long time. His letter is interesting in itself but even more as an echo of that Haileybury Prize-Giving speech, a vignette of the tricky demands the British emissaries faced as they juggled the policies of their distant masters and the touchiness of squabbling local rajahs fired up by 'deadly personal animosity… mutual insults and religious feuds', compounded by a profound distrust of the rule of London. In Sattara this was alleged to have gone as far as inept anti-British plotting by the Rajah with Portuguese emissaries in Goa. The latter denied any involvement and, on the evidence of that marble memorial, the incident does not seem to have cramped Peter Lodwick's career. But, like Grandpapa's 'impassioned' letters to his future father-in-law, the pamphlet is an early example of what John Lodwick claimed rather proudly over a century later was the family's 'tendency towards belligerence, a lack of tact in private relations'. We shall see much more of it as we go on.

2

Captain Courageous

Slipping Anton Walbrook's scarf around our narrator's shoulders for a moment, we can now crank the wheel of the Roundabout and shift the setting from the Raj back to Cheltenham, the domestic centre of gravity in the inexorable British–Indian life cycle from infancy to senility.

Cheltenham College was founded in 1841 in the classical 'high noon' of high-minded new 'public schools' (another British euphemism; attracting pupils from the general public was far from any of their thoughts). Its promoters were a group of army officers and its location and its syllabus, as well as its fee structure, were a direct response to the demographics and financial position of the British–Indian parental base. Its declared aim was to educate 'the sons of gentlemen', though the subtext was the sons of decent families who would have to make a living and a career in the overseas Civil Service or the armed forces rather than drift languidly, by way of more exclusive schools such as Eton or Harrow, into Parliament, the Bar or managing the family estates. Like India it is a clear strand in our story; two generations of Lodwicks were pupils there. John's father, Captain John Thornton Lodwick, entered the School as a day boy in 1892, when he was ten years old. There was an unexplained gap – money, sickness, behaviour, some parental duty overseas, we can only guess – between his leaving again in December 1894 and rejoining in September 1897. Reflecting the spirit of the age and the make-up of its local parental base, the College operated for many years with a Classical and a Military side in tandem, and the records show that the future Captain Lodwick followed the Military stream. He was 19 when he was commissioned into the Royal Lancaster Regiment in 1901; in Lodwick's later memory, much against Grandpapa's wishes. He fought, fought well and gained medals in the Boer War and transferred to the Third Gurkhas, then part of the Indian Army. John Lodwick tells us in *The Asparagus*

Trench, without a date but no doubt connected with this transfer, that the Captain, 'never a punctual man, had once hired a special train to take him from Waterloo to Southampton, because, awakening in loving arms, he had discovered himself to be in imminent danger of missing a troopship for India.' It cost Grandpapa £100, a sizeable sum in those days.

He was appointed Military Instructor in the Bombay Presidency where Grandpapa Lodwick had once served as British Resident. When World War I began, the Empire and the Dominions rallied to the call of King and the Mother Country on a scale and with a loyalty unimaginable in today's post-colonial times. Captain Lodwick shipped back to England as a machine-gun officer in the Indian Corps. On 16 November 1914, three and a half months after war was declared, he and Kathleen ('Kitty') Frances Halsted Crump announced their engagement in *The Times*. Kathleen too came from a 'Raj' family: her father, Sir Henry Ashbrooke Crump, was then serving as Financial Secretary to the Central Indian Provinces.[1]

By March 1915 the Captain was floundering in the freezing mud of northern France, where between 10 and 13 March the Indian Corps under Sir James Willcocks fought alongside the British Fourth Corps at the Battle of Neuve Chapelle. Time has all but erased the ink and the date on what seems to be a letter he wrote to his father, though the word 'Kitty' can just be made out, and a barely legible phrase about 'a narrow squeak from sniper fire' that 'parted my hair for me all right'. It was an early example of a doubtless unfair, *Blackadder* vision of the war: corpulent generals on both sides, comfortably distant from the front lines, moving flags around a map to orchestrate bloodshed and destruction on a huge scale and usually accomplishing little more than gaining or regaining a few yards of muddy territory. There are photographs and flickering newsreel shots of the killing fields. None of those black-and-white images – of heaps of bodies, skeletons of buildings, tree stumps and booted shinbones jutting out of the mud, a solitary crucifix retrieved from a ruined church, a group of Indian troops at prayer, so far from home – can possibly tell a twenty-first-century viewer what it was like to face death in the ooze, tormented by lice and bellowed at incomprehensibly by red-eyed sergeants and whey-faced officers.

The records do not make a clear distinction – if one could ever be made in the middle of the confusion and carnage – between 'casualties' and 'losses' but, in another reminder of the Empire's commitment, while British losses were some 7,000, Indian forces suffered 4,200 killed and wounded, against 10,000 German lives. Twelve Victoria Crosses were awarded, one to an Indian soldier. Captain Lodwick received the Distinguished Service Order, or DSO, for his cool reconnaissance of briefly recaptured German positions and the 'immense number of German casualties' who fell to his 22 strategically placed machine guns. In the aftermath the battle was 'spun' to the press as 'a striking British advance' which would 'cheer and invigorate our Army in the field', and the War Office cabled the Viceroy in Delhi praising the 'great gallantry' of the Indian Corps, whose 'tenacity, courage and endurance were admirable'.

Later comments on the battle were more measured – a French general was heard to mutter that 'it was a success with no follow-up' and another pundit saw it as 'a tactical success but the strategic intentions were not met'. They bring to mind the hoary medical quip that 'the operation was a success but the patient died', not least because the Allies' artillery found themselves woefully short of shells. It is one of the curious twists of this tale that later on in the narrative we will encounter an officer who died at Neuve Chapelle and whose family became linked to the Lodwicks by the happenstance of love.

Even though war was not far away, and ferries still criss-crossed the Channel, it comes as a slight surprise that just a few weeks later, on 1 April 1915, Captain Lodwick and Kathleen married in the 'Cheltenham Roman Catholic Church', probably the neo-Gothic St Gregory's. The incense, the robes and the choir's melodious messages to the heavens are an extraordinary counterpoint to the tang of cordite, the smell of blood and the shrieks of the wounded and dying in his passage through hell in Flanders just a few weeks earlier. How could they have known what fate had up its sleeve, in the person of 'Blue Max' Valentiner.

After a ceremonial visit to Buckingham Palace to receive his medal from the King's own hand, Captain Lodwick decided to rejoin the Gurkhas in India, leaving a now pregnant Kathleen to follow him later. On 16 December 1915 he boarded the SS *Persia* in London. Were it a red London bus, rather than a black-hulled, twin-funnel steamer, the 8,000-ton Peninsular and Orient liner, built in 1900, might have been dubbed the 'Routemaster' of the India run. Not just a workhorse of what Kipling, in an early poem, called 'The Exiles' Line' but an enduring emblem – the Kipling Society's current website page for the poem has an image of the *Persia* as its masthead² – it had already made over 70 round trips between London and India, calling en route at Gibraltar, Marseilles, Port Said and Aden.

This time there were 519 men, women and children on board, 184 of them passengers, the rest 'crew'. Much like the British distinction in cricket between Gentlemen and Players, or in *The Times*' casualty lists between 'Officers' and 'NCOs and Men', the *Persia*'s manifest divided the crew tally between 'European' and 'Native'.

London was cold, across the Channel men were being blown up, crippled or gassed, and when the wind blew from the south the thump of heavy artillery could be heard like a distant Guy Fawkes Night as far away as Surrey. Assuming the Gloucestershire casualty lists, indexed by the local newspaper and drawn from what was still a largely rural area, are a rough proxy for the country as a whole, they rub home that in those early years of conflict there can have been few families anywhere left untouched by official notices that loved ones were dead, wounded, or – in a way worst of all – 'missing in action', a phrase which offered a cruel blend of forlorn hope and hand-wringing despair.

As *Persia* weighed anchor yet again, its siren trumpeting the long, single blast of farewell, the passengers must have felt relaxed, even if relief was diluted by slight twinges of guilt as they looked forward to the sun, decent food, decorous dancing or less decorous dalliances down below. There was another strand too, nicely captured in a quote by Elizabeth Buettner from a memsahib embarking on an earlier return voyage. 'It was a Bombay ship full of Anglo-Indians. I looked up and down the long saloon tables with a sense of relief and a solace; I was again among my own people.'³ The Christmas and New Year rituals would delight the English families aboard, though they might have had less significance for the several rich and royal Indian families who were travelling home. The festivities over, *Persia* sailed from Marseilles on 26 December.

On the 30th, as it ploughed steadily ahead some 70 miles south of Crete, passengers were taking their seats for lunch when the ringing of the steward's gong was drowned by a rumbling explosion, the sound of shattering glass, screams and a slow-motion sideways lurch from which, like a crippled mare, its guts blown by one jump too far in the hunt, the stalwart *Persia* could not right itself.

Captain Lodwick had won his DSO for gallantry in open conflict. As the commander of German submarine *U-38*, Max Valentiner, then in his early twenties, was in a profession for which bravery and nerves of steel were also essential ingredients. But whether his attack was gallant or open is, to put it charitably, debatable.

It took only one of Valentiner's battery of six torpedoes to send *Persia* to the ocean floor in less than ten minutes. But as one survivor wrote: 'The conduct of the passengers and crew was splendid. There were no struggles, nor was there any panic.'

It was, after all, a British ship.

Captain Lodwick, a strong swimmer who could certainly have saved himself, yet again showed his courage and calm, throwing wooden chairs, cushions – anything that could float – to those floundering in the water until the ship slid beneath the waves, tragically taking him with it. He was swallowed by seas through which his filibustering son John would later navigate into and out of danger from a new generation of Germans on his bloody missions for the SBS.

The Germans had unilaterally renounced the Prize Law which demanded that submariners should attack passenger vessels only after giving due warning and allowing those on board to take to the lifeboats. So Valentiner was only obeying orders when he gave no warning, then made no attempt to pick up survivors or even put out a 'Mayday' call to bring other ships to the rescue as *U-38* slipped away.

It was, after all, a German ship.

Valentiner went on to notch up one of the top tallies of tonnage sunk by the Germans in World War I, and in December 1916 the Kaiser awarded him Germany's highest military honour, the 'Pour le Mérite', a creation of Frederick the Great (and nicknamed from its glossy enamel background the 'Blue Max'). After Germany's defeat, he melted back into the tweedy anonymity of a gentleman farmer's life and successfully avoided prosecution as a war criminal.[4] Not that it took much doing. After much political posturing and fruitless searching for alleged culprits, only 12 individuals, all officers, actually faced a court, and a German court at that. The commander of another U-boat which had sunk a British hospital ship was found 'not guilty' on the familiar grounds that he was only following orders. Other verdicts struck British opinion as too lenient, though the German public thought them harsh examples of 'victor's justice', while German military men bristled at the slur to army honour implied by compelling officers to serve their sentences in civilian jails.

The official toll of those who died was 335, made up of 119 passengers, Captain Lodwick among them, 50 of the European crew and 166 'Natives', most of the latter engine hands and stokers hopelessly trapped below decks. The list of passengers who died is shot through with sadness: 'Major Hutchinson, Mrs. Hutchinson, child, infant and nurse' gives a sense.

A mystery which continues to interest treasure hunters today, about whether *Persia* took to the seabed a high-value cargo of gold and jewels for an Indian rajah, need not detain us. Another sideswipe of grief which is unrelated to our story but does deserve a brief mention is that among those drowned was the 35-year-old Eleanor Velasco Thornton (the name is a coincidence; she was born in Stockwell, daughter of a telegraph engineer and a South London girl), torn by the waves from the arms of her lover, John Douglas-Scott-Montagu, Second Baron Montagu of Beaulieu. First reported as missing, then discovered to have survived, he is remembered for public service and his early and energetic advocacy of the newfangled motor car. It is characteristic of the moral double standards of the times that, though they were well known (by those who needed to know) to be 'a couple', indeed had a daughter and were travelling together, he was a married man, so she was listed separately on the passenger manifest as his Private Secretary, and no hint of the liaison was printed for years. She lived on as the original model for the 'Spirit of Ecstasy' emblem which crowns the gleaming bonnets of Rolls-Royce cars.

Captain Lodwick too was remembered. First, by a former Company Commander who wrote that 'in the course of 30 years' service, after intimate knowledge of many hundreds of officers I have not come across more than half a dozen of his equals… there is no man that I would rather have had with me in a tougher place than him.' He was also a fine horseman and polo player, a good shot and big-game sportsman and, ironically, 'a splendid swimmer'. There is irony too in the reference to polo; John Lodwick was later to suggest that the cost of that private train to Southampton was only a fraction of what Grandpapa, long-suffering, somewhat of a skinflint but at heart indulgent, had paid out for his son over the years, not least 'a fortune' in the bills for the Captain's string of ponies.

A second, if more arcane, memento is an *Instruction Manual on the Hotchkiss Machine Gun*, which John Lodwick recalled had been written by his father. There are in fact several different editions of this guide to efficient killing, and authorship is hard to determine, but the most elegant version is the hardback version attributed to an anonymous 'Instructor' and sold at two shillings and sixpence by the military publishers Gale and Polden; its availability to the general public suggests a rather more relaxed attitude to firearms than today. It would be nice to believe it was Captain Lodwick's work if only because of a coincidental discovery on the back cover, to which we shall refer later.

But the saddest note of all – so far – is the announcement in *The Times* of the birth of John Lodwick, on 2 March 1916 at his Grandpapa's Cheltenham home, delivered to a grief-torn mother, with a ghost for a father. A ghost of whom the only image we can find is a yellowing page headed 'For King and Country: Officers on the Roll of Honour' in the *Illustrated London News* of 29 January 1916. Perhaps because of the receding hairline and the obligatory brisk moustache, the studio-posed image, too faded to be reproducible here, makes him look far older than his years. Even older in real terms was Grandpapa, who now had to do his best to stand in the dead Captain's Crockett & Jones calf-length leather boots. It was a decidedly rum ménage. But Lodwick enjoyed it. And so did Grandpapa.[5]

3

Schooldays with Grandpapa

John Lodwick tells us that Grandpapa did not like to be reminded that a witch lurked somewhere in the leafy branches of the family tree, if only as the result of a short-lived marriage. On their refugee journeying the Lodwicks and other Huguenots had put down their first British roots in Essex. Harwich, conveniently just across the North Sea from the Hook of Holland, had been a busy port since the Middle Ages. According to a local historical society[1] the name first appears in Essex in the late 1600s when a Peter Lodwick was recorded as a 'yeoman of Shopland' and the owner of the 380-acre Great Borwood Farm and ' Littlehouse' on flood-prone, inaccessible Foulness. The family's interests grew – they bought 'fowling' and fishing grounds and grazing land. The name lives on. The porch of the charming Church of St Thomas in Bradwell St Mary displays the headstones of two Peter Lodwicks, Senior and Junior, moved there after a nearby church was demolished in 1954. And even today there is a smart street of 'executive homes' in Shoeburyness, near Southend-on-Sea, named Lodwick (South Shoebury is inscribed on the Indian plaque as the birthplace of a much earlier John Lodwick).

But a witch? Up in the North in the 1820s the first jittery passengers were being carried on the Stockton and Darlington railway, the start of a speculative mania for railroad building, but goods, people, news and ideas still travelled by packhorse, carriage, stagecoach or canal barge. So they moved slowly. Even though Essex was not far from the capital as the crow flapped eastwards, it was light years from the sophistication and madding crowds of London. Its country communities were inbred, uneducated and uncouth, still steeped in ancient superstitions, primitive beliefs in the black arts. They were not alone. Almost every rural community believed in powers way beyond those of the Church – the supernatural healing gifts of the seventh son of a seventh son, a brook with magic powers, the 'evil eye' attributed to some harmless old crone.

Eliza Frost Kersteman – her surname suggests a Huguenot background – married her cousin Jeremiah Lodwick of Canewdon, Essex, in July 1825. A brief notice of the marriage appeared in the comprehensively titled *Bury and Norwich Post, Suffolk and Norfolk Telegraph, Essex, Cambridge and Ely Intelligencer*. It used the now archaic term 'sennight' to indicate that the wedding had taken place a week before the announcement appeared. She was 42, may already have been a widow and was said to belong to 'a local landed family'. Jeremiah had lost his first wife and, in contrast to Grandpapa, was doomed to die young, after only 15 months of marriage. Eliza Lodwick found herself running a sizeable farm, with a fine home at Lambourne Hall, and another in Royal Crescent in the then fashionable resort of Southend. She farmed 500 acres, employing 25 labourers, a shepherd and four maids, and when she died peacefully aged 78 she left 540 sheep and lambs, 17 bullocks, 18 cart horses and colts, 23 'head of swine and poultry', and sheds full of machines and implements; the catalogue for a separate sale in the Southend house listed furniture and effects of distinctly high quality.

Why, then, should she be remembered as 'Widow Lodwick, the Witch of Lambourne Hall'? Why did the villagers seek the help of James Murrell, 'The Witch Doctor and Cunning Man' of nearby Hadleigh? His claim to fame was that simply by whistling a secret melody he could force witches to reveal themselves, unable to resist the urge to leave their hovels and their covens and dance in the local churchyard. Or so he claimed.

In that closed and backward community it was all too easy for muttering and finger-pointing to escalate, tinder sparked by visceral peasant jealousy of a rich landowner, a spinster who lived in 'The Big House' with her sister. The locals resented the tough jail sentences meted out by magistrates – landowners themselves – for poaching on her fields and copses, and the more obvious causes for a series of accidents to her farmworkers were dismissed in favour of whispers that dark forces had been at work.

The villagers soon convinced themselves the Widow was a witch and the call went out for Murrell. But despite his carefully burnished local reputation as a seer and witch-sniffer, the local vicar refused to let him work his whistling wizardry. It was an understandable decision on theological grounds, as well as pragmatic; the vicar was Eliza's brother-in-law. She lived on, untroubled and unexorcised.

Grandpapa sounds like, indeed probably was, an ogre, but even though he wrote of him as 'a gross and sensual old hypocrite' John Lodwick had considerable fondness for him. And vice versa. Grandpapa was a life-enhancer trapped in an old man's body, surrounded by faded paintings and photographs of his children – the three who had died with their images biblically turned to the wall – interspersed with the moulting heads of equally dead animals. On his desk stood a jar in which a two-headed mongoose had been pickled for posterity in yellowish fluid, alongside a chunk of the chocolate said to have been issued to troops in the Crimea and an Indian blowpipe. For an old man, his Raj-thinned blood kept warm by hot water bottles tucked under his waistcoat, living on his memories, the irruption of a high-spirited young boy must have been a more powerful stimulant than brandy or cheroots.[2]

How did a young and highly impressionable fatherless child come to be living in a Cheltenham household creaking with old age, the aroma of tobacco, mothballs and patent medicines hanging in the upstairs corners? Its epicentre was Ashley Lodge in Shurdington Road, an area realtors today tout as 'highly desirable' (which means expensive and that most homes have names rather than numbers). Tracking old addresses is not always reliable, but the best evidence suggests that the Lodge has long since gone, replaced by a row of smaller houses and maisonettes in faux-Georgian style. In its day it was no doubt much in the mould of the eight-bedroom home nearby recently offered for sale, spacious and dignified with panelled walls in the downstairs rooms, and enough accommodation for children, guests and staff, but sadly with no trace, at least in the agent's snapshot, of an asparagus trench on the brick-walled lawn. It was nice enough as a setting but Grandpapa, its curmudgeonly master, was long retired and set diamond-hard in his ways. He hadn't had any dealings with young people for many years, and tyrannised a supporting cast of his browbeaten wife, a justifiably timorous maid and a chauffeur-cum-handyman, an ex-serviceman who drove the General's 'Model T' Ford. The UK production line had shut down around 1927, after churning out some 250,000 vehicles, and the car was already something of a vintage rarity, though the General may not have known that over the years his loyal chauffeur had almost completely rebuilt it as various parts failed or fell off. Trembling in the kitchen when she was not playing cards with the chauffeur was the long-suffering cook, whose inability to prepare a curry up to Raj standards made her a frequent target for abuse; if she served up what her irascible boss thought was a poorly cooked leg of lamb he had been known to hurl it out of the window. When his eldest son by the General's first marriage, already an old man in John Lodwick's time, and a Colonel, came to visit, he had to stand to attention and address Grandpapa as 'Sir'. As one of Lodwick's cousins wrote to him rather bitterly – the letter is undated – Grandpapa was 'a man whose children were to him little more than a projection of himself. Their glory was his. In your father he had something to be proud of, but mine – in his opinion – let him down.' In a line which might have been used in a *Downton Abbey* script, he is said to have boasted that, as the late Captain Lodwick had held the DSO, Kitty as his widow would be entitled to take precedence at dinner over a General, if the latter did not have one.

But the death of another of his children and the birth of a fatherless grandson cannot have left the grouchy old man unmoved. It crystallised the 'special relationship' he had with John, who listened in awe to his stories, came running when the old man summoned him to his bedside by thumping his stick on the floor, and shared his passion for stamps and geography. He told John that he slept only three hours a night; when he woke up he stared at the framed family photos on his dressing table. 'They were changed each week like the programme of a repertory theatre.'

No Grandpapa is immortal; John was with his grandfather in the hours before the old man's death, when he was 'confronting the expected, now in the coalescent shadows of approaching death. I represented no more than a tiresome, and inconsequential interruption, but he smiled and took the ritual half-crown from beneath his pillow. "Well, boy, at least you have known me."' He steps off our narrative Roundabout after a life fuller than most people, even most novelists, could have imagined. He was 99. As the Cheltenham headmaster told John when breaking the news at school a little later that the old man had died: 'We all wish he could have reached his century.' Only the English could use a cricketing metaphor for consolation.

It is the fatherless John whose trail we now follow to his own connection with India and his grandfather's home. What John does not tell us in his *The Asparagus Trench* is that in June 1921, five years after Max Valentiner launched his

'Widowmaker' torpedo, his mother Kitty announced her engagement to Major C.L. Ruck. The announcement says he was an officer in the Indian Signal Service, but that may not be the full story. Again we come up against the wall of that unfinished memoir. In his opening 80 pages John Lodwick's stepfather barely rates a mention, no doubt because for a professional writer Grandpapa made a better opening subject. Would Major Ruck have come onto the page later? If so, what would Lodwick have written? John's eldest son remembers Charles Ruck well but as a much older man, a dentist, practising in Southsea. Further investigation by the British Dental Association tells us that Charles Frederick Lyson Ruck qualified as a dentist at the Dental School of Guy's Hospital in 1910. It would follow that his role in the Signal Service was as a dental officer rather than an expert in Morse, telegraphy and the use of signalling mirrors.

The scythe that had been swung countrywide by World War I, cruelly followed by the ravages of an influenza epidemic, had accelerated a relaxation of the strict Victorian and Edwardian codes of etiquette about how long a widow and her family should wear mourning and 'weeds', and how long she had to sit around embroidering cushions and playing the piano before she could remarry. (The customs must have been a trial for those subjected to them, but a business boon for West End milliners.) For John to adjust to 'Your New Daddy', when he had never known the real one, is something of which we could make too much, but it must have been a tricky passage for all of them. By the summer the Major had transferred to the Royal Signals, presumably in the same professional role, and he and Kitty were married on 8 June at Bombay's Roman Catholic Cathedral of the Holy Name, a place of architectural exuberance, its Gothic structure embellished by Indian admixtures in the roof tracery and the mini-cupolas above the organ loft. The Major was not just taking the important walk along the aisle into marriage but as a Protestant he would also have had to go through a period of instruction in the Catholic faith and also agree that any children of the marriage would be baptised and brought up as Roman Catholics. Quite where a stepson fitted in canonically doesn't matter, since Kitty's faith was too strong to leave any doubt about John's religion.

Whether John was initially left behind at Grandpapa's and how long he spent in India as a child is uncertain. He writes loosely of passing the first eight years of his life 'mostly' in the Raj. Like the *bindi*, the red dot carefully applied to a girl's forehead on marriage as a mark of love, prosperity and the 'third eye', it left its indelible mark, as it had on his ancestors and so many thousands of British children and adults. He remembered it as a land where

> magic abounded, awaiting discovery at every instant of the day, in the muttering of an *ayah* [nanny], in the creep of a scorpion, in the odour of markets, even in the dripping ice-pads intended to relieve my frequent sunstroke. In that lost world I learned to believe in the marvellous. I found it again in my Grandpapa's study.

The savagery of the land also made an impact: a moment in tranquil Kashmir when he saw a bearded thug chop off another man's lower leg. The axeman ran off, and, in Lodwick's childhood memory, the victim 'picked up his leg and crawled after him'. When he told his mother and stepfather and dragged them to the lakeside to show them the bloodstains, they said it was cruel. 'I found it interesting.' That same reaction to violence comes back at least twice, in totally different contexts but with the same grim resonance, much later in his life. So does another marble memorial.

We have already noted that 'moral and physical' health risks were a major reason for shipping children home. Making sure they spoke 'proper' English was another, a point borne out by Lodwick in one of his lightly fictionalised flights about his boyhood, claiming that his mother and stepfather thought he needed to get to grips with his mother tongue, as he spent all his time 'in the Compound jabbering away in Hindustani'.

Though his writings give the impression that he appeared, slightly bronzed and flustered, straight from India at Cheltenham College's imposing gates, this was not his first stop, nor indeed his last 'fudge'. College records show that when she wrote the application letter, his mother Kitty gave their address as Silverdale Road, Bickley, in Kent. Rolling the timeline and landscape backwards a century or more, the aggressive General Peter Lodwick had a 'gentleman's home' with spacious acreage just a few miles away in what was then the gently rolling countryside of Beckenham.

Modern images show Silverdale Road as an enclave of 'decent' rather than grand, semi-detached homes which could be in the leafy suburbs of any major UK city. Whether the Rucks owned or rented we do not know – probably the latter, as capital was scarce – but the general sense one gets is that, like so many in the British–Indian diaspora, they were neither rich nor poor, but hovering, not always comfortably, in-between. The Bickley address and Lodwick's later disparaging reference to a flat in Earls Court are reminders of the point made by Elizabeth Buettner that not all those who retired from India could afford Cheltenham or other 'British–Indian' catchment areas. Caught between the realities of the deflated purchasing power of their pensions and the inexorably rising UK cost of living, they found themselves squeezed out into suburbia or the (then) less expensive terraces of West London. In E.M. Forster's words they would 'retire to some suburban home and die exiled from glory'.

The whiskered discipline of Shurdington Road, Cheltenham was either not an option as a home for a remarried former daughter-in-law and her new husband, or, more likely given John's picture of Grandpapa's household, something both Rucks preferred to avoid. Again, it is a slice of his life on which John might have expanded had he lived to finish his work.

John was a pupil at Bickley Park, a prep school opened directly after World War I by an ex-officer, Richard Brandram and his wife, combining 'progressive foresight' and a 'sporting ethos'. Lodwick the infant, wearing the almost universal kit for boys of that age – an Aertex shirt in summer, Viyella in winter, a cap, grey shorts held in place by a snake-buckled belt – would not recognise the school in its twenty-first-century expansion. He was too late to have been taught by one of Brandram's former assistants, who was later to become rather better known as an author than he ever was, the young Enid Blyton. In a letter commending her to her next employer, Brandram wrote that 'To be able to lead small boys, and to understand their ways, is a gift given to few, but Miss Blyton has the secret.'[3] A decision by an earlier school administration means that early archives, which might have given us some facts on Lodwick as a child, have been shredded.

With his family hoping he would add another link in Kipling's Imperial 'chain gang' the eight-year-old John Lodwick first appears in Cheltenham College records in the autumn term of 1924 as a 'weekly boarder' in the Junior School. So he was free some weekday afternoons, a large chunk of each Saturday afternoon and every Sunday. He spent most of his free time at Grandpapa's since a weekend commute to see his mother and stepfather was expensive and a time-consuming diversion from the games and dreams of a schoolboy. The weekly plan was a sensible way for the College to align its fees to parental financial capacity, knowing too that a gallimaufry of grandparents, cousins, uncles and aunts in the British–Indian community was ready and willing, with real or feigned enthusiasm, to look after exiled young children out of school hours. They understood all too well the pangs that went along with the transient pleasures of the Raj system. And as John wrote, with a slight curl of the lip, being with Grandpapa in Cheltenham was preferable to his 'distressingly bourgeois' life in Earls Court.

Philbeach Gardens, which he suggests in one of his novels was the Ruck home at the time (he does not mention Bickley), was built in 1876, and is still anchored by St Cuthbert's Church, its Gothic Revival architecture heavily laden with the 'Arts and Crafts' decorations celebrating its early years under Anglo-Catholic influence. As Lodwick remembered it, the family had a fourth-floor flat with a view over the damp slate rooftops of West Kensington.

On one side the red-brick street backs on to the rattling of a spider's web of rail lines where various Underground routes poke their heads above the surface, and on the other opens into the busy Warwick Road. The area has seen many changes over the years, not all of them for the better. What Grandpapa might have remembered as scrubby former farmland, centred round what is now the Underground station, could not withstand the tides of London's growth in population and its infrastructure needs. The ownership of large swathes of the area by wealthy absentee landlords – notably the de Veres, whose earldom and family home gave the area its name, and by the Gunter family, redeploying the money generated by their fabled tearoom and high-class catering business in Berkeley Square – encouraged development for profit. Its canal and muddy creek have long since been buried by road-widening, tunnel-digging, rail-laying and the building of glassy offices, private hospitals, a supermarket, even a massive exhibition venue, in its turn now being demolished for another bout of redevelopment. In the 1920s the area was probably still clinging on to some of the 'bourgeois' gentility Lodwick evidently despised but by the 1940s, as described so well by Patrick Hamilton in *Hangover Square*, it had become a rookery of shabby squalor and was already turning into a waystation for generations of new arrivals to London. In 1954 Lodwick let his novelist's pen fly free with a vision of what life held along the Cromwell Road once the westbound traveller had passed through the stuccoed straits of South Kensington. 'Gloucester Road… Few men see that sign and return to civilisation without grave impairment to their health and enduring chaos to their soul. And this is but Purgatory. Hell is still a mile away in Earls Court.'

Lodwick would have felt more at home in Grandpapa's spacious household with its bizarre echoes of the bazaar, and, much as he may have rebelled, the British discipline and friendships of his school, even though Cheltenham was a staunchly Anglican Foundation; the head of the Preparatory School when John was there was the son of a Church of England bishop. When his mother asked the headmaster of the College itself to provide John with cubicle space for his rosary, crucifix and missal, he told her, according to Lodwick, 'We don't cater for fancy religions here', a statement at which she burst into tears. But John was at least excused chapel services and allowed instead to attend Mass in the town. Though his comments on religion in his writing and to his children in later life tend towards the sceptical, even mocking, much of what he absorbed stuck with him, and in the macabre *Brother Death*, for instance, he shows a familiarity with saints and rituals which was clearly not simply lifted from an encyclopedia.

In this context his Roman Catholic maternal grandmother's Limerick land-owning background is another puzzle, since the majority of Anglo-Irish landowners, 'The Ascendancy', were Protestants who had spent centuries in what hankerers after Empire called the 'Last Lost Raj in the Rain', excluding and extirpating Roman Catholics, the 'Taigs'. But those roots, and Lodwick's years in Dublin, may explain a later Whitehall speculation that some of John Lodwick's own traits, especially his 'agin'ness' (*À rebours* again), might be explained by his Irish roots.

Lodwick's story of his schooldays could be cut and pasted from any of the thousands of preparatory school tales of the period – exploiting teachers' foibles, doing the minimum amount of work, faking illness to avoid classes and sport, playing fanciful war games – though seemingly without the bullying and sadism others of his age reportedly experienced elsewhere.

He gives the impression in his books that his end-of-term reports were generally bad to critical, though the records do not bear this out. Even allowing for the careful prose teachers adopt when writing to those who pay the fees, they are not that bad, even though when taken together there is an undertone of hope periodically deferred: 'Most of it to his credit', 'Quite a good performance', 'Promising well again', 'The outlook continues to improve'. There is no trace of the comment he recycled in *The Asparagus Trench* that he 'Makes no progress. Continues to employ his intelligence in extra-curricular activities', a quote which may have been misremembered or embellished for effect. The detailed exam results are equally hard to read but suggest, not surprisingly given his future profession and his fondness for quotations, that English and Classics were among his stronger suits. In the autumn of 1928, a year before he left, a plunge to low positions in the main subjects hints, if we play at idle amateur psychology, at a period of particular turbulence or truculence; perhaps both. His prolific use of literary and philosophical references in his books suggests that some at least of what he absorbed in Classics must certainly have stuck with him.

John was mischievous and inventive, although most readers of *The Asparagus Trench* would award the prize for 'worst boy' at his school to 'Storey'; not necessarily his real name, though the book is a memoir, and a character with echoes of the rebel Lodwick. One of his many strikes against authority was to herd a sheep wearing a mortar board and gown into his classroom before lessons began. Rewarded with a beating, he took a carefully planned revenge on the punisher. Part of the masters' duties was to take the head of one of the boys' tables at lunch. Storey spent days sitting next to his victim, 'pestering him with loving attentions, watching fear spread from the man's eyes to his quivering jowls'. At last he struck:

'I say, Sir, I'm glad you like that meat. It's dog: I killed it myself for you.'

As John Lodwick vividly recalled, such was Storey's well-earned reputation for malevolence, the teacher believed him implicitly and, staggering to his feet, he vomited. 'Really, Sir!' Storey sneered. 'Have you been drinking again?'

In later years Cheltenham College was one of the principal though (by mutual agreement) uncredited settings for the 1968 film *If…*. It was directed by Lindsay Anderson,[4] one of its former senior prefects, himself a 'Child of the Raj', born in India, son of a Major General and a broken marriage, and a rebel from an early age. Its anarchic theme, and its culmination in a machine-gun shoot-out on the hallowed, hand-trimmed quadrangle of his old school, would have appealed to John Lodwick, and Storey might have been a model for the Malcolm McDowell role. One reviewer's comment on the film, 'a happy mixture of wrath and absurdism', might even be applied to John's life, bouncing between school, Earls Court and Grandpapa. Had he lived to see it, Captain Lodwick, a machine-gun expert, might have wondered how McDowell manages to rake the quadrangle for several minutes without reloading. In reality, his gun kept jamming, probably because he was using 'blanks'. What we see in the film is an editor's spliced-in 'loop'.

Many years later Lodwick would face and fire real bullets, not blanks, and, truth be told, rather enjoy it. But Dartmouth, Dublin and Provence lay ahead first.

4

Carry on, Sailor

Lodwick's final report from Cheltenham in 1929 told his mother and stepfather that 'His Royal Naval College success is a most creditable performance, on which I congratulate him.' Whether it was written with a slight sigh of relief, we cannot tell.

Though some accounts claim that it was as a Cheltenham schoolboy that Lodwick developed an interest in going to Dartmouth as the first step to a career in the navy, in fact his mother had indicated on the original application form that she was looking for him to follow a naval career. Why? Certainly Grandpapa had a profound aversion to seafarers. 'He must have suffered much from pursers and apple-cheeked officers in those first long voyages around the Cape,' John wrote. And with its military traditions Cheltenham was not a school which put a naval career at the forefront of its boys' ambitions.

Some of the answers might be found in his fictionalised account of his Dartmouth years, *The Cradle of Neptune*, which he wrote in the South of France in 1949 and 1950. The 'father' he invents for the story works as a Mincing Lane tea merchant. As we have seen, the real-life Captain Ruck had been a dentist attached to the Indian Army; on his return to England he practised first in the West End and later in Southsea. But dentistry may have been a profession to which Lodwick, with his disdain for the 'bourgeois' tone of Earls Court, would not have given much prominence. In the days of Empire, Mincing Lane and its tea, coffee and spice merchants – let alone its former historical role in the opium and slave trades – had more of a Lodwickian ring about it.

In the book Lodwick's 'father' is portrayed as having set his heart on a naval career as a young man but fails the Dartmouth medical because of poor eyesight. This leads him to encourage the boy as a surrogate, giving him seafaring novels from the age of seven. Here again fact and fiction blur and several other factors seem more likely. Maybe when she told Cheltenham in the original application that she and his stepfather had a naval career in mind for Lodwick, Kitty Ruck had the first forebodings of the need for discipline in a potentially wayward son. And they would doubtless have believed that, although the career might not end in a blaze of gold braid at the Admiralty, it gave men social cachet at a time when ships' movements and naval promotions – even amendments to the 'Dress Code for Officers' – were given respectful column inches in *The Times*. In an age when Britain still claimed to rule the waves, but opportunities to run the Empire in India were in sharp decline, it took young men to interesting places across the world; places where there were still magnificent dockyards over which the Union Jack fluttered, and where governors set the social tone in a style Jane Austen would have recognised. In an age of increasing economic uncertainty it was also a career which carried a decent if not outstanding pension. That lower deck life still maintained some of the traditions pithily summed up by George Melly[1] – of whom more later – as 'rum, bum and concertina' was not something to which genteel middle-class parents of potential officers gave much thought. If they did, it was with the conviction that nothing so beastly (reports from the divorce courts of the era referred euphemistically and chauvinistically to 'Hunnish practices') could ever involve 'my little lad'. Across England, at all levels from cottages to castles, the Royal Navy was far more than bell-bottoms or gold braid, or even unpleasant folk memories of Nelson-era 'press gangs'. For centuries – even before the Spanish Armada had been scattered to the four winds – the navy had been an integral element of the country's psyche, shielding the island and its Empire against enemies and challengers. A contemporary photograph by Fleet Street's Press Association of four towering battleships steaming in line, signal flags fluttering, guns menacingly ready for action, would have stirred the hearts of many parents, the Rucks among them, and their impressionable sons. The navy was a key component of a patriotism that is now long gone, even derided. Since the carnage of World War I had ended just 12 years earlier, it is no surprise that the fallen of the Great War were remembered with massive respect. Nevertheless, it takes a jaded twenty-first-century viewer aback to see another Press Association overhead shot of a crowd, for once described correctly by the caption writer as 'vast', standing bareheaded for two silent minutes outside the City of London's Mansion House on 11 November 1930.

Most are men – no doubt City workers. The sense of respect, the poignancy, are palpable, intensified by the viewer's knowledge, denied to those standing there mute and remembering, that in just nine years' time the whole bloody business would start again.

His mother may even have been swayed by a cunning marketing ploy by the navy's exclusive tailors, Gieves & Hawkes in London's Savile Row. Realising that once they had a customer they probably had him for life, and for civilian clothing as well as navy uniforms, they promoted through *The Times* a brochure with the straightforward title *How To Become a Naval Officer*, and even offered face-to-face personal advice if needed.

John Lodwick attributes his 'most creditable' performance in the Dartmouth entrance examinations – he was among the 44 who passed out of 200 applicants – less to aptitude than to the fact that he was 'a well-trained dummy', coached heavily in mathematics by a Cheltenham teacher who accurately predicted four out of seven of the exam questions. And family members fluttered about offering guidance about how to handle himself with the Interview Board: 'sit up straight', 'don't mumble', 'look them in the eye', 'try to mention India and the family', we can hear them say. Another key to his success, he remembered, was that for his compulsory essay he chose to write about Warren Hastings, of East India Company fame, whose trial records he had been reading with Grandpapa. 'Some truly stupid boys, unwisely sycophantic, chose Nelson. They did not pass.' Unlike the army's future leaders at Sandhurst, the cadets at Dartmouth, at least as seen through Lodwick's eyes, were less from the landed gentry than the 'solid middle class, with father struggling hard somewhere in the background on a thousand a year, and not too much nonsense about extras such as music lessons'. Lodwick remarks that because 'the nomenclature of the British middle classes' tended not to change with fashion, 125 of the boys in College during his time were named John.[2]

His fictional picture of Dartmouth is at its heart a study of the effects of authority on young men; whether to go along with the system or to rebel against it, as Lodwick, assuming him to be largely 'Roffey', evidently did. He arrived in September 1929, a 13-year-old overawed like most new cadets by the College's grandeur, an Edwardian confection whose exterior was replete with architectural hints of Hapsburg admiralties, lunatic asylums or the Surrey country mansions newly built by those 'hard-faced men who look as though they have done very well out of the war'. In fact it had been built by the distinguished firm of Higgs and Hill, who had constructed London's Tate Gallery and much else besides, and in what might be called their crowning achievement was the main contractor for the post-blaze restoration of Windsor Castle in 1996.

Despite its solid terrestrial magnificence, navy tradition deemed the College to be a ship, its address listed officially as 'HMS *Britannia*'. Its interior, with 'decks' rather than floors, was a maze of 'gunrooms', 'wardrooms', 'mess-halls' and a 'quarterdeck' built on the half-landing of the sweeping staircase. The cadets' cabins each had 20 'bunks' separated by 'sea chests' rather than lockers, where, as Lodwick remembered, the boys' 'slops' – 'clothes' to the ordinary mortal – were neatly arranged, socks across vests, reefer jacket folded, shirts in neat tiers, cap perched above, 'crowning all'.

As all schoolboys do, the cadets detested the monotonous diet of institutional food: bloaters and porridge for breakfast, barricaded by mini-mountains of white bread with little butter; haddock, mutton or beef of dubious origin for lunch, leaving them hungry for 'fryups' in the tuck shop. They were served cocoa (made not from familiar Cadbury's or Rowntree's tins but powdery blocks of bitter chocolate) as their mainstay drink rather than tea, and had to absorb the naval dialect, or 'Jackspeak'; entering the front door was 'coming aboard' and cadets and staff alike did not just leave, but went 'ashore'.

Lodwick was neither the first nor the last cadet to write about Dartmouth, though his was more a character-related narrative. But like the battle of Neuve Chapelle, the sharpest images are visual, such as the Pathé newsreel clips from the 1930s: almost impossibly neat young men parading in long white trousers and navy-blue jackets, the senior cadets marked out by white lanyards looped around their collars. Just a few minutes earlier, by Lodwick's account, they would have been woken by yells of 'Show a Leg!' This was yet another Jackspeak phrase, said to have originated in Nelson's time when sailors were not allowed shore leave but could bring their 'wives' on board to share a connubial if less than private hammock. When the men were rousted out for morning duty the girls could snooze or snore on, and would wave a more or less hairless calf to show who they were. It seems rather out of place for an all-male Naval College, but traditions die hard, and when the Petty Officer bellowed the boys rushed (or more often dawdled) to the cold water plunge pool and pulled on their uniforms. A few film frames and a quick change later sees them in the gym in shorts and long socks, vaulting, climbing ropes or going through endless and painful exercises. Yet another change of gear and locale, and we are watching earnest groups in their classrooms. Though French was still taught, there was the relief of no more Latin or Greek. Instead, after the basics of knots, rope splicing, semaphore signalling and Morse code had been drummed in, the cadets were indoctrinated into the deeper mysteries of their chosen calling. They built model boats, and furrowed their brows over textbooks on dynamics, electricity, mechanics, trigonometry, chemistry, draughtsmanship, even welding and metal moulding; every skill the Admiralty believed they needed to understand how a ship was put together, how it worked, how to make sure it went more or less in the right direction and what to do if something went wrong. There were lessons in practical boat-handling; Lodwick recalls, or creates, a harrowing scene in which through his own clumsiness Roffey (curiously the name of a cadet who, according to a report in *The Times*, had died at the College shortly before John joined) is responsible for the drowning of a fellow cadet on a 'Man Overboard' drill. The boys were kept fit in the gym, where they also boxed, and outside, whatever the weather, they played hockey, soccer and rugby, and puffed and panted over the hills in cross-country races. A taste of what the future might hold if they were successful was provided by sorties on sloops and destroyers, where wonder and bewilderment were mixed with terror at 'letting down the side' by being noisily seasick. Lodwick writes elsewhere about eating cucumber sandwiches 'as a child in uniform' on board the cruiser HMS *York* and the aircraft carrier HMS *Courageous*.

Lodwick had been a natural rebel at his prep school. Roffey fights authority at Dartmouth, and it seems highly likely that it is his mother, as 'Mrs Roffey', to whom Lodwick attributes some well-meant, if nervously delivered, remarks over the breakfast table:

> 'We think there may be something in you – something you perhaps don't know about – which is resisting the Navy, resisting its discipline, resisting everything in the last resort just for the <u>sake</u> of resisting.'

So they had arranged for him to see a psychiatrist.

It didn't work. Roffey stonewalled the attempt to analyse, and even hypnotise him and the best the consultant could murmur to his mother as he took his fee was that his parents shouldn't worry. 'You could call it a refusal to grow up. There's confusion in his mind between the real and the unreal. He probably has a very intense secret life.' (Lodwick may well have based his image of the consultant's rooms on a memory of Charles Ruck's surgery, which was then in Upper Wimpole Street.)

That 'secret life' began with the games Lodwick and his friends had invented in the walled gardens of his Cheltenham school, and had evolved far beyond the conventional schoolboy rites of 'Roundheads and Cavaliers' to Lodwick's invention of a new country of the mind, confusingly called 'Liberia': 'A rugger-playing monarchy in whose highlands and forests lurked armed bands ever at variance with each other, united only in opposition to the central authorities.' As the adult Lodwick wrote, 'One way and another I have lived there ever since.' When the boys picked sides for one or other of their freetime games he claimed he had nothing against the British. 'When they were fighting the French I was loyally upon their side, but on the private plane they represented authority and were therefore to be opposed implacably', a childhood sentiment which, as we follow his life, will explain much about him. It is a sentiment echoed in reverse in a manual issued to British soldiers kitting up for the invasion of in 1944. They were cautioned that

> The French... are not tolerant of authority... Their first reaction to a uniform or regulation is not to obey unquestioningly but to ask whether it is necessary and make disrespectful comments if they decide it is not. This is all part of the Frenchman's deep belief in the individual. He is convinced of the right to think for himself and voice his criticisms aloud.[3]

Little wonder that in later life Lodwick felt so much at home in France.

Imagination and wide reading must have played equal parts in his Dartmouth book, *The Cradle of Neptune*. In a plot which revolves around purloined postal orders, the story has hints of Rattigan's *The Winslow Boy*, of Graham Greene in the conscientious, homespun local parish priest and the faith-troubled Carnell, a sneak thief *malgré lui*, and of Evelyn Waugh's *A Handful of Dust* in the sidebar story of Captain Bouchard held hostage in China by a mad missionary. (In another sleight of pen, 'Bouchard' is the name of a Company Commander under whom Lodwick would later serve in the Foreign Legion and, as we shall speculate later, the rather obvious borrowing from Waugh may have prompted the latter to a literary side-swipe soon after *The Cradle* appeared.) Lodwick's Catholicism, shared by Roffey, also set him slightly apart. Like Cheltenham, Dartmouth was Church of England to its core. But it did at least acknowledge, though not necessarily embrace, Roman Catholics, who were excused from church services and sitting though what were then known as 'Divinity' lessons.[4]

When the College Chaplain opened his prayer book at morning parades it was the signal for a Petty Officer to bellow, 'Roman Catholics… fall out!' and 20 or 30 boys would hurry away behind a wall 'to gabble a few Hail Marys… and recite the unenthusiastic orisons of the Papists'. In their wake trailed two or three Jewish boys and 'the occasional Mohammedan' (in Lodwick's words) who, though not officially recognised, were also tacitly excused rites they might well find confusing if not actually blasphemous.

Jumping ahead for a moment, since George Orwell and his chum Georges Kopp appear later, this element of Lodwick's story brings to mind Orwell's dour picture of his own time at prep school (a picture disputed by many fellow pupils) and his attitude to religion. As he wrote in 'Such, Such Were the Joys', he believed in God until he was 14 'but I was aware that I did not love him… in the New Testament my friends, if any were Ananias, Caiaphas, Judas, and Pontius Pilate.' (For those without the benefit of a Divinity Prize Bible, the first was struck dead for holding back part of the proceeds of a land sale instead of giving it all to the church, and then lying about it; the second was the High Priest who accused Christ of blasphemy; the last pair neither need nor deserve an introduction.)[5]

Lodwick appears in the College Passing Out List in April 1933, admittedly amongst the tail-enders academically, in Class 3 of Division 2, but there is no trace that he followed the career path ordained for Dartmouth alumni: spells at sea and at the Old College in Greenwich. Given what he suggests were his critical reports and his rebel streak, it would be no surprise if his mother and stepfather were politely discouraged from keeping him on. Formal expulsion, as Lodwick noted wryly, was an 'irremediable step rarely applied… reserved for gross indecency and for crime which would have sent the boy, had he lived in another walk of life, to Borstal.' But Borstal – the generic term for correctional centres intended to give wayward young men 'a short, sharp shock' – was happily not the next stop on his personal pilgrimage, though in later life he saw the inside of far more unpleasant houses of detention and made do with 'food' which would have made the Dartmouth fare seem like the Ritz.

But that is jumping too far ahead. Our next sighting of him is in the damp dreamland of 1930s Dublin.

5

Dublin's Fair City

Lodwick's life between leaving Dartmouth in 1933, aged 17, and turning up a year or two later in Dublin brings to mind Lytton Strachey's comment about Queen Victoria's widowhood: 'With Albert's death, a veil descends. Only occasionally, at fitful and disconnected intervals, does it lift for a moment or two.' So too with our less regal subject. His claim that he knew the Channel Islands and the Brittany coast well through service with the Merchant Navy, made to the British authorities when he was pushing to join the clandestine services in World War II, may relate to these 'gap years' or equally to his post-Dublin drift towards France. But since the claims were never checked and are thus not documented, their time frame remains a mystery.

We get a clearer view of his tracks on Dublin's rain-slicked streets, where barefoot boys scampered between the donkey carts, hawking apples and newspapers as Lodwick looked for lodgings, carrying his cardboard suitcase of half-written stories, dreams and spare collars. The Dublin turns of the Roundabout's magic wheel are the background to some fascinating professional and personal stories and introduce us to several larger-than-life characters and one sad riddle, whose real explanation is likely never to be known. It is even harder to find why he actually went there. One account claims that it was the advice of his then literary agent. But how could a young, unpublished striver have attracted the attention of any commercially minded agent? It is hardly a surprise, at this distance in time, that the successor to the firm which acted for him in his heyday has no record of any such dialogue or advice.

His grandmother on his mother's side was from Limerick and he had enjoyed several months with an uncle in Omagh 'during the Troubles', but claiming deep Irish roots would be a stretch. Writing many years later, he said that 'by lumping my grandmothers together and combing the family tree on both sides' he could claim to be five-eighths Irish. Given its turbulent history, Ireland seems a natural fit for a bred-in-the-bone rebel like Lodwick, but his later attempts to break into the world of Dublin theatre, with the support of his maternal grandfather, General Ashbrooke Crump, suggests that what really prompted the move was a family effort, after Dartmouth led nowhere, to get the boy on a new tack, a new start in a new place.

But there he was. Who then drew him into the liquorish world of letters, many of whose garrulous illuminati he got to know well? Where and how he met them is hard to pin down, since he never completed his autobiography. Did he meet Yeats, George Bernard Shaw, Synge, Sean O'Casey or Samuel Beckett? It would need only one or two of the notional 'degrees of separation' to allow us to state with some confidence that he did.

To extend the Lytton Strachey reference, glimpses of Lodwick in Dublin are just that: glimpses. A recent commentator on one of the poets who wrote for the arts journal *Ireland Today*,[1] a short-lived (1936 to 1938) but important periodical, mentions Lodwick in passing as 'a shadowy name' amongst its contributors. It was so long ago that we are left to speculate whether Lodwick's contribution was a poem, a story or a piece about the theatre.

We get a clearer view of Lodwick in April 1937 when he wrote to Sean O'Casey from 18 Upper Fitzwilliam Street, an elegant and as yet unviolated building in the heart of Georgian and literary Dublin, asking his permission to stage the writer's dark drama *Within the Gates*. This was an early step in a Lodwick venture – ambitious for a man in his twenties – to launch himself as a playwright and producer. In February that year he and two partners, one of them from an Irish theatrical family, had launched the Stage Society ('yet another', the *Irish Times* sighed), which planned to use the Peacock Theatre, in fact a space inside the better-known Abbey, 'to present plays of a controversial nature not seen hitherto in Ireland'. Against the grain, again.

O'Casey's play had been produced in New York, with Lillian Gish in a starring role, and in a London theatre club, but though Lodwick was concerned that in Ireland it would attract the hostility of the Church, he felt, in typical Lodwick style, that it was something he could deal with. O'Casey replied:

It isn't a question of the Catholic Church's opposition – though believe me, the Catholic Church in Ireland won't 'hump off' as easily as you think. And I have as much experience of its opposition as any other playwright. I am sorry about *Within the Gates*. But it can't be helped – I can't give the play to you.[2]

Despite this setback, the new group's ambitions were considerable. Its first production would be Lodwick's own *The Basket of Fruit*, followed by what their publicity claimed was James Joyce's only play, *Exiles*, and C.S. Forester's *U 97*. The latter is set in a German U-boat officers' mess in 1918, where the impending Armistice raises fears that some of them might be arraigned as 'war criminals'; Lodwick may have chosen it with his father's oil-soaked drowning at the hands of Max Valentiner in mind.

A later venture was Shelley's *The Cenci*, whose tale of Beatrice, beheaded along with her mother, stepmother and brother for the murder of her abusive father, would have appealed to Lodwick but not, one might think, the matrons of Dublin. Written in 1819 but long blacklisted by the Lord Chamberlain, Britain's home-grown censor, because of its subplot of incest, it finally had its first public performance in England in 1922, but a private production in 1886 had a neat Irish connection, with Oscar Wilde and George Bernard Shaw among the audience at the Grand Theatre, Islington. In July the *Irish Times* drama correspondent noted tartly that the Stage Society's future productions included *Going Off Gold*, the title of which explained itself (no doubt a reference to Britain's 1931 abandonment of the Gold bullion metric for sterling), and Lodwick's *This Hot Hereafter*, 'which does not'. Lodwick himself admitted later that his own plays were 'a tiresome constrictive form of art necessarily divided into acts and scenes within a creaking framework'. O'Casey had a better sense than Lodwick that the Irish Censors were not a body which it would be easy to 'hump off'. The Censorship Board met in secret and never explained how it determined what books and magazines were 'indecent' or 'obscene'. Later on, as we shall see, it would target Lodwick, among a host of more prominent literary notables. Presenting avant-garde plays and poking fingers in the eyes of the Establishment must have been great fun, but in the absence of 'smash hits' it is hard to see it paying the rent and food bills, let alone for evenings in saloons like Toner's or Kennedy's, the cosy comfort of the well-rubbed wood panelling and the Victorian bevelled glass bar screens, reinforced by thick glasses of Guinness, the fug from Sweet Afton cigarettes and the booming surf of the endless chatter. His other earnings must have been meagre. We can only point to anecdotal evidence of Lodwick as an occasional contributor to the now-defunct *News Chronicle* in London, and working as an advertising copywriter. The homespun style of Irish advertisements suggests he was more likely to have been working for media in Britain, but whatever he was doing it must have been a hand-to-mouth existence.

We can conjecture about whom he knew or didn't know in that hotbed of writing and drama. We are on firmer ground looking at the men who in their different ways influenced him then and later. There was a woman too, but that is a separate strand of our story.

Francis Stuart (1902–2000), Walter (Fitzwilliam) Starkie, CMG, CBE, LittD, (1894–1976), Georges Pelorson (as he was then known) (1909–2008) and John Collins (1883–1954) are men whom we can describe as Lodwick would have known them at the time, and again as they reappeared in his later life.[3] Take Stuart. To know him back then was to know a struggling but already much talked-about poet and playwright, whose early work was described by the *New York Times* as 'mystical and talented' but whose postwar recognition as one of Ireland's 'men of letters' was always grudging, bedevilled by controversy over his World War II broadcasts from Nazi Germany. How and where he became one of Lodwick's close friends, evidenced by warm mutual book dedications and conversations Stuart had with one of his own biographers, is lost in the sands of time, and though they must have run into each other in the convivial confraternity of literary Dublin life, letters surviving in Lodwick's papers show the relationship was warmly rekindled after World War II.

Stuart's childhood – an alcoholic father who committed suicide, a jolting return from Australia to the chilly rituals of an English public school – segued into an Irish life, mainly devoted to writing but with diversions into chicken farming, horse racing and breeding, together with a complicated marital and extramarital life, the whole overlain with a strong spirituality and horrendously complicated by his German connections in 1930s Dublin and his aberrant behaviour in World War II. His life and work have been put under the microscope in innumerable research papers and three biographies. Kevin Kiely's study, based on many talks with his subject and the family, and backed by solid research, probably gives the fullest picture of this enigmatic, mystic, reckless and promiscuous talent, though over everything written about him there hangs a nagging sense of elusiveness and even casuistry.[4]

Stuart had been a Republican militant and spent time in jail for a minor foray into gunrunning, all of which is understandable in the context of Ireland as it was. One of his early books was published in the US, with an accolade from the Jesuit head of America's Catholic Book Club, his poems appeared in the Irish press, and he also found time to write *Racing for Pleasure and Profit*, a one-shilling guide to the Irish Turf; he followed horses with an informed passion until the end of his life. In contrast to the thrills, spills and disappointments of the Leopardstown Racecourse there was the *Irish Academy of Letters*, more cerebral than racing but just as prone to heated arguments about form, style and staying power. Stuart wrote years later about how he became involved. It was a chance encounter on a Dublin pavement with W.B. Yeats,[5] who told him he and George Bernard Shaw wanted Stuart to become a founder member of 'an association we are establishing to oppose the censorship introduced by these nonentities of ours in their effort to establish a safe parochialism here'. Quite a mouthful for a meeting on the street, but then this was Dublin. The anecdote blithely begs the question of the emotional cross-currents which flowed murkily between the two men. The years of Yeats' barrage of marriage proposals to Maude Gonne, all of them rejected, have been fully described by others, as has Yeats' volte-face in proposing to Maude's daughter Iseult, who also refused him. In 1920 Iseult, conceived on a French tomb and born out of wedlock, had eloped to London with none other than Francis Stuart. If the story had played out in Italy, it would have ended with a duel.

But this was Dublin, and Stuart's later retelling of this tale says only that while his instinct was to decline on the spot, he didn't because 'because of a reluctance to appear disrespectful'. Rather an understatement. Yeats was widely considered one of the greatest poets of the twentieth century, had been awarded the Nobel Prize for Literature in 1923, and was a prime mover behind the Abbey Theatre. It was as if in an earlier, foggy age a struggling London poet had been stopped in The Strand by Dickens and asked to join a new literary group pushing for more press freedom.

So Stuart joined, and in March was one of the 13 members – the 'genial, versatile' and ubiquitous Walter Starkie among them – who dined well and verbosely in the Blue Room of Jammet's Restaurant with Yeats in the chair. (In a city not renowned as a gourmet Mecca, Jammet's stood out as a beacon of French cuisine. Like much of Georgian Dublin, Jammet's is long gone and much missed. It closed in 1967 and is now a gastropub.) Stuart was also called into polemic action, writing to the *Irish*

Times to refute the arguments of a Jesuit priest that the Irish Academy of Letters might better be called the Anglo-Irish Academy and implying that real Irish literature should be written in Gaelic, and about Ireland. As it happens, Lodwick's first novel takes as its title *Running to Paradise*, a borrowing from Yeats himself. But there is more. The Dublin literary world was a tiny, self-obsessed community and Lodwick must have been acutely aware of the emotional ties which connected Yeats, Stuart and the two powerfully temperamental Gonne women, adding another shamrock leaf of seasoning to this Irish stew of intellect and passion and beginning a saga of alleged espionage, infidelity and unhappiness which would not end until Iseult died in 1954.

Men Crowd Me Round, a Stuart play presented at the Abbey Theatre in 1933, drew what was described as 'harsh criticism'. An anonymous correspondent for *The Times* told its London readers that 'many may be found who think that Mr. Stuart has failed utterly. Attempting the fantastic in terms of the realistic, all that he could do was make his characters seem absurd.' Little surprise, then, that it ran for only seven performances.

We find Stuart contributing to *Innisfail*, a new magazine about Irish life (its title is a poetical name for Ireland), writing poetry for the *Irish Times* and working on the screenplay for the 1935 film of Synge's play *Riders to the Sea*. He was given second credit for the adaptation. The producer was Brian Desmond Hurst, an Ulsterman and Gallipoli veteran who after a bohemian spell in Europe became a Hollywood film-maker to be reckoned with. The film was part financed by the much-loved singer and music hall star Gracie Fields.

Georges Pelorson, another of Lodwick's Dublin friends, was a man whose real persona slips through the fingers like mercury through a fork. He had been a Reader in French at Trinity College from 1929 to 1931, but came back often in the years that followed, not least because of his close friendship with Samuel Beckett, once a pupil. Pelorson was remembered and much admired as a lecturer, and captured for posterity by the Dublin press for sporting a 'huge bent pipe', his fondness for bridge, his excellent tennis and his ability to 'mix a neat cocktail'. He also acted, playing the title role in a College production of Jean Giraudoux's four-act drama *Siegfried*, based on the author's novel *Siegfried et le Limousin*. But he was more vividly remembered for two Peacock Theatre performances of *Le Kid*, a parody by Beckett of a play by the French dramatist Corneille. Pelorson contributed heavily to the script and played an onstage, albeit back of stage, role, moving the hands of a prop clock which was key to the narrative. The first performance, the review of which suggests it was a dress rehearsal mainly attended by students, had the audience cheering. The second, played to a more staid audience of academics and critics, fell flat, and Beckett was berated by the University's Corneille 'expert' for putting on a 'frivolous, irresponsible and juvenile' play. But as Pelorson told an interviewer many years later,[6] though his time in Dublin came to an end, Ireland had become his second home, 'my homeland of the heart. And sometimes I find myself needing Ireland, taking an airplane and going to stay for four or five days in the West.' He was hardly the first to contrast its magic with the 'terrible weight of Catholic censure' and the 'medieval power' of the Church, which had driven the country's greatest writers into exile. A postwar letter, written under his new name, Georges Belmont – a complicated story we shall come to later – tells us that at some time in 1936 he and Lodwick had found themselves discussing the world's need for a modern-day Aristophanes, the classical writer of comedy with a gift for ridicule. Though Ireland had much to admire, it also had aspects which even then deserved to be mocked, through there was a price to be paid.

In 'Sailing to Byzantium' Yeats declares, 'That is no country for old men', a phrase used not so long ago as the title of a fine novel and equally fine movie. Nor was Ireland a country for free spirits, who often faced the choice of knuckling under or emigrating, one of the messages in Yeats' poem. The Censorship, which we look at later, was a prime example of the country's costive attitude and made its British near equivalent, the Lord Chamberlain, seem like a libertarian paragon in comparison. The harsh, in many cases savage attitude of the Church – and it has to be said a large cross-section of the public – towards unmarried mothers and their hapless babies was another harsh feature of Irish life; both have their place later in our story. In fairness we have to remember that Ireland was not England. It had gone through more than one revolution against British rule, and its own Civil War, and had emerged in Lodwick's time as essentially rural, Church-dominated and conservative. Writing of its early history, one British academic commented that 'few countries… had been more actively misgoverned' by London, which in the seventeenth century had destroyed the natural leaders of the Catholic Celts and given their lands to 'a garrison of alien landlords'. Even in the later eighteenth century 'Protestant ascendancy remained unimpaired. The gates of political power were still closed on the Catholics and the peasants tilled the soil to pay tithes to an alien Church and rent to an alien squirearchy.' Folk memory went back centuries: the abortive French attempt to land 14,000 troops in 1796, in support of a planned rebellion, which was savagely put down by the British; the famines; the power of the Ascendancy landlords; the savagery with which the British put down the Easter Rising; and the brutality of the 'Black and Tans', though the extremes of Irish nationalism and factionalism were hardly blameless.[7]

Radio programmes in Britain at the time were hardly a feast of fun and laughter but a random sample of a day's Dublin programming, which on one station did not start until 5.30 p.m., gives the flavour. It offered listeners 'A Talk for Women on Loose Covers', music, a talk on 'The Irish as Missionaries' followed by another on 'Great Irishmen – Roger Casement', 15 minutes of harp music, Gaelic Poetry, 'Have a *Céilí* in Your Home', and a Jesuit priest earnestly laying down the rules for 'The Good Citizen'.

Putting Ireland behind him, but not out of his memory, back in France Pelorson became a *littérateur*, busily contributing poems and reviews to avant-garde Paris journals such as *Transitions*, 'an international review for Orphic creation' and the far more distinguished *La Nouvelle Revue Française*. We shall meet him again with Lodwick on the postwar French Riviera, by which time his world, like France itself, had been turned upside-down, as indeed had Lodwick's. By then Pelorson had changed his name and brushed over his ambiguous war years, much as a golfer takes the handy rake to smooth out any dips and bumps in the bunker sand, walking backwards to erase his footprints too. Not, however, those of Lodwick, whom he used as the hero, or anti-hero, of a 1966 novel, again a subject for later. Meantime, there are other people we need to introduce, less controversial perhaps but in their own way no less gifted, and in the case of John Collins, someone whose family relationship with Lodwick left lasting scars.

6

Faces in the Rain

Walter Starkie, for instance, was a personality who must have made a powerful impression on the young Lodwick. While he and Lodwick moved in the same Dublin circles, the latter was a small but fiery comet whirling through a larger galaxy in which Starkie was already a recognised planet. Under British rule, Starkie's father, a Greek classicist, had been Resident Commissioner for Education in Ireland, and his children grew up in the genteel upper stratum of Edwardian Dublin; a French Governess ensured that they also grew up Francophone and Francophile. Walter's sister Enid became a distinguished French scholar[1] and although his prodigious talent on the violin won him a scholarship at the Royal Irish Academy of Music, he decided against a professional career and gained further honours at Trinity College, Dublin, in Classics, History and Politics before being appointed the College's first Professor of Spanish. As a colleague wrote, 'men of this kind are rare; but they should be treasured when they do appear'[2] and, to judge from the columns of the *Irish Times*, he appeared as a prominent figure in every area of 1930s Dublin society, civic as well as literary and artistic. He had served as the government-nominated director on the Board of the Abbey Theatre and, uncharacteristically, as a member of the Film Censorship Board, set up in 1923 to counter 'the menace of Hollywood'. Starkie was steeped in Irish, Spanish and Romany history, and was a man of consummate energy, translating Spanish classics, broadcasting, one month roughing it with Gypsies across the Hungarian *puszta*, the next ferreting for folklore in Romanian villages before steaming off on a lecture tour of the US and Canada. He also pushed, unsuccessfully, for a Chair at Oxford. Some claim that his two books about his wanderings with the Romany people are closer to 'real' travel writing than the poetic transports of others, and among many other books and translations he wrote the introduction to the reprint of George Borrow's classic Gypsy tale *Lavengro*.[3]

Starkie, who was married to an Italian, was briefly attracted to her home country's model of a corporatist state, but though in later life he also mixed with the right-wing Croix de Feu in France, as did Lodwick, there is no trace of his taking sides in Irish polemics or the debate about Spain. Starkie too has been much written about, notably by Jacqueline Hurtley,[4] and we can leave him for now until his path crosses Lodwick's again in Franco's Spain.

On the face of it John Collins personified much that Pelorson, Lodwick and the bohemian world of central Dublin so profoundly disliked about Irish attitudes. The son of a borough constable, he was an upright, staunchly Roman Catholic career civil servant. Born in 1883 and educated by the unyieldingly tough Christian Brothers at their Mount Sion school in Waterford's Barrack Street, he made little career headway under the Anglo-Irish administration, until the creation of the Irish Free State in 1922 gave him more opportunity to move slowly up the Civil Service hierarchy as a specialist in public health and local government, and he is remembered by one of his family as a weekend, beach-strolling confidant of the canny Irish leader Eamon de Valera. Though Collins had a strong interest in the theatre and literature, was widely read, and was much influenced by John Stuart Mill's philosophy of utilitarian government, he is also remembered as a man who was 'deeply religious but whose mind had an astringent, sceptical cast; in private life he was unworldly'.[5] That may be so. He may also have been rather perceptive. John Collins was one of the first to open Lodwick's eyes to the world of literature. Of more relevance to our story – at least for now – he also had a son and two daughters, one of whom moved centrally but all too briefly and sadly into Lodwick's life; and, possibly, his heart.

These were the 1930s when stronger winds were again gusting across Europe. Many were the consequences, unforeseen by short-sighted statesmen, of the treaties which were supposed to draw a line under 'the war to end all wars'. One which had its home-grown roots was the Civil War in Spain. Among those involved were George Orwell – for whom the conflict collapsed with a nasty wound and deep disillusion with Communism – and Georges Kopp, the Belgian chameleon who was Orwell's commander in Spain and whom Lodwick was to meet a few short years later in the polyglot embrace of the Foreign Legion, and again after World

War II.[6] Like several others in this story, the Russian-born Kopp (1902–51) was a man who buffed up his record. There is no doubt, though, that he was a hero in the Civil War and its bloodstained internal sideshows. He was later a less than successful entrepreneur and an 'asset' for British intelligence. His life has been well sketched by Marc Wildemeersch.[7]

This is Lodwick's story, not a history of prewar Europe. At the time he and his friends were more preoccupied with the fight for personal fame and – hopefully – fortune against the backdrop of Dublin's literary fads, feuds and 'talk' rather than what was happening in the cities and olive groves of Spain, and the atrocities committed by both sides. That said, it would have been impossible for Lodwick to ignore what was going on. In Britain and across Europe, furious debates and the taking of sides over what was happening in Spain overwhelmed the generation of the Thirties with what the historian A.J.P. Taylor called 'the emotional experience of their lifetime'. Irish public opinion, led by the Church – one priest told his congregation that 'the rifle is a holy weapon' – and most of the press leaned heavily towards Franco and protection of the Roman Catholic Church against Republican and Communist anti-clerical attacks and brutality. The 'Irish Christian Front' laid on special excursion trains to Dublin from every corner of the country for a national demonstration which would show that 'Ireland Rejects Communism'.

The Irish government prudently decided to support non-intervention and to discourage overt involvement. Officially, that is. On the ground in Ireland, there were volunteers aplenty. Their support had the perhaps rather typically Irish feature that factions who had fought bitterly on opposing sides in Ireland's own Civil War, and in later street battles, went to Spain to fight each other again.

Supporting Franco, battling for their Church and to prevent Communism taking hold in Spain were the 700 Roman Catholic men of the *Brigada Irlandesa*, selected from a much larger number of volunteers and led by Eoin O'Duffy, who had commanded Ireland's extreme right-wing Blueshirt movement, and later the Greenshirts, who made no secret of their Fascism. The *Brigada* went off to Spain amid cheers, blessed by the Church, their banners held high.

If they were in the Blue corner, in the Red was the smaller but equally passionate Connolly Column, commemorating James Connolly, executed by the British for his part in the Easter Rising, and not surprisingly made up in the main of supporters of the IRA or the Republican Congress. It went off to war with far less fanfare, and fought bravely but ultimately in vain with the larger International Brigades.

Surprisingly perhaps, given his appetite for risk, we can't find a trace of Lodwick anywhere in the imbroglio. A few years later, like a moth to a flame, he would be dangerously attracted to larger wars. For the moment he had more domestic concerns, which, though far removed from the battlefront, must have weighed hard on him. The first clue was found in a passing reference in an SOE file, and it was later given substance by family sources. It will bring us back again to the power of the Church.

In a nutshell, Lodwick got married. As usual, the story is far from simple and 'nutshell' does it less than justice.

7

'A Marriage has been Arranged'

John Collins left his mark on Lodwick's life and on his mind. As Lodwick did on his. Lodwick remembered him as 'almost the first person I met who taught me about good literature and it was fascinating to listen to him'. Though it would be easy to typecast Collins by schooling, religion and profession as an instinctive supporter of The Censorship and other Irish moral straitjackets, he introduced Lodwick to the works of, among others, the essayist de Quincey and gave him a pocket edition of the erratic Mancunian genius's collected essays, neither a book nor an author which at first blush one would have thought would appeal to a conservative Catholic civil servant. Collins was a loyalist, but might actually have shared de Quincey's dim view of Ireland, admittedly dating back to the 1840s, as a country whose 'luxury of excess indolence' had led it into 'a savage life', one out of four of its people 'fierce, famished and without prospect of regular employment', a country which exported 'the contagion and causes of pauperism amongst their neighbours'.[1] But of more relevance for us the collection included not only the *Confessions of an English Opium-Eater*, and his satirical essay 'On Murder Considered As One Of the Fine Arts' must have affected Lodwick's *noir* fiction.

We turn back to John Collins' family and specifically his elder daughter, born in Dublin on 27 December 1914. She was christened Dorothea ('God's gift' in Classical Greek, but perhaps her literary father was remembering the heroine of *Middlemarch*) but soon changed it to Dorothy. She entered Lodwick's life – and maybe his heart – irreversibly when she married him in the Roman Catholic Church at Booterstown, on the southern outskirts of Dublin, on 30 October 1937.

There were two witnesses, one an Edward Jones, the other a lady whose name is unclear. Despite, or perhaps because of, his rather precarious life in the theatre (his approach to O'Casey about the Stage Society had been just a few months earlier)

Lodwick described himself as an 'advertising agent', rather than a copywriter or theatrical producer, and gave his address as 18 Herbert Street. Despite the depredations of developers and the crash of the wrecker's ball, Herbert Street, close to the heart of Dublin, has retained many of its fine Georgian facades, including No. 18, now the office of a digital media company. Intriguingly there may also be links to Pelorson, Beckett and the French scholar Enid Starkie – Walter's sister – since at the time No. 18 also housed the French Cultural Centre, forerunner of the modern *Alliance Française.*

Whom Lodwick told about the marriage and its background is as unclear as one of Dublin's nicknames: 'The Big Smoke'. Lodwick family memory has it that even though his mother made no mention of it in the scrupulous family tree she drew up for her grandchildren, she did in fact know, but by background and religion was inclined to be prudish and above all anxious to bury any hint of scandal.

The lichen of time and memory has long since overgrown the paving stones on John and Dorothy's pathway to the altar. Perhaps that is just as well, since even if we could scrape away at it for longer it would involve pain and conjecture far outweighing the unlikely prospect of actually finding the truth, not least as the principal actors are dead.

Dorothy was pregnant, a fact which in much of the West today would likely cause no more than a puzzled and pained parental frown, a slightly embarrassed conversation about whether she wanted to go through with it, and, whatever her decision, a resigned shrug. But in 1930s Ireland it was the equivalent of Hester Prynne's 'Scarlet Letter'. The options for an unmarried mother were few and grim. Even more so for her child. It was not unknown, though not at the Collins' social and urban level, for a newborn infant to be killed at birth, hastily buried in a ditch or distant wood. If a child was placed in a chilly Catholic orphanage it might also die young, whether out of neglect, hard work or something more dreadful and systemic because of the deep-rooted conviction that illegitimate children had no place in society. The Church held fast to its dogma that an unwed mother and her child (but not, it seems, the father) were to be excised from the mainstream of Irish life. Unless the family or the father stuck by her the mother had a stark choice. She could give up her baby and find an uncertain future as a 'skivvy' in some rich household. Or she could wrap herself in a shawl of shame and take the ferry across to England, have the baby in a public hospital and try to eke out a living in a factory or domestic service, either keeping the child or sending it back home to her family as a 'cuckoo in the nest', whose background was never fully explained.

The story of John and Dorothy, fuzzy though it is, has some of these elements. We have a few hard facts: the marriage certificate, a couple of ambiguous letters from Lodwick to Dorothy, the redacted family tree drawn up by his mother, and hazy family memories, including a conversation with Dorothy's son, who did not take the Lodwick name. Do they give us the facts? Far from it. We are left to ask: was it Lodwick's child, and was the marriage his way of 'doing the decent thing'? Or was the father, as Lodwick later claimed, a friend of his who took fright and scarpered when told a baby was on the way, and Lodwick stepped up to the plate and the altar as a courageous or foolhardy surrogate?

Bizarrely, the only written version we have dates from much later and is refracted through the imagination of Georges Belmont, formerly Pelorson, who took as the central theme of his 1966 novel *Un homme au crépuscule* a story he claimed he had been told by a Dublin friend thinly fictionalised as 'John', a painter. The title translates as 'A Man at Twilight', a none-too-subtle echo of Lodwick's 1949 book *Just a Song at Twilight* and, as we shall see later, explicable only as a thinly disguised and embroidered retelling of Lodwick's spell in the South of France. True or false we cannot tell: a Lodwick alibi confected or enlarged by self-justification, an embroidery from Belmont's fertile mind, or bits of both. But the main elements are broadly in line with what we know, and with family memories, though the overall tone of the book is one the family rightly find distasteful. In Belmont's novel, he and John argue, swagger and often sway, drinking, as someone once remarked in another context, 'like the Russians – to get drunk'. Belmont writes that when the two men chatted about marriage in the late 1940s 'John' claimed he could not remarry, because he had exchanged marriage vows in a Catholic country, where divorce, always anathema to the Church, had been officially declared illegal in 1925, and was simply not an option. He had married – Belmont's version again – because the girl was pregnant by his best friend. When the 'friend' found out he suddenly discovered an urgent need to go 'home to the Antipodes' (whether Australia or New Zealand, we are not told) and Lodwick had taken his place at the altar. The 'friend' never returned. Lodwick had gone through with it because he had made a mistake in giving his friendship and his trust to a 'coward', and it was up to him to put it right. Belmont claims that his fictional hero didn't know his bride-to-be, a claim that is hard to believe since in real life Lodwick and John Collins were close, and even if the shadowy 'friend' existed his path would inevitably have crossed those of Dorothy and Lodwick somewhere or other on their closed social circuit. Belmont lets his imagination run even further by telling his readers that when the pair did meet they realised they could never love one another. But she had gone along with the arrangement so her baby could have a legitimate father. They had gone their separate ways after the wedding ceremony and though they kept in contact by letter, and he sent her money, they never saw each other again.

One can pick many holes in this version, not just by asking whether it is actually plausible or inventive Lodwick bravado; or by questioning Belmont's detail, his motives or his memory. Some of the supposedly circumstantial detail isn't quite right, for instance quoting Lodwick's description of the cowardly friend from Down Under as 'a student like him', since Lodwick had long since left Cheltenham and Dartmouth behind him, while Lodwick's later letters make clear that there was some contact with Dorothy and her father long after the wedding. Indeed, if read in one light, Lodwick's 1938 letter, which we shall look at in more detail below, could well be read as implying that she left him. Whatever the facts – a pregnant daughter, a scramble to the altar, thin-lipped, forced smiles for the guests, many of whom would have guessed or even known the truth; even a reception and a wedding cake – they would have been a hammer blow to Dorothy's parents, living as they did by the rules of a prudishly straitjacketed professional, Church and social framework.

It is hard to imagine, whatever the underlying facts and tensions, that Lodwick and Dorothy would have parted unceremoniously and stony-faced at the church door. The Collinses were a family of standing, and the expectations at the 'top end' of society would have been for a solemn black and white procession of top hats and morning coats, with bridesmaids in tulle and organdie. To have had a 'quiet' ceremony in that close-knit community would seem practically impossible. The Church of the Assumption in Booterstown was hardly the place for a quiet wedding. Built in fine Regency style in 1812, it looks more like a rather grand town house or a library than a place of worship. It reflects yet another quirk of Irish life. Since the local landowner, the 7th Viscount Fitzwilliam, was paying for it, he was able to instruct the architects to design a structure that would not offend his local Protestant tenants and Dublin Ascendancy friends. This was a prominent church and the wedding of the daughter of a prominent member of the community. The banns would have had to be read from the pulpit on the three Holy Days of Obligation before the wedding. Bride and groom would have called on the priest for a quiet homily about what marriage meant, and his blessing. Invitations must have been sent out well in advance, rooms booked for the reception, a cake and flowers ordered, wedding presents delivered. So for Lodwick to have been slipped in to substitute for his friend as a last-minute 'ringer', to use the jargon of the cloth-capped punters at the Leopardstown racetrack, would have been impossible.

So whatever happened – and why it happened – was carefully orchestrated and no last-minute scramble. Were this a Lodwick novel we might suggest an even more complicated storyline, in which the hero went to the altar freely and in love, not knowing that his bride was already pregnant by his chum. But it isn't and we just don't know. One perhaps exaggerated memory that has floated down the years is that the marriage hit John Collins so hard that in its aftermath he and his wife retreated into many years of mutual silence. Who knows? But if Dorothy's mother knew, and didn't tell her husband until it was too late, that might be one explanation for glacial non-communication.

It is equally plausible that, faced with such a personal dilemma, John Collins would have found his conscience was painfully squeezed between the upper mill-stone of his faith – and the granite rules of Irish morality – and the lower one of his admiration for John Stuart Mill, who for a man of his times (1806–73) was an early advocate of the rights of women to equality and 'liberation from the shackles they are raised voluntarily to impose on themselves'. If indeed John and Dorothy maintained the facade, and lived together at least for a while, it is tempting to see glimpses of *The Ginger Man*, J.P. Donleavy's rollicking saga of the impecunious, bottle-scarred Sebastian Dangerfield and his long-suffering wife, Marion.[2]

To Lodwick's cronies among the city's writers, actors and boozy scroungers, plate-smashing, door-slamming spats and casual infidelity called for little more than rueful commiseration and another glass of the same rather than condemnation. John Collins and his colleagues and neighbours, his parish priest – and no doubt Lodwick's maternal grandfather, the General – would have seen things in a bleaker light. Marriages might not always be made in Heaven but they were meant to last.

Whatever the truth, the bizarre circumstances of the marriage must have been the final straw in pushing Lodwick to leave Dublin and put behind him the pall of peat smoke unforgettably blended with the yeasty aroma from the Guinness brewery, the rain, the ever dimmer prospect of making a success in the theatre, and to turn his restless mind to warmer climes where the living was easy, or at least easier, with fewer complications about who knew what and whom he might run into in the street.

Then there's that letter, of which we have a copy. Typed rather than handwritten and dated 8 February 1938, and giving his address as Lloyds Bank in Earls Court Road (the area which as a young man he had found 'distressingly bourgeois'), Lodwick addressed it to 'Mrs Dorothy Lodwick' c/o her own bank in Regent Street, a use of banking channels which would give twenty-first-century compliance officers the vapours. 'Dear Dorothy', he begins,

> As the position is at the moment somewhat obscure, will you please tell me whether your decision to part from me is quite final. As I have already said to you personally and by letter, I am willing and anxious for your return but cannot allow things to remain indefinitely in their present state.

He gives her until 22 February to think the matter over and adds, 'I hope that for your own sake you will consider it <u>very carefully</u>' (his underlining). The copy we have, from family files, is signed simply 'John', with no mention of a child, no grace note of affection or cordiality, reinforcing the overall tone of *froideur*. There may even have been a lawyer's pen at work, though Lodwick does not seem a man who would seek outside help on much, and certainly not on his private life. Nor does it read like the aftershock of a 'marriage of convenience'.

We don't know what she replied, if indeed she did, though the reality seems to have been that they remained apart. When anonymous men from SOE interviewed him in May 1942 as a prospective agent, they noted that 'he is married, living not with his wife but with a woman to whom he is very attached', so by then at least the marriage had not been formally dissolved. Just to add to the confusion, when he enlisted in the Foreign Legion in 1939 a clerkly hand added in pencil on his file '*célibataire*' (bachelor). Another copy letter, which we will look at more closely in another context, shows they were in touch, rather neutrally but not without residual affection, when John Collins died in 1954, and there must have been some sporadic contact in the meanwhile. We know that Lodwick and John Collins kept in intermittent contact by letter (all long vanished), suggesting that whatever the rift may have been it was not a total rupture. Picking up what Belmont claims to have been told, we haven't been able to trace any record of a divorce. It could not have been registered in Ireland, where, barring a few extremely narrow judicial loopholes, divorce was not legalised until the 1990s.

The press report of John Collins' funeral in 1954 shows she attended as 'Mrs Dorothy Lodwick', so by then at least she had not remarried. A 'Dorothea Mary Lodwick', born in 1914, is registered as having died in London in 1991, at an address which fits with the last known sighting of her as a housekeeper in a Bayswater hotel. For many years she maintained the fiction that she was her son's 'Aunty Dot', until one day she told him in London, 'Enough of this. I'm your mother.' As he told this author sadly, who his real father was he never knew. Nor do we know what happened to a portrait of Collins by Sean O'Sullivan, presented by his Civil Service colleagues to mark his retirement. O'Sullivan (1906–64) was the pre-eminent Irish portrait painter of his time and it is another sign of the closeness of Dublin society that his other sitters included W.B. Yeats, Maude Gonne, Eamon de Valera and, rather later, Brendan Behan.

But who was the woman to whom Lodwick was so 'very attached'? Her name was Sheila Legge, and she opens another chapter of his life.

8

The Leg and the Legionnaire

Sheila Legge, with whom Lodwick had two children, was a beautiful and talented woman, of whom SOE noted warily that 'her influence on him and his career is a great deal stronger than one usually finds. The association colours his whole attitude towards life.' Years later Lodwick wrote in a private letter that he had 'the great good fortune' to live with Sheila for one-fifth of her life. 'And I need no other compensation.'

John Lodwick being John Lodwick, the story of when and where they met yet again comes in contradictory versions. Family legend, which must have had its roots in what either or both of them told younger generations, has it that they met in London around 1936. If so, it might go part of the way to explaining the problems he evidently had with Dorothy or she with him. Though only part. The contradiction comes in the circumstantial account of how they met, which Lodwick himself gives in his autobiographical account of his World War II experiences, and which puts a much later date on their meeting. For our immediate narrative it does not matter.

Our picture of Sheila is a collage. First, Lodwick's sad reflections in his books, especially in *Bid the Soldiers Shoot* and *Somewhere a Voice is Calling*, and his portrayal of her in *Brother Death*. Perhaps her most offbeat credit is in *Just a Song at Twilight*, when he borrows her name for a salt-caked tramp ship, the *Sheila Inglis*, 'the "Marks & Spencer" of the Pacific', ferrying copra, cheap tin trays and every conceivable household need between the tiny islands of Micronesia. Then there is what we know of the facts, not least from the painstaking research of Silvano Levy[1] and from press cuttings. What the suspicious minds of SOE claimed. The memories of an artistic friend. A second-hand but authoritative reference by George Melly to her and one episode in her love life. A short essay she wrote. The hazy recollections of one of her children whose only tangible mementoes of her as a mother, one whose diaries and library were lost to sight long ago, are a shopping list and fading photograph. What emerges is the image of a highly intelligent and well-read woman, whose life, like Lodwick's, was that of a wanderer – Cornwall, Scotland, Tahiti, Australia, London and the South of France. A life which also ended far too soon.

The SOE files tell us that she was born in St Ives as Sheila Chetwynd-Inglis on 25 June 1911. In a rather typical comment ('typical' in the sense that its security arm was always sniffing for weak points) the file noted that her background was 'disappointingly respectable'. Indeed it was. Her father was James Chetwynd-Inglis, 31 years old, nicknamed 'Laddie', son of a well-placed Edinburgh family with a military and colonial history; her mother, Ida Evelyn Kerr, was Australian, and with their backgrounds they had the cachet and cash to marry in London's fashionable St George's Church in Hanover Square. Laddie, Ida and the infant Sheila made the long voyage to French Tahiti, where he had a job as a mining engineer, and their second daughter, Lorraine, was born. When war broke out in August 1914 he shipped back to England to enlist; and also to earn a ghostly mention in the Lodwick story.

When they were sniffing into Sheila's background SOE failed to make the connection with the World War I Battle of Neuve Chapelle, where John's father, Captain Lodwick, won his DSO. Had they done so, they might have spotted that among the uncountable dead was Sheila's father Laddie, by then a young officer attached to the Seaforth Highlanders. *The Times* noted that his wife Ida had been working at a Red Cross hospital in France when Laddie was killed. A touching notice appeared five years later in the paper's *In Memoriam* section. It read: 'To our very dear Daddie, from his daughters Sheila and Lorraine, "*They Need No Bier Who Died At Agincourt*".'

Ida Evelyn remarried and Sheila was 18 when she moved back from Australia to St Andrews in Scotland to join her mother and stepfather, James Sutherland, in his family home. In January 1934, as Levy recounts, Sheila, already pregnant, married 'the son of a South African Brigadier General', but divorced him after 'he ran off with another woman'. In *Brother Death*, Lodwick's portrait of 'Fiona Lampeter' seems to have the lipstick traces of Sheila's early years – her father killed in the Great War, an Australian mother, a 'good' school where she was bullied and from which she was kicked out for indolence, finishing schools in Melbourne and

Lausanne. Reminding us a little of Elvira in *Blithe Spirit*, she also hovers importantly as the recently dead 'Norah' in Belmont's strange novel *Un homme au crepuscule*.

We get another glimpse in the archives of the Victoria and Albert Museum's photograph collection, which has a stiffly posed image of Sheila's father-in-law Brigadier General Reginald Legge in the uniform of the Leinster Regiment[2] and his Turkish second wife, a reference to their messy divorce in the 1920s and then a note that one of the four children of the marriage, Rupert Maximilian Faris Legge, married Sheila *Shetywnd*-Inglis [*sic*] in 1934. It did not last long, since, according to the catalogue entry, they were divorced the same year, and their baby son was adopted by one of her husband's relatives. An odd, distant echo of what happened in Dublin. The SOE files claim 'he ran off with another woman'. Lodwick embroiders this in *Brother Death*, portraying the husband as a poker player and second-hand car dealer, albeit of good family, and gruesomely but characteristically centring the plot on a child's murder, so that its mother could get her hands on an inheritance. Our next finding – or, more precisely, sounding – comes from another London institution, the British Library, whose Sound Archives include interviews by Mel Gooding with the poet David Gascoyne, a key figure in the Surrealist movement.[3]

During a spell in Paris Gascoyne had met many of the 'modern artists' working there, and had a brief flirtation with Communism and the Spanish Civil War. When his *A Short Survey of Surrealism* was published in 1935, with a cover design by Max Ernst, Sheila Legge wrote him a 'fan letter' from her bed-sitting room in Earls Court, an area about which, as we remember, Lodwick had mixed feelings but where he also placed the lodgings of the fictional 'Fiona' in *Brother Death*. As Gascoyne remembered, in real life 'she was an attractive woman and we got on very well'. She went to Paris for a while, hoping to model for the photographer and artist Man Ray,[4] but was disappointed to find 'she was not quite his type'. That may have been just as well. Man Ray was a modernist artist and portrait photographer – his subjects included almost every artist, novelist, composer and sculptor of renown – creator of the far more abstract images known as Rayographs, avant-garde film maker, and, to judge by his photographs for a book of poems published in 1929, not afraid to shock with material that was explicit even by Parisian standards of the time. Lodwick translates this episode into fiction as a spell in Paris with 'an American photographer' who tried to get her a job as a mannequin, which she refuses because she lacks confidence. 'My style was the politely tatty, not the mink.'

In the non-fiction world of the spring of 1936, with Edward VII newly, confusedly and only briefly on the throne and the Nazis trumpeting the build-up to the Berlin Olympics, Gascoyne and the painter Roland Penrose were the leading lights of a group of artists and critics, Sheila somewhere amongst them, working to organise the International Surrealist Exhibition, which would run at the New Burlington Galleries in the West End at the height of the summer season. Surrealism as a topic has enraged, captivated and baffled many authors who have tried to explain, praise or condemn it. One pithy version of its aims is 'to resolve the previously contradictory conditions of dream and reality'. So pithy it actually tells us little, and the artworks – unnerving, illogical, often turning everyday objects into strange creatures – command ever higher prices more because of fashion and canny marketing than because of a deep understanding of their meaning by the oligarchs and tycoons who bid for them.

The artists listed in the catalogue, produced by the Women's Printing Society in Brick Street, would make a twenty-first-century auctioneer purr. They included Arp, Brancusi, Calder, Ernst, Giacometti, Klee, Magritte, Miro, Moore, Picabia, Picasso, Man Ray himself, Sutherland and Tanguey. There were also unspecified 'objects', one produced by Sheila herself. (From a sketch made by Man Ray for some of his friends, perhaps as a greetings card, Sheila's 'object' seems to have been a 'pillow', though what it was made of, and what message it was meant to convey, we have no idea.) It was not just an exhibition. A central element of Surrealism's self-created mission was to shock, so spectators found themselves watching performance art, coming face to face with the poet Dylan Thomas offering cups of boiled string, asking 'Do you prefer hot or cold?' In an act she had performed for press photographers in Trafalgar Square as part of the pre-exhibition publicity, Sheila appeared as a Surrealist 'Phantom of Love' in a flowing white dress, her head swathed in paper roses and ladybirds; in her rubber-gloved arms she carried an artificial leg and, by some accounts, a pork chop, the latter soon abandoned because of the heat. The costume was the work of The Motley, three talented female designers, sisters Margaret and Sophie Harris and Elizabeth Montgomery Wilmot, who, as Alan Bennett remembered when reminiscing about the theatre, then and for many years later produced stunning effects from the cheapest materials.[5]

Though some of the several (not surprisingly conflicting) reports of the event claim the limb was borrowed from a Bond Street window display, Gascoyne remembers that he had in fact bought it from an orthopaedic supply house, his idea being that it was a visual pun – a Legge carrying a leg. Not many saw the joke. There were also several 'lectures', the last by Salvador Dalí (1904-1989), the Catalan artist whose career and moustache cannot be reduced to a footnote. His chosen topic at the exhibition was *Fantômes paranoïaques authentiques* ('authentic paranoid phantoms'), for which he dressed head to toe in a thick canvas diving suit, holding a billiard cue in one hand and in the other a leash to which were attached two Afghan hounds belonging to Edward James, a super-rich Surrealist aficionado.[6]

Two minutes into the 'lecture' (one wonders how the audience could hear through the closed glass porthole in the diver's helmet) Dalí began to totter and to mime that he could not breathe. Again, there are two or three versions of his rescue, an event which may in any case have been a scripted 'happening' within a 'happening'. Passed down through the Lodwick generations is the story that John, already in a relationship with Sheila, was in the crowd and quickly unscrewed the faceplate. David Gascoyne's account is that he came to the rescue himself, after scurrying around nearby buildings to find the right tool. ('And to find a spanner in Bond Street is not easy.') Since Lodwick's *Bid the Soldiers Shoot* is categorical that he and Sheila met in France only several years later, the story that he saved the day may not be correct; equally for Dalí to lie suffocating, while Gascoyne bustled round Bond Street shouting for a spanner, like King Richard for his horse, does not ring quite true either. So the story leaves us just as intrigued as the exhibition audiences, who are said by one reviewer to have left each day 'amused, scared, or just bored'. The *Daily Mail* was alarmed by the 'distasteful revelation of subconscious thoughts and desires' while *The Times* dismissed Picasso with the sideswipe that 'though an eminent designer, he is not a painter'. The author and broadcaster J.B. Priestley grumbled that the Surrealists were 'truly decadent… there are far too many effeminate and obscene young men lisping and undulating. Too many young women without manners, balance, dignity – greedy and slobbering sensation seekers.'[7] At least they achieved their aim of attracting attention.

George Melly had been bitten by the Surrealist bug as a precocious Stowe schoolboy. Towards the end of World War II he joined the navy, as a lowly rating rather than a well-scrubbed and drilled Dartmouth product. His personal leanings and trim uniform drew him like iron filings to a magnet towards London's gay milieu, uninhibited experiences recounted in his early autobiographical sketch.[8]

In 1975 he also produced a sympathetic TV film about Edward James' life and amazing creations.

From the rather dismissive way Melly writes about Sheila it seems he never met her, but he certainly seems to have known a lot about her at second hand from his Belgian-born mentor and employer E.L.T. Mesens (1903–71), the self-appointed leading light of the British Surrealists. Melly's first job was working for Mesens in the London Gallery on Brook Street, in those grey postwar days when England was lurching back to its feet. Multi-tasking, it would be called today, since Melly's duties covered not just hanging, packing and selling but also sweaty couplings *à deux* with Mesens and occasionally *à trois* with him and his wife, Sybil, hence the title of another Melly memoir, *Don't Tell Sybil*, to which we are indebted for these memories.[9] It was the first step on Melly's idiosyncratic escalator towards reincarnation as a zoot-suited jazz and blues singer, art collector, author, critic, cartoonist, placid fisherman and much-loved media personality.

But where does Sheila fit in? Mesens had first tried to hire her as a sales assistant in the gallery, but his other shareholders preferred someone else. According to Melly, Mesens introduced Sheila to René Magritte, an introduction which led to a relatively brief but passionate affair. The dates are vague, but the narrative suggests this was before the war, maybe around the time of the exhibition and thus firmly pre-Lodwick. Mesens, 'who was on the spot and feverishly interested in everybody's sex life', never spoke to Melly about what had happened, remaining 'as silent as the confessional'. It was an atypical muteness which Melly attributes to Mesen's sense of guilt as the 'treacherous enabler' of a liaison which had been a 'traumatic lapse' in the Magrittes' otherwise completely uxorious relationship, and one which had put the marriage at risk for some years. To judge by today's rather overheated modern market, Mesens and his supporters could at least claim they were right about the lasting value of the art, and Priestley was wrong. Works by Magritte now command millions of dollars.

Melly describes Sheila as 'a beautiful Surrealist groupie'. From Levy's painstaking research she emerges as more than that, with a real interest in the movement, though despite her appearance as 'The Phantom' she left little tangible evidence of her pretty presence. We know from Levy and from Lodwick memories that she read widely and voraciously. We also have one remnant of her writing, a one-page prose poem called 'I Have Done My Best For You', in the December 1936 'Double Issue' of *Contemporary Poetry and Prose*, a magazine which flourished briefly under the editorship of Roger Roughton,[10] another of those literary shooting stars making a transient passage through the night sky of the 1930s arts world. A poet and friend of Dylan Thomas and many in the British Surrealist movement, Roughton had short spells as a Hollywood extra, and a reviewer for the *Daily Worker*, and through it all remained a staunch Communist. He gassed himself in Dublin in April 1941, two months before the Nazi invasion of the USSR.

Sheila's one-pager can be analysed, as Sylvano Levy has done at length, and mined for its deeper psychological import and its veiled reference to her failed first marriage. After so many years, a more cynical eye less attuned to how the Surrealists thought and felt might see it as not much more than a disturbed pastiche of Lewis Carroll, but 'groupie' still seems unfair for a woman who read widely and discriminatingly, spoke several languages and knew more than many about the work of the Danish philosopher Kierkegaard. Some of the latter's thoughts rubbed off on Lodwick himself, for instance when he borrows as an epigraph for *The Cradle of Neptune* the Dane's somewhat obscure observation that

> If anyone were to say this is a mere declamation, that all I have at my disposal is a little irony, a little pathos, a little dialectics, my reply would be: 'What else should anyone have who proposes to set forth the ethical?'

It is also pleasing to see that as recently as 1990, in an enthusiastic commentary on an American study of Surrealist displays, *Eye*, an international quarterly focused on the graphic arts, suggested that the Turner Prize should be renamed the 'Sheila Legge Prize' because the message of that now celebrated image, for the author of the commentary, was not 'I have been here before' but 'I have been here since'. It is a shame neither Melly nor Mesens are here to interpret for us what that means.

Many of the fans of Surrealism vociferously embraced Trotskyism, Communism or anarchism and this may help explain the rather jaundiced view MI5 and SOE took of Sheila. No file notes have come to light to substantiate this, but, as Levy has noted, in 1937 she attended a May Day demonstration organised by the British Artists' Congress in support of 'democracy and social advance'. Amid the political clamours of the times, meetings of that flavour, under a banner which proclaimed, in an adaptation of William Blake's phrase, that 'A Warlike State Cannot Create' would inevitably have attracted the attention of Special Branch detectives, taking surreptitious notes of who was there and what was said. Photos too, in all likelihood, though in one found by Levy in the National Galleries of Scotland, other than the banner the small assembly has far more of the air of an outing of a suburban bridge club.

The fictional Fiona and the real Sheila converge in the South of France, in the later 1930s, the area where Lodwick claims the romance started and where Sheila's mother was then living. What was he doing there? To get at the answer we need another creaky turn of the Roundabout, to take us to the travails of Lodwick the Legionnaire.

Among the stack of British official files, press extracts and books – not least his own – which tell us about Lodwick's adventures and misadventures in World War II, the one document we might least have expected to have seen is his Foreign Legion dossier. The Legion is rightly proud of the many honours it has earned for France, but also of the anonymity it is said to grant those who have chosen for whatever reason to enlist in its ranks. So to see the name LODWICK in the dossier's clerkly copperplate suggests he was not joining up to hide. The terse notes record that he signed up in Marseilles on 9 September 1939 'for the duration of hostilities', along with his physical details, the fact that he was 'a writer' and 'bachelor' (as we have seen, an economy with the truth), rounded out when the hostilities came to their painfully premature end in 1940 by his discharge certificate, attested by the whorls and loops of prints of his left and right index fingers.

But what was he doing in Marseilles, 'the fundament of Europe, the last port of the emigrant, the whorehouse of the sailor, the haven of the card-sharper, the clearing house of every venal and some mortal sins', as he later remembered it? Lodwick does not tell us so we are left to guess. We have already wondered whether the earlier move to Dublin was a gesture of family support, a fresh start after Dartmouth and whatever drifting followed. When that didn't work, support would have turned into frustration, a collective view that, whatever he did, he and the family would be better served if he did it at a discreet distance from England. His maternal grandfather, General Ashbrooke Crump, who had lent his name as a director to the Stage Society venture, had a retirement home in Alassio on the Italian Riviera, about 200 scenic miles from Marseilles via Cannes, Nice and San Remo. 'Nice weather, cheap, can't get into too much trouble, and if he does, I know the right people down there,' the

General might have tried to reassure John's mother. Whether this followed the gap year in which, as he later claimed to a British inquisitor, he had been a merchant seaman in and around the Channel Islands, is a question left unanswered as we yearn for that permanently unfinished autobiography.

Why join the Legion is an easier question to answer, but we also have to look at where it led: Lodwick's experiences as a fighter and a fugitive, what happened when the tumult and the shouting died and the France he knew died with it. How did he get back to Britain, how did he enter the clandestine world of the British secret establishments, and what happened then? And where did Sheila fit in?

Lodwick presented his own 296-page version of the story in his *Bid the Soldiers Shoot: A Personal Narrative*, published in 1959 and described by the historian M.R.D. Foot as 'a frivolous and entertaining war autobiography'. Less well known is a fictionalised version of the same tale, *Running to Paradise*, in which Lodwick, thinly veiled, Roffey-style, as 'Adrian Dormant' is a sculptor and the adventurous narrator. How it came to see the light of day in 1943 is another curious tale in itself, to which we shall turn later. ('Dormant' is a surname which Lodwick used in several books. Whether it was a hidden allusion or a joke he does not tell us.) For the broader context of the Legion, its history and the events of World War II for which Lodwick volunteered, Douglas Porch's history[11] is unrivalled. The broader context was less relevant for Lodwick, however, whose view of the mayhem was more the often frightened and confused squint of 'the toad beneath the harrow'. As to what happened afterwards we have the benefit of the once 'Most Secret' British archives to see what Lodwick accomplished, and how his armchair masters judged him.

Bid the Soldiers Shoot, the title of the book in which Lodwick told his story, is the line that brings down the curtain on *Hamlet*. Had florid epigraphs still been part of a publisher's toolkit in 1959 the book could have been better described by Horatio's earlier lines:

> So shall you hear
> Of carnal, bloody and unnatural acts
> Of accidental judgements, casual slaughters
> Of deaths put on by cunning and forced cause,
> And in this upshot, purposes mistook

But the accurate, if chilling, foretaste that these lines offer for Lodwick's wartime service is part of the difficulty in retelling it. There is no point in our simply rehashing Lodwick's tales of derring-do, or trying to better his descriptions of those he met in the process, each one of them worth a short story in its own right. Even a partial listing gives the flavour: a 'bent' London policeman on the run, an insurance fraudster, several grades of conmen from cheap tricksters to sophisticated men who knew the best hotels and their wine lists, a car thief, the London bookie's runner now literally on the run as some of his curiously prescient wagers came under close scrutiny, a senescent and suicidal 'flasher'.

This turn of the Roundabout begins in Provence in the autumn of 1939. The bruising heat of summer was easing off but it was still warm enough for the hard-up 23-year-old Lodwick to sleep in the back of a car owned by his chum Titin Blanchin. Short of money he may have been, but after helping pick potatoes he could still join Titin and his friends ('all rich peasants, which in that part of France meant very rich indeed') at bullfights, bars and the local brothels, one of which boasted caged parrots with the ability to curse in Siamese.

On 3 September France joined Britain in declaring war on Germany. As men in berets and blue overalls plastered the walls of local town halls and gendarmeries with notices calling reservists to the colours and urging men to enlist, Lodwick astonished his friends by announcing he was off to Marseilles to join the Foreign Legion. When they asked why, his answers may have made sense to him at the time, though not to his bewildered peasant pals. Lubricated by several glasses of the rough red wine they knew as *pinard*, he declared that, first, it would be a long war, and he wanted to serve in a field 'uncovered by literary compatriots'. Second, he wanted to test himself; was he as brave as his heroic, sadly invisible father or even his Grandpapa? Third, if he made his way back to Britain it would take at least a year before his age group was called up; better to join the fray now. We have no grounds to question what he said, though on the face of it in those early days of war he could have reached England and enlisted, rather than wait to be called up, putting to practical use some of the basic skills he had learned at Dartmouth. He gave substance to the first motive by mining his experience for at least two books and parts of others. He was also unconsciously channelling at least two other writers. The first was Ernest Hemingway. Writing in December 1925 to F. Scott Fitzgerald, then still to reach the dizzy heights of success, Hemingway, himself nastily wounded as a Red Cross volunteer on the Italian front in the closing days of World War I, asked:

> Like me to write you a little essay on The Importance of Subject?
> Well, the reason you are so sore you missed the war is because war is the best subject of all. It groups the maximum of material and speeds up the action and brings out all sorts of stuff you have to wait a lifetime to get.[12]

Another model was the quirky de Quincey, whose essays Lodwick had been given by John Collins, and who once observed that 'War has a deeper and more ineffable relation to hidden grandeurs in man than has yet been deciphered.'

Looking back on Lodwick's life we can speculate that the driving motive – captured perhaps as he was peering blearily at his reflection in a steamy French shaving mirror, casting his hyperactive mind backwards and forwards – was how to prove to the world and, more important, to himself, that he had as much of the 'right stuff' as his father, his grandfather and all those bemedalled and bewhiskered forebears. Maybe. Sometime later a phlegmatic British assessor for the British clandestine services put it more succinctly and probably more accurately: Lodwick had enlisted out of 'emotional enthusiasm'.

Whatever drove him, off he went. Not quite a lamb to the slaughter but an innocent abroad who had no idea what to expect. Forms to be filled in, the endless barking of orders, a brusque quartermaster's clerk measuring him by eye and chucking over the flat-topped *képi* hat, rough-cut trousers rather like jodhpurs, webbing belts and straw mattress, off to a rudimentary clinic for every orifice to be unceremoniously probed, to the team of barbers with clippers poised to shave the recruits' heads to the bone, all the – universal, not just French – military preliminaries to another, and this time danger-laden, lurch of the Roundabout.

1   The young John Lodwick.   2   John Lodwick relaxed.

3   The Lodwick Memorial in India.

4   The tools of Captain Lodwick's trade.

5   War as Captain Lodwick would have seen it.

6 The SS *Persia*.

7 German U-boat, the same type which sank SS *Persia*, taking Captain Lodwick with it.

8 'The Cradle of Neptune' – Royal Naval College Dartmouth.

9 Hermann Görtz –
German agent in Eire.

10 Iseult Gonne, the face of poetry.

11 W.B. Yeats – Irish poet of genius, and unsuccessful lover of Iseult Gonne, who eloped with Stuart.

12 Francis Stuart, maverick genius.

13 Eoin O'Duffy, Irish Blueshirt Leader, with a few right-minded friends.

14 Jammet's restaurant, Dublin, where the Irish literary elite met to compete.

15 Eamon de Valera.

16 Getting ready for the London Surrealist Exhibition,
Sheila Legge seated second from right.

17 Sheila as the 'Phantom of Love' in Trafalgar Square.

18 Sheila by Man Ray.

ICI REPOSE
SHEILA LODWICK (1911 - 1949)
LA FEMME BIEN-AIMÉE DE JOHN LODWICK
QUE LES ÉTRANGERS QUE LES ESTIVANTS
QUI PASSENT SE SOUVIENNENT QUE MORTE LOIN DE SON PAYS
ELLE REPOSE DANS CE TOMBEAU
GRÂCE AU GESTE SPONTANÉ D'UN CATALAN

HERE LIES SHEILA LODWICK 1911 1949
THE BELOVED WIFE OF JOHN LODWICK

19   Sheila's bilingual memorial.

20   Selwyn Jepson, SOE
talent spotter, author and
friend of Lodwick.

21 Evelyn Waugh
in martial mode.

22 George Jellicoe.

23 First Special Boat Service, 'K' Patrol.
Lodwick is in the back row, second from left.

24 Chetniks with Wehrmacht prisoners, whose subsequent fate is unknown.

25 'Have fiddle, will travel.'
Walter Starkie, genial polymath.

26 A young W.S. Merwin as Lodwick
and Belmont would have known him.

27 Georges Pelorson, later Belmont, as a Vichy Youth leader,
cheerleading a group of hikers in the mountains of the Valloire.

28 W. Somerset Maugham, an admirer of Lodwick's work.

29 A hidden aspect of Franco's Spain – budding bullfighters practise in the backstreets.

30 Old and new in Franco's Spain.

31 Josep Janés (standing, right) with Spanish composer Federico Mompou (left).

32   Peter de Polnay and Dodo.

33   Rebecca West, author and sharp editorial reader for Heinemann.

34   Gregory Ratoff, the archetypical image of a movie director, including the cigarette ash on his coat.

35 Building the tower or *castell* at a Catalan folk festival, an event Lodwick and his friends never got to see.

36 *Calsotadas*, a coincidental link back to Grandpapa's asparagus trench.

9

One Step Forward, Two Steps Back

If this chapter of the story were a film, it might be neatly framed by two 1660 forts which still stand on either side of the Old Port of Marseilles; like the Scylla and Charybdis of Greek mythology, both were destinations to be avoided. Lodwick started his brief Legion service in St Nicolas, and marked its completion, though not the end of his adventures, locked up in Fort St Jean. What happened in-between were experiences few would care, or be mentally and physically able, to live through.

If he had been looking for colonial legend and glory, he was not about to find them. Though he was often teased in later life, and enjoyed it, about taking on a *Beau Geste* persona to do brave battle against the Tuaregs at Fort Zinderneuf, he was just one of the mongrel multinational group who made up the Legion's 12th Foreign Regiment and ended up fighting the Germans in Northern France before being forced into disorderly retreat as France itself crumbled. He never served in the deserts of North Africa or the jungles of South-East Asia.

His Legion *fiche* shows that two days after he enlisted on 9 September 1939 he was sent on his way for basic training at the Legion's Camp de La Valbonne, some 20 miles outside Lyons. It was the time of the 'phoney war', a period in which Lodwick spent his first spell in jail, for an offence which in the British system would have been closer to 'insubordination' or the catch-all 'dumb insolence', an almost farcical spat with an officer on a muddy firing range; another minor act of a rebel. The Legion took things more seriously and charged him with 'Mutiny and Incitement to Mutiny while on Active Service', which could have led to a court martial and a possible five-year sentence; but a civilised and lenient commanding officer decided that three weeks locked up in the Camp *gnouf* (British squaddies of the epoch would have called it 'the glasshouse') was punishment enough.

Inside and outside the *gnouf* he was in colourful company. Napoleon had first introduced 'Foreign Regiments' in an era when mercenaries were an accepted if heartily feared element of most European armies, but he would have been rather taken aback by the make-up of the 12th, in which Lodwick now served. In 1886, a French officer had drawn a harsh contrast between the 'good little French soldier' who just wanted to get his military service over and go home, and the legionnaire who, 'while he often has a military vocation… is sometimes a *déclassé*, an adventurer, someone made bitter by life, a bandit'. The 12th had been hastily cobbled together from what one historian has described as 'very heterogeneous' elements: there were Poles (some of them Catholic coal miners who had been working in the seams of Northern France, others Jews whom viscerally anti-Semitic Polish émigré units refused to accept) as well as suddenly stateless Jews from across Europe who were hoping that military service would set them on the path to French citizenship (after Vichy came to power it was a hope that, like many others, came to nothing). There was also a phalanx of Spanish Republicans, bloodied but not bowed after being crushed by General Franco with the help of his Axis allies; they stood out by their taciturn solidarity and their fondness for the knife as a swift and efficient way to settle scores. There were Croats, generally men of extreme religious or political views, a Turk or two and several Englishmen. The Legion, which even before Vichy had itself discreetly sought to reduce the intake of Jews, leavened the amateur foreign ranks with men who had been indoctrinated with the right spirit and discipline in the sands of North Africa propped up by tough NCOs, many of them German. Even finding a common language for training must have been next to impossible, let alone forming ties of comradeship between groups of men who had nothing in common other than a hatred and fear of Fascism, often based on brutal first-hand experience. To make matters worse, they were poorly armed. Though Lodwick at one point followed in his father's footsteps by manning a Hotchkiss machine gun, some of their rifles had last seen service in the Madagascar campaign in 1859 and others were leftovers from distant French operations in Morocco. They had no artillery, and after the Germans took some prisoners and saw their equipment held together by frayed cords, they nicknamed the 12th 'the String Regiment'.

On 10 May 1940 Hitler launched his 'Case Yellow', combining air power, tanks and infantry with ruthless efficiency to convert the 'phoney war' or *Sitzkrieg* into a *Blitzkrieg*, a lightning strike at the Low Countries and France. The same day, in a confused, scared London, Winston Churchill took over as prime minister.

On 11 May the 12th Regiment was hustled out of Camp de La Valbonne in a frenzy of barked, often contradictory, orders, bugle calls, the crunch of boots on barrack squares, kitbag stuffing, postcards scribbled to loved ones. By the 24th, rumbling lorries, the cattle cars of slow, jolting trains and marches on dusty roads brought them to defend the town of Soissons on the River Aisne, about 100 km north-east of Paris. Many of the foreign volunteers would have had no idea where they were; most, including their officers, had only a hazy notion of what they were supposed to do. It was not a time for indulging in memories; had the French among them known, cared or had a moment to reflect, they might have remembered that Soissons had been the centre of one of the last big battles of World War I. Now some of the sons of those who died were fighting the same enemy in the same place, and the local farmers, whose ploughs still gouged up dragon's teeth, the rusty relics of that early 'War to End Wars', would once again cower from the roar of shells and bombs, and wait for their homes to be shattered once more. The Regiment did not make much of an effort to dig in, as rumours were already spreading that the General Staff did not plan to make a stand. But when German tanks could be heard in the distance, Wehrmacht mortars began to find their range, their bombs exploding over the legionnaires' heads in a deadly shower of shrapnel, and Stukas screamed down into dive-bombing runs out of a sky from which French and British planes were conspicuous by their absence, they set about cobbling together some rudimentary defences. By 8 June the legionnaires risked being outflanked and surrounded and, as Lodwick remembered, his unit had twice been ordered to fire on fellow French units on their flanks in a bid to stop them abandoning their positions. It had no effect. The retreat began.

Among those trying to escape the tightening German noose was a now bearded Lodwick, never far from the line of fire or the risk of capture, sporting, according to his memoirs, a black leather 'biker's' jacket, a checked Lillywhites flannel shirt (which he must have bought heaven knows when in Piccadilly), his French uniform trousers and boots, waving a German submachine gun and a Luger pistol. Little wonder that he came within a centimetre of being shot by a jittery French officer as a spy, saved at the last minute by a fellow legionnaire, who was himself soon to be wounded and later shot dead as Lodwick tried to push him to safety, folded painfully over the luggage rack of a bicycle. As the German machine crunched inexorably ahead, the Legion could be found trudging dispiritedly homewards, wherever home was, along dusty, poplar-lined country roads clogged with the human debris of war – terror-stricken families, overloaded prams, farm carts, and here and there dusty cars, mattresses slung over the roof as a flimsy shield against bullets from marauding Luftwaffe fighter planes. Many had long since run out of fuel and had to be stolidly pushed by their passengers or pulled by a weary horse.

Tying two of his separate stories together, it was during this terrifying exodus of old, young, the halt, the lame and the blind that Lodwick later remembered machine-gunning refugees 'who were getting in the way of military operations', adding that he had squeezed the trigger 'with a feeling of satisfaction'. We will come later to the circumstances in which this ghoulish or boastful (or both) comment was made; it comes from a British secret file. In his biography he also tells us that around this time he evened the score with a Toulon pimp who had tried to assault him in their first Legion days while in shared lodgings awaiting space in the barracks. 'Nine months later on the Ourcq canal, I shot this man dead – not from personal animosity, but because ordered to do so; he was proceeding with too great speed for the taste of our section leader in the direction of Paris.' Another boast? Or are these tales and the style in which he tells them distant echoes of his childhood memory that he found the sight of a man having half his leg chopped off in Kashmir merely 'interesting'?

Not all that far away, the British Expeditionary Force which had been ferried across the Channel with such high hopes in September 1939 was painfully regrouping towards the beaches of Dunkirk, from which between 17 May and 4 June they were snatched from defeat and surrender, mainly by a flotilla of small craft, a page of history which defies both belief and description. Among those who made it home was Lodwick's future boss and nemesis at SOE, Maurice Buckmaster.

On 22 June France metaphorically broke its sword of honour and signed an Armistice in a musty railway carriage at Compiègne, the setting vengefully chosen by Hitler because it was there Germany had formally capitulated in World War I.

This is not the place to write an epitaph for the Legion, the Regiment or France, but the conclusion seems to be that despite being poorly trained, poorly armed and poorly led, with no air cover, no artillery support and no anti-tank guns to fight back against the otherwise unstoppable German panzers, the performance of those foreign units ranged from 'very credible to spectacular'. As one French veteran wrote: 'With equal arms we were easily worth our adversaries… an enemy which certainly dominated us materially but never morally.'

Many Croix de Guerre were awarded, some to units, some to individuals. French military records show Lodwick's was awarded on 25 July 1940 in the name of 'Jean Lodwick, Legionnaire 2nd Class, 12th Foreign Infantry Regiment'. In characteristically deprecatory Lodwick style he tells us it cited 'a heroic action involving the defence of our Colonel's command post, with which I was totally unconnected'. Buried in a different silo of French history, or more likely lost, the citation cannot now be traced. As the Germans strutted and the French cringed at Compiègne, the 12th were trying to regroup in Limoges. When the rolls were called they could only muster some 300 men of the 2,800 who had left La Valbonne a few weeks earlier.

Lodwick was just one of the hundreds of thousands who slouched into captivity, not knowing whether it meant futile and frustrated years behind barbed wire, forced labour, deportation or even summary execution. The Wehrmacht had not expected to take so many prisoners but while they could not resist gloating over their victory, they were as efficient in setting up temporary POW enclaves as they had been in their attacks, putting a cathedral and a brickworks to good use. It was from the latter that Lodwick shuffled out to a brief spell of freedom, helped by loyal French workers who created a diversion as he merged casually into a crowd of workers finishing their shift, a half-eaten baguette tucked under his arm to add authenticity.

He trudged warily and wearily south through the Nivernais into Burgundy, covering 20 to 30 miles each day, heading for the Demarcation Line which, for now but not for long, separated Nazi France from the Unoccupied Zone. Peasants gave him scraps of clothing and food and he slept rough. And one night not so rough, even though it was a hayloft. A rich family had agreed to put him up in the barn, accepting his presence with a mix of fear and condescension. Lodwick describes what happened with tactful opacity, but it is clear that one of the family's daughters sought him out in the straw, and human nature took its course. He dangles the intriguing postscript that when she wrote to him after the war she urged him to stay away from that part of France, since she now had a son, born nine months after he passed through. A son named Jean. Lodwick tacitly acknowledges him again in an aside in *The Asparagus Trench*, telling his readers that he had two French children, not just the one shown in his mother's detailed family tree. In each of their births he had been 'no more than a humble agent of transmission, a worn and much chafed link between the capstan and the anchor'.

Finally crossing the Line, after swimming across a canal, he found himself without papers, temporarily housed in a centre for 'military waifs and strays'. He was desperate to get back to the Legion depot and sort out his papers, since like so many thousands of others he was in military limbo, neither combatant nor prisoner, not released from whatever obligations he owed the State. So he did not hesitate when another squaddie suggested he take a bike from the many racked up by the wall. He did. Though it got him on his way it was the start of 18 months of aggravation pursued by a system which, though now that of a defeated country, retained the bureaucratic methods and records established in the Napoleonic era for dealing with bicycle thieves and wandering soldiers.

The next stop was Marseilles, where Lodwick managed to retrieve his British passport from the Legion filing cabinet, declining an offer to have him listed as 'Dead on the Field of Honour', partly because a fellow legionnaire counselled him not to claim he was dead till he had collected any demobilisation gratuity which he might be due. He may also have thought that to be declared dead, while offering certain advantages, was an irreversible step with unforeseeable consequences.

Orwell's friend Georges Kopp had a 'now you see him, now you don't' persona, well suited to the claims, often self-fostered, that at various times and in various roles he had been an asset of several clandestine services, including MI5 and the French and Belgian Resistance, and perhaps even the Germans. He had been Orwell's commander in Spain. He had then joined the polyglot platoons of the Legion, and Lodwick had last seen him wounded by German bullets as he manned a Legion barricade. To Lodwick's surprise he popped up yet again in Marseilles when, still wheezing from his wounds, he was working as a clerk in the Legion office. He wangled Lodwick a travel warrant to Perpignan, and told him where he could find a *passeur*, one of those fleet-of-foot mountain men whose dangerous profession was to guide escapees over the Pyrenees on their way to comparative safety in neutral Spain. (It could also be dangerous for their 'passengers', whom some guides had been known to abandon well short of safety, or even betray.) Kopp himself was making for North Africa (and will turn up again later in our story). Meantime he would fix the records so that Lodwick would not be listed as a deserter for two months, but simply logged as 'absent without leave'.

Through no fault of Kopp's or Lodwick's the attempt foundered on the high screes of the border itself. Lodwick and his fellow escaper, a British Army sergeant, were first chased by a Spanish patrol and then captured by French gendarmes. Lodwick himself describes it as 'a textbook example of an unsuccessful escape story'.

Making light of what must have been extreme discomfort, Lodwick says of his next jail that 'the quieter parts of Bedlam or the Newgate debtors' prison must have been very like Perpignan. Hogarth would have enjoyed himself there', not least because the gloom was alleviated by impromptu accordion music, cards, *pinard* and another oddball cast about whom Lodwick writes with affection. When his case came to trial his 'gaunt, crow-like' attorney bombarded the bewildered three-man bench with references to Lodwick's youth, his aged mother (a stretch), the London Blitz, Voltaire and the Bible, and secured his acquittal, saving him from further detention in a refugee camp by agreeing to act as surety.

He went back to Marseilles, where another brush with the law arose from a police claim that, whatever his papers made him out to be, he was a deserter. A spell in that forbidding Fort and a provisional release gave a temporary respite in which he was again drawn to the wilder shores of life, mixing, so a later British file note records, with black-marketers and 'friends from the Croix-de-Feu milieu'. Though academics still debate whether Colonel de la Rocque's Croix-de-Feu movement, originally built around World War I veterans who had been awarded the Croix de Guerre, was actually 'Fascist', it was certainly on the less than democratic end of France's unfathomable political spectrum.

In his own memoirs Lodwick also claimed he was one of a trio who made a living bilking money from impressionable American girls of good family waiting to get safely home to neutrality and apple pie, snatching overcoats and sheepskin jackets from unattended racks in cafes and hotels or wheedling tea and sympathy out of stranded and lonely English widows. The trio had dodgy papers and dodged about themselves – at one point Lodwick was bedding down on a deserted yacht in Villefranche harbour. But the clock was ticking.

Generations ago, when British schoolboys looked forward eagerly to the next of their weekly adventure comics, many an aspiring writer cut his professional teeth plotting the thrilling deeds of comic-book heroes such as 'Rockfist' Rogan, Wilson

'The Wonder Athlete' (alias 'The Man in Black') or even, may we be forgiven, 'Cripple Dick' Archer, as they outwitted the Hun, cannibals, school bullies, Chinese opium smugglers, pirates or several in combination. One young hack is said to have got his hero into such a complicated tangle that, slamming both hands on the typewriter keys in despair, he turned for help to a veteran colleague at the next desk. 'What do I do now? How do I get him out of it?' 'Simple,' said the voice of many years' experience. 'You start the next instalment: "With one bound, Jack was free."'

For Lodwick that 'bound' was the Mixed Medical Commission, a creation of the postwar Geneva Convention, whose laudable aim was to examine those male foreigners stranded in France, less than 48 years old, who claimed to be unfit for military service and who wanted to be sent home. On what leafy branch of his extensive grapevine Lodwick heard about it, and how he thought he could get away with it, he does not tell us. But on 12 January 1942, fortified by a hefty glass of cognac and after memorising an eloquent speech, he reported for examination by three doctors. All were French, but one had been nominated by the Germans and a second by their Italian allies. Lodwick met none of their criteria. In fact he cheerfully admitted that there was nothing wrong with him. But what seems to have won the day more than his rhetorical flights was a simple appeal to Gallic logic. He argued that the French had agreed to return all their soldiers home after hostilities ceased. He had served France, and the fact his home was in England made no difference. He should be sent back. The medical gods smiled, or perhaps the dice had been loaded, the wheels greased a little, and the doctors lost little time in agreeing that he was unfit for military service because of 'concussion', a hypothesis invented by the independent French representative. He was luckier than several others.

At this point in Lodwick's book, we are introduced again to Sheila Legge, and it shifts into a new gear; we might almost be beginning a second volume. It is a story of love and war.

10

Orange Blossoms

Though family memory has it that Lodwick had first met Sheila in London at or around that bizarre Surrealist show, in Lodwick's version they first set eyes on each other in the South of France the day after his successful exercise in blarney in front of the Medical Commission. What was she doing there, among the many trapped in France by the randomness of war?

The simpler explanation is that she had gone there, probably from Paris, to join her mother Ida, yet another in our band of strolling players who had been drawn towards the sun, in her case Avignon, where she died in 1941. Lodwick's version is that Sheila, fictionalised as 'Fiona', had drifted south from Paris and found herself embroiled in an affair with a handsome, married fisherman in St Tropez, one of those he called 'the confraternity which exists to pleasure English ladies on the loose'. While the French Civil Service passed the files and the buck to and fro, not keen to tackle the vexed issue of trapped foreigners, the gendarmes had exiled her to the Romanesque quiet of Orange, some 175 miles north of the Riviera. An Irish friend who was part of Lodwick's Marseilles circle told him she was unhappy there, and they agreed to get her to join them and somehow tweak the system so she too could get back to England.

Protected by his 'Get out of Jail Free' card from the Medical Commission, Lodwick and Sheila travelled slowly by train though Barcelona, Madrid and Lisbon – as did the fictional Fiona. Sheila was held up in Lisbon by the Kafkaesque intricacies of visas, especially in Portugal, which as a fierce guardian of its neutrality was extremely wary about admitting foreigners in transit, and Lodwick had to wait a month after his return to London on 6 May before they were reunited. Foreign Office and MI5 archives have several references to 'financial assistance' given to her on that difficult homeward trek, as well as the interception of her letters.

In telling how, after his return, Lodwick descended into another underworld of danger, violence and yet more prisons we again have several – almost too many – sources on which we can draw. There are Lodwick's own memoirs and fiction. There are the files of SOE and the SBS as well as the official histories of both organisations, though even official material needs to be treated with care. The often weeded, culled and, on at least one occasion, partially incinerated records of SOE make a 100 per cent accounting of its achievements and failures virtually impossible. Moreover, the SOE and MI5 judgements and comments which we quote here need to be read as the reactions of men under stress, with little collective experience of the clandestine world, who knew they were trafficking in human lives and whose own background and upbringing made their 'default setting' one of acute suspicion when faced with someone not cut from the same cloth, especially glamorous women; the shadow of Mata Hari took many years to fade.

Much has been written about SOE, Lodwick's first brief employer in the secret world. Again, some context is needed. Set up in the first grim, even panicky moments of World War II to strike back at the Germans by subversion and sabotage, the Special Operations Executive is seen today as a characteristically Churchillian initiative to 'set Europe ablaze'. It was in fact a reincarnation of the network of spies and oddly named agencies created by William Pitt's government in Switzerland, Holland and France to combat the menace, as they saw it, of the French Revolution and later of Napoleon. Because SOE had been hastily cobbled together, more established elements of the British clandestine world, each with its own objectives, secrets, budgets and needs, immediately saw it as an interloper, so that while doing its best to take the fight to the Germans and their allies it had to spend too much time battling in Whitehall about lines of demarcation, agent recruiting, the allocation of scarce air and radio resources, and its supposedly lax internal and signals security.

These aspects of its struggle to carve out a role are fortunately beyond our scope since Lodwick was involved in only one of its operations, codenamed BOOKMAKER, for the F or French Section, run by Maurice Buckmaster, who became its head in March 1941 after he had been evacuated from Dunkirk. Before the war he had worked as a manager in the French branch of the Ford Motor Company. Some of the notes on Lodwick's file are his; others were written by various of his senior colleagues. Buckmaster had a tough job. Praising his 'boundless enthusiasm', the official historian of SOE's considerable achievements in France – and its inevitable and costly blunders – saw him as 'a colourful and often controversial figure; he had considerable gifts of leadership and some of his most successful agents long admired him. Other did not. He was by no means universally popular but no better Section head was ever in sight.' On SOE itself, the same history remarks that it 'was not a place where fools were suffered gladly... Many of the staff were uncomfortable companions, dead keen on their work but proud and petulant as prima donnas.'[1]

How did SOE come to recruit Lodwick, what did they think of him, and what was the BOOKMAKER story about?

The first official British record of Lodwick the ex-Legionnaire was when he turned up on 22 May 1942 at one of the central London 'cover addresses' used by the secret world, to be interviewed by the urbane and multilingual Major Lewis Gielgud, less well known than his actor brother John but in his way just as powerful a talent.[2] After Eton and Oxford, he was wounded in World War I, and later held senior posts with the International Red Cross until he was 'attached to the War Office' in 1940. From the Bayswater address he gave Gielgud, Lodwick had prevailed on an uncle, a Lieutenant Colonel 'until recently in charge of recruiting for Southern Command', to give him the introductions he needed; it was often, and not unfairly, said that joining the secret world was more a question of whom you knew, rather than what you knew. He had been sent on to Gielgud by MI5's 'Front Office', usually known by the rather Orwellian designation of 'Room 055' in Northumberland Avenue, and had already seen, presumably using the same family introduction, MI19 (the intelligence unit tasked with gathering information from enemy POWs) and the Ministry of Economic Warfare, and had also called on the Free French HQ in Carlton Gardens.

After listening patiently to a long and, from the record of it, overblown and overconfident Lodwick lecture on the state of affairs in France, Gielgud summed him up as 'an impetuous and impatient Irishman [*sic*] who is anxious to find some-thing to do quickly', adding (with a deftly combined pat on the head and rabbit punch) that 'he impressed us as a man with guts and good powers of observation and he has a pleasant manner, which tends to obscure the fact that his judgement is thoroughly undependable'.

His potential value seems to lie in the fact that he claims an intimate detailed knowledge of the Channel Islands and a good knowledge of the Brittany coast and that he served in the Merchant Navy before going to France. He consequently should be of interest to SOE for their operations in this area. His French is not good enough to pass as a Frenchman and I do not think he has the mentality of an Agent for intelligence purposes.

There is no evidence that anyone took the trouble then or later to question or check Lodwick's claims about his knowledge of the Channel Islands, the Brittany coast and his service in the Merchant Navy, but at least they fitted with the seafaring skills he had learned at Dartmouth. His time in Dublin and his connections there, not least with Stuart, were also left unexplored. So too his marriage. At that low ebb in the war, the British secret world was only too happy to consider any adventurous candidate; even a criminal record was not necessarily a bar provided the offence was not too heinous. In some cases such as safe-crackers and forgers, proven skills, even if proven in court, were more of an asset than a liability.

Following his instincts, Gielgud sent Lodwick to SOE, with some help from Lodwick's friend and fellow novelist Selywn Jepson, whom we quoted earlier and who is named in the files as one of his references. Jepson was recognised as far and away the best of SOE's 'talent spotters', though not everyone liked him. The brave and ebullient SOE agent Nancy Wake,[3] who was no respecter of rank when training in England and took no prisoners when fighting in France, dismissed him as 'a creep… so sarcastic that I decided he either had an ulcer or was constipated'. The initials SJ appear on the note we earlier described as making a 'snide' comment about Sheila, though in a rear-view mirror exercise, after Lodwick and Sheila came under closer scrutiny there were veiled suggestions that Jepson had short-circuited the process by which all SOE recruits were checked with MI5.

So Lodwick was taken on in the usual shroud of mystery and ritual signing of the Official Secrets Act, and given a rail warrant to travel to one of the SOE's training centres on the Beaulieu estate of Lord Montagu, whom we last saw floundering in despair through the flotsam and jetsam of the SS *Persia* as it bubbled to the seabed. To judge from the reports, whether on or off duty the trainees were kept under much closer physical and psychological scrutiny than they might have realised, and there seems to have been at least one MI5 or police informer in every London pub, club or cocktail party.

Lodwick's trainers assessed him as 'good and strong. Plenty of guts. Extremely fit.' Not surprisingly, given his Dartmouth schooling, he was highly rated for map reading, boat work and navigation skills, and scored well – 'fearless, strong and very fast' – in close combat. A deeper concern that runs through several reports was the man beneath the skin. An instructor with a sharp eye thought Lodwick a 'semi-keen and efficient soldier; semi-vague and unreliable artist'. The anonymous course commander of STS 23 summed him up in September 1942 as

> Extremely fit and tough… clever and well above average. An objectionable type himself who is conceited, arrogant and intolerant of others who do not do as well as himself. He would be completely ruthless and would make a first-class commando. Has little or no fear of anything and would make a good tough.

An undated comment from the School's overall commander noted that Lodwick 'won't be bothered with written exams… but nearly always on top when physical energy and endurance are required'. He appraised him as 'a typical dauntless devil-may-care individual, fundamentally I should think a weak character and an easy tool for others; disarming manner'. It was to one of the trainers that Lodwick told the story about machine-gunning refugees who were getting in the way of military operations in the helter-skelter French retreat.

More fretting about what might lie below the hard shell comes through in the reports on his parachute training at RAF Ringway, which has long since morphed into Manchester Airport. Although in the 'two days of nervous tension' before his first jump 'he frequently unbent and became quite human', the reports sent to Buckmaster tended to stress Lodwick's 'sarcastic, rather aloof mood', which one observer archly thought might be because he had little to spend on drinks and cigarettes: 'he sends four fifths of his pay to his lady friend'. He summed up with the comment that

> Frankly I don't know what to make of him. Quite apart from the question of security-mindedness I would hesitate to say that I trusted him. He certainly

needs to be kept under observation… I rather suspect he still considers security as a bit of a joke.[4]

To Buckmaster and his colleagues at SOE, the 'lady friend', Sheila, was just as much a headache as the perceived lack of 'security-mindedness' of her headstrong partner. Her earlier life in the art world does not seem to have come to the notice of the stiff-collared men at SOE or MI5, who, if they ever thought about paintings, would tend to prefer Munnings over Magritte. But she had set bells ringing even before she got to London, as F Section brooded balefully about an 'undesirable' association she had formed on her way to England. Lodwick had to pitch in on her behalf before he left on his BOOKMAKER mission to explain that the 'association' had begun with a chance meeting on the train out of France. The man concerned, who at this distance sounds a stereotype from a 1930s novel, was an Englishman who had settled on the Riviera after World War I in search of 'a better climate, a better exchange [rate] and a more sophisticated moral code'. He was now trying to reach Bermuda, for much the same reasons. It also turned out, the wartime world being a small one, that he had been at Cheltenham with John's father, so they found they had a lot in common. When they reached Lisbon it was soon evident that Sheila's visa issues would take some time to sort out, so Lodwick had asked his new friend to keep an eye on her. Old school ties or not, the security mavens at SOE had a low opinion of this new friend, verging on suspicion of disloyalty, which Lodwick defended as the blustering of a man who needed to justify to himself why he had left his homeland for the *dolce vita* of the Riviera.

As the SOE file note from which we quoted earlier had recorded, Lodwick

is married, living not with his wife [i.e. Dorothy] but with a woman [i.e. Sheila] to whom he is very attached. Her influence on him and his career is a great deal stronger than one usually finds… Their association colours his whole attitude towards life… and I believe she is in the process of having a child by him.

Something only a man of his era would write. So SOE and MI5 were fretting about Sheila, hardly helped by episodes such as Lodwick leaving a chunk of SOE explosive in his room (we might wonder who searched it), the young couple's bold but unauthorised attempt to order an Intelligence Corps officer's uniform for him from the Austin Reed menswear store in Oxford, and their indiscreet chatter in pubs and at parties since they had been reunited. Seen through the prism of a relationship between two carefree spirits, one can – just – understand it. Although SOE did its best to smooth over the uniform incident – MI5 noting that 'it was not entirely his fault', merely a matter of not having the right clothing coupons – when refracted through the bottle-glass lens of Baker Street it was unforgivable. Jepson had already arranged for MI5 to give Sheila a heavy warning about indiscretion on the London social scene; one officer suggested they should try to 'prise' them apart.

At various points in his books Lodwick admits to three marriages, one to a Frenchwoman, but says nothing about Dorothy, and he is reticent on names. Nor does he say when and where he and Sheila married. On an SOE form he completed in May 1942, and which was used to run candidates' names 'across the cards' for clearance by MI5 and the police, an admittedly ambiguous question which seems to call for the full names, nationality and place of birth of 'Father/Mother/Husband/Wife' is answered with the single word 'British'.

But despite the doubts and hesitations, SOE selected him to be parachuted into the action in France. Perhaps he was simply expendable cannon fodder, since the odds against BOOKMAKER proved rather high. To find out what happened, we turn first to the official history of SOE as a whole.[5] Because its scope was SOE worldwide, this study, long suppressed in Whitehall, does not mention what was, after all, just a pinprick operation. But it provides some context by making the point that these *coups de main*, a phrase redolent of the Nelsonian era, which had begun in SOE's earliest days, were essential to what modern marketers would call 'building the brand'. Until SOE had built up a field organisation of networks, agents, couriers and radio operators in occupied territory, the only way it could fulfil the sabotage element of its mandate to 'set Europe ablaze' was through 'miniature military operations' from British bases, though with the key difference that the men they sent in wore civilian clothes and were thus not protected by the laws of war. The official history advances a second and probably even more compelling argument: that SOE was anxious for tangible results as ammunition to justify its existence in the Whitehall turf wars.

Looking more narrowly at France, we find that Michael Foot's detailed story of SOE's successes and nasty missteps there does have a succinct account of BOOKMAKER, though it implies that there were two parallel missions under the same codename.[6] But what they were supposed to do? And what happened to them?

11

Beating the Bookmaker

As Foot wrote:

> All through the year [i.e. 1942] F Section toyed with coups de main; several were proposed, but only three men actually left the country, and they all failed. Norman Hinton, a wild and unpunctual Australian art student of 28 with a good deal of skill in fieldcraft, parachuted into France late in November on a lone wolf mission of which no trace remains in his file but a note that 'he did quite well'… The other BOOKMAKER party, J.A.P. Lodwick, a youthful novelist who had fought in the foreign legion in 1940, and Oscar Heimann, a Czech Jewish dentist of forty, were dropped blind on 29 December near La Rochelle to attack a factory that was working for the Germans. Heimann hesitated before he left the aircraft, and consequently fell rather wide of his companion; neither could find the other in the dark. As Heimann had all the explosives and Lodwick had all the information about the target, neither could attack it alone. They made, separately, for a safe house in Paris where they quarrelled sharply; returned through Spain having accomplished nothing, with Hinton, and were all posted out of SOE.

'Posted out of SOE' will prove to be a typically British euphemism. We can fill in many of the blanks from Lodwick's own narrative and from those 'Most Secret' after-action notes in the SOE files. Some will remain forever a white space, like the redactions on Hinton's personal file. Heimann's makes more emotive reading and, as he was Lodwick's parachuting partner, we can start with him. His family were Hungarian, spent World War I in Switzerland, and after the Armistice moved to Czechoslovakia where Heimann served for two years in the army. In civilian life he became a dental technician, and later qualified as a dentist (reminding us, and perhaps Lodwick too, of Captain Ruck). Vaulting frontiers and the Channel with evident ease, he practised near Bordeaux for four years until in August 1939 he turned himself in to the police after entering Britain illegally on a French fishing boat, served ten days in jail and was sloughed off to the Royal Pioneer Corps. In the early days of World War II, before some of its men moved on to frontline duties, the Corps was the polyglot ditch-digging, tree-felling, sandbag-filling 'dustbin' into which were shovelled émigré musicians, bemused anti-Nazi journalists, mid-level foreign bankers without family or City connections, and harmless long-naturalised German waiters. It was there that SOE's radar picked him up. His training reports are sprinkled with comments about his enthusiasm, 'bounce', physical fitness (in another segment of a nomadic career he had coached a football team in Luxembourg) and found him 'cunning and clever'. His handlers worried that he might attract hostile attention in the field because he looked too Jewish, something he dismissed since he claimed he was generally taken in France for a Basque. Anti-Semitism was not confined to rural France or the Wehrmacht. In an off-the-cuff note sadly representative of the British officer-class mindset of the time, one of Heimann's own course commanders wrote: 'This Yid seems keen enough and works hard', though another more balanced observer concluded that 'I think he would prove ruthless and a completely reliable man provided his obviously Jewish origin did not land him in trouble.' (Buckmaster himself thought nothing of tagging another of his teams, all of them Jewish, 'The Palestine Express' and even Lodwick makes a throwaway reference to Heimann as 'hook-nosed'.)

Heimann was not an obvious choice for a sabotage mission. He was undoubtedly brave, but on the face of it this was a man who in his professional life was unlikely to have seen much real danger beyond the removal of an impacted wisdom tooth, and who if captured was in double jeopardy, as a saboteur and a Jewish refugee.

Why were they dropped into an area which would have been crawling with German patrols in the aftermath of a commando raid on the St Nazaire U-boat pens? Why fit them up with aliases and cover stories which would not stand up to five minutes' questioning by the Gestapo or the French gendarmes? Lodwick was reincarnated as Robert Mason, the Cairo-born son of a French ironmonger, and a ne'er-do-well who, after enlisting in the French Army but never firing a shot before the Armistice, had drifted into working on the Riviera as valet for a rich, homosexual

American who had now gone back to the USA; they had parted on bad terms after his employer accused him of stealing his cufflinks. Not, one imagines, a character with which Lodwick would have felt comfortable. The men and women sent out into the field by SOE also had a 'field name' so that they could be identified in its own radio traffic. Once again we might see Jepson's sly hand at work, in choosing to cast Lodwick as 'Arsène', a name which in those far-off days was usually associated not with a north London football team but with Arsène Lupin, a fictional French 'gentleman burglar' in the style of E.W. Hornung's Raffles. Heimann was allowed to keep his first name and his profession but was rebranded as a Lebanese named Leclerc; an implausibly long way from Prague.

The ill-matched pair were parachuted into the hostile dark at 500 feet from a Wellington bomber, one of SOE's sturdy workhorses. The factory they failed to destroy was at Aytré and had been building locomotives since 1918. Today it is the biggest manufacturing plant in the area, producing everything from body shells for the French superfast TGV to tramcars for St Petersburg. We can also confirm Foot's comment that Hinton's mission, though also sent in under the BOOKMAKER heading, was a slightly earlier, separate operation, a bid to set fire to a nearby plant building U-boat hulls. He made two abortive attempts, managed to evade the Germans and made his way – painfully, walking much of the way along railway tracks – to Paris. His family was in Australia, where he had been born, and like Lodwick and others in this story he had come to Britain from the South of France and Spain, describing himself as a 'photo retoucher and artist'. His SOE training reports were mixed, though a 'natural instinct' for fieldcraft was highlighted. In a nice example of SOE's unvarnished internal language, a note on his recruitment says he was 'ultimately to be employed in France as an agent (thug) [*sic*]'.

But we need to stay with Lodwick, for whom in his memoirs BOOKMAKER, although 'a pearl, perfectly planned upon the bureaucratic level, by us a hundred times rehearsed', was stillborn.

Who knows why? Freezing fog – literally – plus fear, the awful difference between rehearsal and the real world, in short the immutable operation of what soldiers call 'Sod's Law', which tells us that if something can go wrong, it will, and at the worst possible time. Amplifying Foot's account, the SOE files tell us that the reasons the mission was abortive are difficult to analyse… what happened after [Lodwick and Heimann] landed is not quite clear. Reports have been rendered by both men which are very contradictory, particularly about the early stages of the operation. It may be that they lost confidence in one another before it began, but it culminated in each ditching the other on reaching the ground. Lodwick is by far the stronger character and we know that he was doubtful about his companion's capabilities, but not to the extent that he ever refused to work with him.

Yet again we are at a narrative crossroads. How fast do we turn the Roundabout? Do we follow Lodwick's telling of their escape under stress and threat, via a safe house in Paris and eventually Spain and another prison – a story which is full of colour – or do we stay with SOE's more prosaic version? For the same reasons as before – why should we venture to recycle or improve on Lodwick's own words in *Bid the Soldiers Shoot*? – we will stay mainly with the SOE paper, written by one of F Section's officers to an SOE senior who had requested 'an objective picture of the case' after Lodwick returned to London under a cloud rather bigger than a man's hand.

But let's begin at the beginning. Lodwick 'made his way', a bureaucratic elision which makes it all sound much easier than it must have been, from the Atlantic coast to the 'safe house' in Paris, actually a small flat in Rue du Bois de Boulogne, between the Arc de Triomphe and Porte Maillot. There, after giving the ritual password – *'Je viens de la part de Michel'* – he found himself once again at close quarters with a nervous Heimann. Too close. They began 'arguing and recriminating'. Hinton, whose French SOE thought was weak, and delivered with 'a very Cockney accent', despite several years spent in Paris as an art student, turned out to be staying in a nearby fleapit hotel. They had money, liberally supplied by SOE along with their false identity papers, and could afford to eat in black-market restaurants, but it was a 24-hour high-wire act and time was not on their side. The fear of capture, bickering with Heimann over the mission's failure and what Lodwick perceived as the latter's pessimism, along with Hinton's risky fondness for picking up impressionable French girls, all made the 'safe house' less and less so; it was, he later told SOE, 'obviously impossible for the three of us… to sleep on a mattress on Cardanelle's kitchen'. (Cardanelle, not otherwise identified, was presumably the brave host of the 'safe house'.) Lodwick turned for help to a woman named Nadia, opening yet another sidebar story, another episode in our version of *La Ronde*. Twenty-eight years old and born in Deauville, Nadia Hamelot was a jewellery designer who had inherited money and whom he asked for help in finding new accommodation. She found him another room on the Boulevard Gouvion-St-Cyr. But he was a man on the run. How did he find her? Was she an emergency SOE contact? Far from it. According to his memoir, 'She had long been a friend of my wife [undoubtedly Sheila, who we know had spent time in Paris] who had guaranteed both her sentiments and her discretion as irreproachable.'

But the story Lodwick told in his memoir about how he met Nadia is not what he said to SOE, to whom he claimed that he had known her in Marseilles before the war. This may well have been an attempt to divert attention from Sheila, since the unavoidable implication of her 'guarantee' was that before he left for the field he had talked to her in detail about the BOOKMAKER plan and the fallback arrangements, another brazen breach of the rules.

Nadia knew people with cars, flats, villas in the country and money. In Nazi-occupied Paris, where even bicycle tyres and matches were scarce commodities, theirs was a rarefied milieu. And she lived at a rarefied address in the *bon chic, bon genre* 16th arrondissement. One of her friends, as Lodwick later told SOE, was a wealthy American, who owned five garages in Paris, 'all working for the Germans and who is also prepared to find cover jobs without recompense'. Another was the French General Manager of the 'Focke-Wulf Factory'; at the time a plant near Paris was working for the Luftwaffe on a design for a multi-engined long-range bomber, subsequently scrapped. Despite the red flags these connections should have raised to anyone even remotely conscious of risk, Lodwick 'took matters in my own hands' and sounded her out in detail about helping SOE by hiding others of their people on the run and working as 'Southern Courier' between the two French zones 'in place of Janine', about whose fate we know nothing, though it is not hard to guess. Put more starkly, as SOE was bound to do, he compounded his indiscretion with Sheila by sketching out to Nadia, maybe with other names, what SOE's basic needs were and how it operated. He told Baker Street, 'I would stake my life on her reliability', reinforcing this with the rather flimsy comment that she had twice been fined by the Police Court for making remarks 'in favour of de Gaulle'.

In his report to SOE, Lodwick, uncharacteristically sensitive to how he was viewed by his employers, added the rider that 'it is perhaps apposite to point out that I have no emotional interest [in Nadia] whatever'.

Apart from an incident when Nadia talked a French policeman out of arresting him for dodgy papers in a late-night Metro raid, Lodwick tells us nothing further about her. He would have been surprised that, though he had yet again broken every rule in the book, another SOE network recruited her in January 1943, through a different connection. Sadly it did not take long for the trap to spring shut. A postwar report written by an SOE officer sent to Paris to find out what had happened to its missing people, especially the brave girls sent out from London, records that the Gestapo snatched her in July, and lost no time in boasting that they had identified her from an intercepted wireless message from London to an SOE operator in France named 'Pierre'. They may well have done – their intercept service was first class – but a core element in their interrogation technique was to demoralise their prisoners by giving them the impression that SOE codes were insecure and that they knew all about SOE from the inside. 'So save yourself the pain and trouble of denying it all.' They were not wrong about the codes, though a key part of the weakness was sloppy message handling at the London end. Another damaging reason was adroit German penetration of the Resistance networks by men and women, one or two British, others French, whom they had 'turned'. Jepson remarks wearily in his postwar oral memoirs that 'the French are rather accustomed to playing both sides against the middle' with their own survival the paramount interest.

In that hyper-watchful world, one small slip was all it took. Maybe someone in her rather attention-attracting circle was indiscreet, or even informed on her to save their own skin or for money. It made no difference. As French internet archives show, she was shipped by cattle car to the concentration camp at Ravensbrück some 50 miles north of Berlin. It was intended mainly for women prisoners, though Lodwick tells us in another section of his war memoirs that after he was rounded up in a police sweep in Marseilles, Cecil Atkinson, the Irishman who had encouraged him to take care of Sheila in the South of France, had been sent there and died. It was a Nazi hell-hole of such vileness that to say Nadia was 'one of the lucky ones' who survived to be repatriated by the Red Cross misses the point of her resilience and bravery. Unless prisoners were shot, beaten till they dropped dead, or subjected to lethal medical experiments and then simply shoved into the camp crematorium, they were worked, starved or, as the Third Reich finally crumbled, force-marched to nowhere to die in the frozen wastelands. Only 15,000 of the 130,000 prisoners taken into German 'protective custody' survived. The available records make chilling reading but suggest that at least Ravensbrück did not indulge the SS' predilection for tattooing its prisoners, and that Nadia's 'registration number', 24729, would only have been inked on a tag sewn into her tattered clothes. She would still have remembered it for a long time. When Captain Hazeldine of SOE interviewed her in Paris after the war he reported to Buckmaster with insensitive understatement that she had little to tell him, 'possibly due to the bad state of nerves she is in following her internment'. We called this a 'sidebar' to our main story. That may be too dismissive. But if a 'sidebar' can have a 'sidebar' of its own, one with Surrealist links appropriate to Sheila will appear later.

In the meantime, picking up our main Lodwick thread again, there is the matter of the code, another potential lapse in security, or at least a blurring of the lines between love and duty, and perhaps another example of sloppiness in the SOE ciphering section. Lodwick does not mention it, nor is it referred to in the SOE summing up which we are using as our main source for this period, but a copy of the original is tucked away in his file. When going 'into the field', SOE officers were given their own code, based on the Playfair/Rimmer cipher system, the origins and relatively easy 'breakability' of which others have analysed at length. (Put at its simplest, it was a box of squares five by five, not unlike a Sudoku puzzle into which the agent inserted as a personal key the name of a person, thing, or place, supposedly known only to the agent and the coders in London; repeat letters were omitted; the blank squares were then filled in with letters of the alphabet in sequence, but with vowels omitted. Lodwick's key phrase was SHEILA LODWICK; so much for prising them apart.) Since BOOKMAKER had no wireless, the code was presumably meant to be used to send word to London if, after success or failure, the agents came into contact with an SOE or Resistance group with their own operator. They didn't and it wasn't.

The Three Musketeers, as one might think of them – though it is hard to envisage a more oddly assorted trio – left France by rail for the Spanish border, clambered onto a truck loaded with refugees, spent a night in another 'safe house', crunched through dense groves of cork trees and finally pushed their way onto a crowded bus which took them thirty miles inside Spain before a spot check by the Guardia Civil revealed them for what they were. Not that they would have blended in any too well with the black-draped Spanish grannies and peasants taking vegetables to market.

Lodwick tells us they were taken to first to Pamplona's grim Fort de San Cristóbal jail, though the SOE file also locates them at the Miranda de Ebro, one of the network of concentration camps, nowadays airbrushed from memory, set up by the Franco regime as handy hideaways to detain their real or alleged opponents, or work them till their corpses could be tossed into communal graves. Along with commandeered hotels, the camp system now had to accommodate a growing number of British escapers. In line with the SOE playbook the trio claimed they were RAF men shot down over Belgium. Though one worldly-wise Spanish officer had been heard to murmur that the number of RAF planes allegedly shot down over Belgium seemed greater than the entire strength of Bomber Command, the Spanish handled each case with canny caution. Processing too many exfiltrated saboteurs along the road to repatriation would have caused diplomatic problems with the Germans; on the other hand, in the background was a secret and probably undocumented understanding under which the Spaniards would release a certain number of detainees, against a British agreement to allow specified quantities of oil to pass through their naval blockade.

Again, as Lodwick told his own stories, we can stay with the London view. His copybook was already stained with blots, and his next steps would spill the entire inkpot over his record. The letter he wrote to the British Consul in Madrid, and which Hinton and Heimann co-signed, struck a raw nerve with local British diplomats and much annoyed London, where it was seen as 'vexing, injudicious, stupid and impertinent'. Even allowing for the stress the men had been, and continued to be, under – an allowance London was not prepared to make, commenting that the letter 'shows a degree of insolence which can hardly be excused even on grounds of nervous strain' – it was a prime example of Lodwick vituperation. To complain to an overworked Consul after only two weeks that they had not been given the 'absolute priority' for return they had been promised, that they had not received their back pay or clean shirts, and to moan about the Consulate's 'lackadaisical inefficiency' was not calculated to win friends and influence people. And it didn't. The Consul minuted crossly that the men 'had been released as a result of my representations [and are] now in Madrid'. And London noted the letter had left a 'very bad impression out there, causing [SOE] a great deal of irritation and necessitating apologies', and prompted Baker Street to signal that the trio were not to be given any priority at all. If air space became available it was to be allocated to Hinton, Heimann and Lodwick – in that order!

Another piece of Lodwick's Spanish jigsaw is the reappearance of Walter Starkie, another of those bright lights in the Dublin firmament in which the young and ambitious Lodwick had tried so hard to become a star. Starkie had been posted to Madrid in 1940 to develop Britain's cultural diplomacy in Spain. As Donald Steury's analysis for the CIA's Center for the Study of Intelligence[1] points out, though often described as 'neutral' Spain was actually a 'non-belligerent power', and in the early years of war had a decidedly pro-German tilt. In November 1940 Franco's Foreign Minister (and brother-in-law) Ramón Serrano Suñer signed a secret protocol under which Spain became an 'adherent' to the Tripartite Pact agreed a few months earlier between Germany, Italy and Japan, and even promised to enter the war at some unspecified future date. And as a minor but symbolic step, not reversed even today, Franco shifted Madrid to Central European Time, to stay in step with Berlin.

Starkie was an astute choice. Though his was a British mission, he was Irish, and thus neutral, and a man who understood Spain and its culture. Moreover, he was a man whose early comments on the Civil War suggested he thought the Franco regime should be given a chance to prove itself rather than condemned out of hand, and who had been a founding member in the 1930s of the Institut International des Études Fascistes, a Lausanne-based group described by one of his biographers as 'right wing and sometimes far right'.[2] As a Roman Catholic he also met one of the post's other important criteria. Scrounging for premises, furniture, books and pupils he set up the British Institute – 'El British' – in Mendez Nuñez Street in Central Madrid, and later opened outposts in Barcelona and Valencia, bridging the cultural divide through concerts, lectures, films and especially its initiatives in English language teaching. In a hotbed of spies and counterspies, it is hardly surprising that there were rumours claiming him to be a British intelligence 'asset' of some kind, but although he and his wife were known to have sheltered escaping refugees and POWs there is no evidence of 'nuts and bolts' espionage. In 1986, in the wake of yet another Spanish press allegation, his daughter denied the rumours vehemently. And recounting a brush with a self-important young Secret Intelligence Service (SIS) officer he met during his turbulent passage back to England, Lodwick wrote of Starkie that 'throughout the war years, it is safe to say that he did more for Allied influence and prestige than any sample of half a dozen of these cloaked but daggerless wonders'. Starkie's Italian-born wife did her bit too, organising the distribution of American Red Cross food parcels to the needy, and dragooning local ladies into fortnightly 'sewing bees' where the empty food sacks were turned into rough and ready clothing for destitute children.

Julian Amery, the 'straight-arrow' brother of the sad and misguided John, has a story to share about Starkie and the Spanish Civil War, on which the ever adventurous Julian, not yet 20, was reporting for the *Daily Express*.[3] When a British diplomat heard that Amery was planning to drive out in search of 'copy' to Avila, the ancient walled city some 75 miles north-west of Madrid, he asked him to give a lift to Starkie, who wanted to get to know one of the local Gypsy tribes. Amery agreed and off they drove, Starkie deflecting questions about the strange and dangerous world which they found themselves crossing by saying he had no interest in politics or the war, just Gypsies. In the middle of the night and of nowhere, the car broke down. A raggle-taggle band of Gypsies appeared out of the dark, prompting Starkie to take out the fiddle with which he always travelled and play some of their own melodies. Delighted, they flourished their primitive guitars and the traditional *bota* bags, goatskin pouches filled with rough wine, and sang their plaintive songs until 3 a.m., when Amery and Starkie finally went to sleep on the cold and stony hillside. In the morning a passing vehicle went off to get help. Other than as a snapshot of relaxed charm and folk music in the middle of a bloody war, the point of the story is that if, as has been claimed,[4] Starkie really was a British agent, SIS had chosen someone who was hardly unobtrusive. Having said that, as far back as Wellington's campaign against the French in Spain, the 'Iron Duke' is said to have used spies 'disguised as pedlars, wandering musicians and suchlike, among whom was a guitar player of some celebrity'.[5] The reality is that Starkie was all too well aware of the fragility of his position – he did not have diplomatic immunity and could be thrown into jail or out of the country at a snap of Franco's fingers, nor was he in any position to get information of much strategic or even tactical value. He was acutely aware that that he was closely watched by the German and other spies in Spain. So we are probably on safe ground to conjecture that at most Starkie was one of the many sources to whom diplomats and SIS officers could talk informally and confidentially as they panned every rivulet sieving for nuggets of information, a man who would allow his flat to be used a temporary hiding place for escaping POWs or refugees but not a formally recruited, let alone paid, 'agent'.

As in other neutral states such as Sweden and Portugal, spying was a cottage industry. One internet listing contains several hundred pages of names, most of them Germans (among them a Jesuit priest whose patriotism overrode his strong anti-Nazi feelings) employed by, attached to or in close contact with the German Embassy in Madrid, its consulates and its commercial 'front' organisations. The list, probably based on US Operation SAFEHAVEN'S efforts to track down Nazi loot, shows they were busy not just with the usual run of overt and undercover work but also less conventional but personally more lucrative ventures involving arms and wolfram trading, smuggling of looted gold, art and wine and high-end cars, all the way down to outright fraud. As another example of the poisonously convoluted world of wartime Madrid, the operations of the American Office of Strategic Services (forerunner of the CIA) were hampered by a US ambassador and staff hostile to their activities to the point where, as Steury's history tells us, most of its operatives in Spain were handled out of Lisbon under non-official cover 'because the (US) diplomatic staff in Madrid made a practice of identifying intelligence agents to the Spanish police'.

In the early days of World War II, when Nazi power seemed irresistible, Franco awarded many Abwehr officers the same glittering medal he had bestowed on Hitler and Mussolini in 1937, and a little later on Himmler and von Ribbentrop. In 1941 he also authorised his provincial governors to make a detailed census of Spain's Jewish residents, not just who they were and where they lived, but where they worked and their politics, well aware it was to be sent to Himmler as he brooded over the opportunity to export his genocidal plans to Iberia. But as one Abwehr officer told his US interrogators after the war, as the times and tide changed around 1943 many Spaniards who had been 'in German service or in liaison' became 'unavailable'. By 1944, mirroring Franco's fleet-of-foot fandango, they had switched their allegiance to the Allies.[6]

Another intriguing tale is worth telling, if only because of its possible link to Lodwick's story, and perhaps Walter Starkie's too. Johannes de Graaf was born in Canada to Dutch parents who moved back to Holland in the early 1930s. Born in a Dominion, he claimed British citizenship, which led the Germans to intern him briefly when they marched into Holland, but he managed to convince them he was more Dutch than English and they let him go. In 1942 he tried to get into England from Gibraltar, claiming he was on his way back to Canada. He found himself caught up in the fine-meshed sieve MI5 deployed to scrutinise aliens and those who had been in enemy-occupied territory. Interrogated for three months in the Gothic rabbit warren of the former Royal Victoria Patriotic Schools on Wandsworth Common and later in the frightening no man's land of Camp 020 on Ham Common – the Model T Ford precursor of Guantanamo's supercharged SUV – de Graaf at first denied having anything to do with the Nazis. Eventually he admitted to being a sabotage agent trained and supplied by them with 'secret writing materials', which he had used from Spain and Gibraltar, though he had never really meant to work for the enemy and had only agreed to do so as a way of getting into England and back home to Canada. In September 1943 a stiff MI5 file note on the case recorded that before he left Europe through Gibraltar, de Graaf had spent nine months working for the Military Attaché at the British Embassy in Madrid,

> during which time he was in contact with large numbers of RAF pilots who had escaped and were making their way back to Britain. Towards the end of this period the Germans succeeded in arresting a young girl who had been responsible for shepherding most of these men over the Franco-Spanish border, and although there is no actual proof, a strong suspicion is entertained that de Graaf was the source from which the enemy obtained their information.

The BOOKMAKER trio also claimed RAF cover, so we can assume de Graaf, who was imprisoned for the rest of the war, knew about their real role, though quite what that might have meant in practice we can only speculate.[7]

The problem for conspiracy theorists is that these stories can always be seen 'through a glass, darkly'. Was Starkie's learned, gregarious, 'have violin, will travel' Irish persona really a brilliant facade, much as no one believed – until too late – that behind the careless demeanour of the brilliant but garrulous Guy Burgess could be an important agent of any halfway competent secret service, let alone Moscow? As regards Starkie, our interpretation seems nearer the mark and we can return to Lodwick, whose real life was the stuff of fiction anyway and about to take yet another tricky turn.

In the Orchard Court flat where F Section was housed, and in other SOE offices in and around Baker Street, there were minutes and mutters about disciplinary action, all the more since Lodwick had enclosed with his letter of complaint the text of a telegram he wanted London to send to Sheila, then staying with a Mrs Brown in Kensington High Street, adding insouciantly, 'I suggest the cost should be put down to my expenses.' The text, which is also on his file in his own capital letters, read:

DARLING. I ADORE YOU. AM WELL AND WILL BE HOME SOON. YOU ARE ALWAYS IN MY THOUGHTS. PLEASE WIRE ME C/O EMBASSY MADRID WHEN THIS RECEIVED. I LOVE YOU. I LOVE YOU. I LOVE YOU. JOHN (LODWICK).

At a human level this was no more than an understandable expression of reassurance and love. But SOE operated at a different professional altitude, with no room for emotion, especially when embedded in secret communications. While all this was being biliously digested, along with another indiscreet letter Lodwick had written to Sheila from Spain but which was intercepted by the British Censorship, Lodwick and his companions returned to the UK via Gibraltar on 2 March. As they passed through Immigration, an SOE emissary sidled up to murmur that they were to report to Orchard Court straight away. Ever cavalier, Lodwick drove the last nail into his SOE coffin by telling his two companions to pass on to Baker Street that 'it was his birthday and he proposed to celebrate it before reporting'.

'This final incident', the SOE officer wrote, 'to my mind typifies Lodwick's attitude towards duty and discipline as far as this Organisation is concerned and probably towards any superior factor in his relationship with the world at large.'

He has got Irish blood in him and with it much of the 'agin'ness' of that race. He is a natural rebel… He is intelligent, clever, a little sly, tactless, selfish and undoubtedly fearless both physically and in spirit. He is very tough and fit. On occasion he is a heavy drinker but as far as I know carries his liquor well.[8]

It is perhaps too melodramatic to see the SOE memorandum as the Prosecution's closing speech, or to imagine that, as in earlier Old Bailey days, the black cap was being pulled out of mothballs in Baker Street in preparation for the judgement on Lodwick. As with headmasters, Dartmouth officers and some of his superiors in the Foreign Legion, he had been pig-headed, tone-deaf to the organisational obsession with security, never mind the practical dictum of 1940, rammed home to the public through mass advertising, that 'Careless Talk Costs Lives'. He knew about SOE training and methods, its codes, its Paris 'safe houses' and escape lines, and could identify some of its officers. He was not given much opportunity to argue his own case; but had he done so he might well have made things worse by yet again behaving crassly, in his superiors' eyes, or, as he might see it, delivering home truths, however unpalatable, and however unpopular it made him. And had he had the chance, afforded to later researchers long after he died, to see several random samples of other SOE files, when what was left of its archives was belatedly released into the public domain, he might have concluded correctly that he was far from the only agent to have been indiscreet on the London social circuit, in the field and in letters sent from Spain.

Writing years later as a fictional character, but surely looking in the mirror, Lodwick observed bleakly that

> It is my hope to remain aloof. That is the lesson my formative years, all spent in the war, have taught me. I despise the world. I cannot accept its conventions. I do not wish to be driven, *cornered*, the victim of chance and circumstance.

The verdict from the Director after reading the memorandum from which we have quoted was scathing.

> This is a plausible, well-spoken but unscrupulous young man. He is only interested in his own skin and that of any woman whom he might admire. He struck me as being a soldier of fortune chiefly for such glamour as might be derived from a lucky VC etc.
>
> His moral integrity I graded as -0%. He is security minded only insofar as it affects him personally or any one he desires. He assesses security in terms of prison sentences and not as a moral obligation to his fellow human beings.
>
> He has written a book and intends to write another. I have no doubt he thinks he is clever enough to cash in on his experiences with us while regarding

the possible penalties under the OSA [Official Secrets Act] as a good gamble or battle of wits. I hope the OSA wins. Perhaps one might arrange a posthumous VC which would make everyone happy...

I gather we are all agreed that the sooner he is disposed of the better and that the disposal, if possible, should take the form of having him posted to a remote place overseas.

It did, but as the suave Selwyn Jepson purred when telling Lodwick his brief SOE career was over, 'Times have moved on. We don't send the naughty ones to the next world, but to Scotland.' Jepson softened the blow by telling him he had arranged an interview for Lodwick with the then Lieutenant Colonel Robert Laycock[9] at the Combined Operations Headquarters. He hoped (which meant he had fixed it in advance through some clandestine version of the old boy network) that Laycock would take him on as a commando. But as Laycock was a stickler for military neatness, not least a tightly clipped 'short back and sides', it would be a good idea if Lodwick took the trouble to get his hair cut beforehand.

Muttering that his hair was short enough after being routinely shaved in Spanish jails, Lodwick for once listened to advice and went to the barber's before he reported to Laycock at his heavily guarded offices in Richmond Terrace across a sandbag-lined, sentry-patrolled Whitehall from Downing Street. Laycock took him on, despite or even because of the red flags in the SOE file which he had on his desk. He added that before he reported to the Commando Depot he needed to get a proper haircut!

He sent him downstairs to a cluttered office where, in another of those encounters which only the confused concatenations of war can create, the ambitious author Lodwick found his travel papers being fussed over by a much more established member of his profession, and fellow Roman Catholic, Evelyn Waugh, then serving inefficiently and bibulously as Laycock's Personal Assistant and Liaison Officer with Combined Operations HQ, in the barren period before he was finally manipulated into resigning his commission.

Waugh's military service, often miserable, sometimes dangerous and disheartening, as in the retreat from Crete with Laycock, has been extensively written about, strikingly by the author himself in his *Sword of Honour* trilogy, and also in his autobiography and letters, and has been combed over closely by researchers and biographers. So we can stay with Lodwick's account of this brief encounter, and consider one trace it might have left.

Lodwick tells us that Waugh did him 'an enormous kindness' by talking to him about books as if Lodwick were his literary equal. Waugh was then 40, Lodwick 27. 'My best book is *A Handful of Dust*,'[10] Waugh told him, adding that he was trying to write another, to be called *Work Suspended*, though he added ruefully that in the circumstances of the war he was unwilling to finish it. (He never rounded it off as a novel, though extracts from it were published by Penguin later in the year as part of a collection of longer and short stories, and 'fragments of fragments' appeared in *Horizon* magazine.)

Though certainly not without private kindness, Waugh could display a nasty streak, not least in skewering and lampooning real people, including his friend Cyril Connolly, *Horizon*'s editor, and borrowing aspects of their personalities, as he built up the characters in his novels. He also had a long memory. Before or after the encounter with Lodwick, brief though it may have been, he would certainly have seen Lodwick's 'Top Secret' SOE file as uniformed messengers hand-carried it to and from Laycock. For the rest, we are not in what the intelligence analysts would have classed as A1 territory, but the speculation is worth an airing.

The three volumes of the *Sword of Honour* appeared in 1952, 1955 and 1961, peopled with extraordinary characters and telling of extraordinary events in peace and war and the power and disappointments of faith. In the second volume we first meet a Corporal Major (an arcane cavalry title, equivalent to an Army Sergeant) who after a nightmare attempt to escape from Crete in a small boat rescues the narrator but who may also (echoes of Dartmouth) have pushed overboard another officer, demented and perhaps past saving. The Corporal Major comes to the fore in the third volume, now an officer and with a personality described by reviewers as 'Faustian', 'saturnine' and 'menacing'. He keeps a daily diary of his thoughts and epigrams, was once the 'valet' to a gay diplomat (echoing some of the 'cover' background foisted on an unappreciative Lodwick by SOE for that abortive BOOKMAKER mission) and after the war publishes *The Death Wish*, a novel which, though he dismisses it himself as 'pure tosh', is well received. Waugh agreed with 'tosh', though he also described the Corporal Major's book more elaborately as turning 'from drab alleys of the Thirties into the odorous gardens of a recent past transformed and illuminated by disordered memory and imagination'. But the comments on the imaginary Corporal Major's imaginary *Death Wish* could apply almost as well to Lodwick's *Brother Death*, first published in 1948.

The only point of this amateur précis of Waugh's depiction of a strange but compelling character in a brilliant narrative is that the Corporal Major's name is 'Ludovic'. Coincidence? A random dip into the grab-bag of memory, or was it a relatively painless professional nip? If so, did Lodwick strike back? *The Cradle of Neptune* was published in 1961. As we have noted, its tale of Commander Bouchard, kidnapped by a mad missionary in China and condemned to endure many months of forced Bible-reading and hymn-singing, has strong echoes of Tony Last's lonely fate in Waugh's 1934 novel *A Handful of Dust*, abandoned deep in the Brazilian forests, reading Dickens aloud to the demented Mr Todd. Lodwick's tale seems almost to have been bolted on to his central Dartmouth narrative. Whether this reflects some minor literary tit-for-tat, Lodwick's response to the thinly veiled adaptation of his name, or whether it was just a regurgitated half-memory of the earlier novel are questions best left to an academic commentator, much like the depiction of the caddish 'Major' (actually Captain) Chipstead in Lodwick's *Contagion to this World*, an older, cannier reincarnation of Waugh's gloriously seedy Captain Grimes. Literary men, and women too, often enjoy revenge. Jumping back to Dublin, in what is claimed to be a blow struck at Stuart and his elopement with Maude Gonne, Yeats wrote in 1936[11] that he had seen

A girl that knew all Dante once
Live to bear children to a dunce.

Before we shift back to the war, and another Lodwick foray into danger, what happened to his two BOOKMAKER buddies?

1 2

Highlands and Islands

Though Michael Foot tells us that all three in the BOOKMAKER party were 'posted out of SOE' the phrase is ambiguous in meaning and vague in date. Lodwick we know about. But the other two?

After disciplinary problems, which may explain the redactions in his file, and an abortive but well-meant attempt by SOE to reposition him as an officer in the Regular Army, Hinton vanished into the civilian world, with the assurance that he would not find himself called up for military service. His unsuitability is encapsulated in the Blimpish reaction of the Major General who presided over the Officer Selection Board. 'Entirely deficient of [*sic*] soldierly qualities or knowledge,' he harrumphed, while another Board member concluded that he lacked 'poise and dignity' and was 'generally lacking in all things calculated to set a good example to anyone in his charge'. The Board's psychiatrist thought him 'a sentimental idealist', though the overall weight of the comments reflects less on Hinton himself than on SOE's own original judgement. It may also indicate an element of instinctive army bias against SOE and its secretive skulduggery.

In Heimann's case SOE allocated him a 'Guest Room' in Hood House, part of the anonymous rabbit warren of comfortable and sporadically notorious apartments at Dolphin Square, overlooking the Thames, and by their account he twice ran into Gaullist Free French officers and chatted to them about BOOKMAKER. Thinking he was about to be sent back to France, he compounded the indiscretion by offering to carry letters for them. (He did not know that SOE had decided that because anti-Jewish measures had considerably toughened in France, he could not be sent back there and there was no other suitable posting available.)

The French officers reported his indiscreet approach, quite rightly, though it can't have been much more than a lonely agent reaching out to men who spoke his language and knew his adopted country. But when, inevitably, the report reached SOE its response was neither a stiff reprimand nor a spell in 'The Cooler', the remote Highland enclave at Inverlair Lodge, where agents judged unsuitable or dangerously loose-lipped were held until time purged them of anything of strategic value they might once have known. Hinton was briefly a 'guest' there. Nor was it a posting back to the Pioneers. Instead, after questioning by SOE's Security Officer and MI5 at Baker Street, where he may have made matters worse for himself by stoutly denying he had said anything untoward, he was slapped with a summons to appear at a court martial in the Duke of York's Headquarters, hard by Sloane Square in Chelsea, orchestrated by Buckmaster and Jepson. Tough Heimann may have been, but this over-the-top demonstration of the power and drumhead discipline of the British authorities, especially to a refugee with the unspoken fear of a long time in jail or even a firing squad, might have reminded him of Kafka's *The Trial*, the story of a man's losing struggle with an invisible and incomprehensible law.

Heimann was sentenced to be 'Dismissed the Service'. The system would never admit that it might have gone too far, though subsequent SOE minutes concede that it had not been the most serious breach of security SOE had seen, and 'he has learned his lesson'. The files also show that Baker Street 'feels some sort of responsibility' for him; he continued to get some unquantified financial support and SOE went out of its way to sort out his immigration status, deflect the Pioneer Corps' bureaucratic attempt to re-conscript him, and to find him work in a factory. Heimann himself seem to have put any rancour behind him, at least as shown by a chatty handwritten letter he sent early in 1946 to Buckmaster, telling him he was now married, had 'a sweet little daughter' and was working as a chiropodist. He did not know SOE had by then ceased to exist and Buckmaster had retired and rejoined Ford at Dagenham.

BOOKMAKER was a bad bet; its failure and the excitable follow-up were a case of poor selection (for neither the first nor the last time), crass behaviour and jittery over-reaction.

But back to Lodwick. Luckily for him, 'Scotland' was not Inverlair but the Commando Depot, at Achnacarry House at Spean Bridge in the county of Inverness, centre of the ancestral estate of the Chief of the Clan Cameron.

He was to make far less comfortable journeys in the life that lay ahead, but a rail trip in World War II Britain was a far cry from the images projected by prewar advertising posters, showing happy families relaxing on almost deserted, implausibly sunny beaches. For him it meant being squashed in a dimly lit and overcrowded train, its corridors crammed with kitbags and the many unlucky enough not to get a seat, its toilets eye-wateringly pungent after Watford and suffocatingly Augean by the time they got to Crewe. Station signs had been removed to baffle any invading Germans, so the passengers never really knew where they were. Or cared. They were just happy to get where they were going.

Lodwick panted, scrambled and shot his way through his commando 'basic training course', a rather euphemistic description of a tough process of indoctrination in survival and killing skills. He surprised himself by doing well, and after more focused training in blowing things up – an art he had mastered in SOE's schools – was taken on as one of the 'no holds barred' men of the Special Boat Service (or SBS), a decision surely suggested by his Dartmouth training.

Again, in our ambitiously adopted role as the *meneur de jeu* we have a variety of sources on which to draw in moving the Roundabout along. The official British history, Volume 2 of Sir Brooks Richards' *Secret Flotillas*,[1] tells us little, in fact next to nothing, about what the SBS did in and around the Mediterranean. Unexpectedly there is much more in Susan Heuck Allen's thorough study,[2] as although its unpromising headline focus is on *American Archeologists... in World War 2 Greece*, it actually gives much operational detail and colour on the SBS and its charismatic leader George Jellicoe, then only in his mid-twenties.[3]

The SBS, 'The Long Range Desert Group', 'The Greek Sacred Squadron', 'Popski's Private Army', 'The Special Raiding Squadron', 'The Levant Schooner Flotilla', 'Pompforce' and 'Force 133' (a cover for SOE) are just some of the units which bounced over the waves between the islands of the Aegean or barrelled their jeeps across the North African deserts. Their forte was the *coup de main* of Lodwick's first (and last) SOE mission, now translated into blunter Anglo-Saxon as 'butcher and bolt' operations, blasting petrol dumps, destroying wireless installations, arming and training Greek resisters, killing Germans; anything that would hurt the enemy, keep his forces tied up in the islands and unable to reinforce Europe, and generally put him 'on the back foot'. And like SOE, though it was a creature of World War II, the SBS could trace its roots back to the reign of George III and English plots, counterplots, coups and deniable assassination attempts, directed mainly against the Revolution in France and its aftermath. Among them was Captain John Wesley

Wright's secret mandate to put together a small flotilla of fast-sailing cutters in the Channel for 'a particular and delicate service of very high importance to the interests of this country'.[4] It was warfare over a scattered seascape of islands that are now mostly tourist magnets; only memorials in the town squares commemorate their savage history. It was skirmishing and quasi-official thuggery over which the 'conventional' military structures of command and control did not readily fit, with the result that who was actually in charge of what remained rather unclear until quite late in the war, a situation which suited the free spirits of the SBS. The strict boundaries of diplomacy were also flexed, with a neutral Turkey turning a blind eye and a deaf ear to German protests about SBS and others sheltering in remote Turkish bays and harbours. Indeed, a large schooner moored in a hidden Turkish inlet was one of the main SBS bases.

The Service also found itself ferrying men and material for other tentacles of the secret octopus such as SOE and SIS, often using the anodyne cover name of the InterService Liaison Department. Their raids could also sometimes be a potential disruption for more delicate landings and exfiltrations; word would filter down that it would be appreciated if 'Jellicoe's bandits' would keep out of the area of this or that island at a certain time. Within the SBS itself, imperious and adventurous types of the likes of Jellicoe, David Stirling, Fitzroy Maclean, Paddy Mayne and David Sutherland were not by nature men who simply obeyed their orders. Energetic improvisation would be nearer the mark. They were in a long-standing British tradition. Back in Boer War days, Stirling's uncle had created the Lovat Scouts, sharpshooters (the term then used for snipers) who were proud of their motto that 'he who shoots and runs away, lives to shoot another day'. The SBS did not run away, just melted back into the hills or puttered away in their clandestine fishing boats. David Stirling, who went on to build the Special Air Service (SAS), was remembered by another brave heart, his friend Fitzroy Maclean, as a man who had 'the ultimate quality of a leader, the gift for carrying those he led with him on enterprises that by any rational standards seemed certain to fail and convincing them that under his leadership they were bound to succeed'.[5]

The main thing was that it worked, but inevitably there was a cost. Into the balance went, on the one hand, many German casualties and much damage to the Wehrmacht supply chain and its ability to move forces to other fronts. On the other hand there was the price paid in SBS lives, and – a much more difficult issue – the many hundreds of killings of Greeks young and old, peasants, priests, fishermen, grandfathers and grandmothers, massacred by the Germans in reprisal for British attacks.

We have a sense of the SBS leaders. Of their officers, dashing, brave and generally surprisingly young, we don't need to reprise Lodwick's pen portraits, except to take as a proxy the Danish-born Anders Lassen, whose reputation – his tally of Germans killed or captured in the eastern Mediterranean was spoken of with awe – is claimed to have directly affected Wehrmacht operational tactics. Lodwick tells us in deliberately flat prose about a raid on Mykonos in April 1944 when Lassen and an unnamed sergeant burst into a barracks in which 48 Italians and 20 Germans were sleeping. Their *modus operandi* was lethally straightforward. First the sergeant kicked the door open, then Lassen lobbed in two grenades and the sergeant, firing his Bren gun from the hip, sprayed the walls and corners. 'Finally Lassen, with his pistol, dealt with any remaining signs of life.'

Just a few months short of his 25th birthday Lassen was killed in an Italian firefight as World War II drew to a close, in an action for which he was awarded the Victoria Cross.[6]

Of the SBS NCOs and men, Lodwick tells us that Scotsmen and Irishmen, most of the latter from the South, predominated. In his words: 'Jocks are deadly in drink and can smash cafe tables more quickly than any other troops, but they can also carry greater loads and carry them farther. Micks are incurably sentimental, obstinate as bedamned, but, well-officered, will go anywhere.'

Lodwick himself earned praise. As George Jellicoe remembered, David Sutherland thought him 'inventive, operationally imaginative with a fertile mind as a planner'.[7] But before we look at what that actually meant in gory detail, we again need context.

This part of the story takes Lodwick through a period and through parts of the world which were then, and for many years after remained, in considerable turmoil. How much does a searcher after the maverick author need to know about the sufferings in Greece as Right and Left battled for postwar power and the people starved and died, or the bloody and debilitating rivalry of the Chetniks and Partisans in wartime and war-torn Yugoslavia? Early on we said this book was not an amateur exercise in literary criticism, but Lodwick's own story. In the same vein, we won't attempt to summarise the course of World War II overall, or even in the Mediterranean. But we need some minimal background. The way to provide it is to guess at what Lodwick would have known at the time, from BBC broadcasts, from SBS briefings, from back numbers of London newspapers, from what the Germans said or did not say, and from Greek prison gossip, often a quite reliable source since some of the Polish POW 'trusties' had contacts outside the barbed wire among SIS and SOE parties hidden in the hills.

By 1944 the tide of war had begun to swing significantly, and though it was hard to discern amid setbacks, in Europe, in the Pacific, on the Eastern Front and in the Middle East, the pressure was on the Germans and the Japanese. With Mussolini overthrown, the shaky new government headed by General Badoglio surrendered, prompting shrill cries of condemnation from Berlin and much confusion on the ground when not all Italian units went over to the Allied side. Some went on fighting alongside their German allies in what proved to be one of the bloodiest and, in terms of losses, costliest campaigns on mainland Europe; many just wanted to go home. True, in July the plot to blow up Hitler at his East Prussia HQ had failed, those involved or even believed to have been implicated had died horribly, and Hitler had snatched the discredited Italian 'Duce' Mussolini to what turned out to be transient safety.[8]

But the field-by-field, street-by-street advance of the Allies into Europe went on, as did the slaughter, tank battles and savage Russian guerrilla attacks on the Eastern Front. August 1944 saw the triumphal liberation of Paris, the city Lodwick had known as an SOE fugitive and, from a few irritatingly fuzzy scraps of memory in his books, as a footless young wanderer on his way South. But the world was reminded of a volley of Churchillian oratory in November 1942. At the time many had privately discounted as no more than morale-boosting rhetoric his prediction after British victories in Egypt that 'this is not the end. It is not even the beginning of the end. But it is, perhaps, the end of the beginning.' But by 1944 many harked back to his words and began to convince themselves he might have been right.

It was still a hard slog. Back in shattered and shabby London, where Sheila was living and waiting, and Evelyn Waugh was drinking away his dejection at being sidelined, the echo of Churchill's brave words and the daily news were often drowned out by the devastating explosions of Hitler's 'Revenge Weapons', the V1 flying bombs, even though intelligence deception, radar and the flying skill of British fighter pilots succeeded in destroying or diverting about half of them before they reached their targets. From September the deadlier V2, the first ballistic missile, almost impossible to track and intercept, brought more death and destruction. But most people heeded the advice to 'keep calm and carry on'. They had little choice.

Down in the Dodecanese, Lodwick and his colleagues were pushing back after operations which some historians have termed 'one of the last major German victories of the war', when they repulsed an Allied bid to exploit the Italian surrender and seize control of the islands. It had been promoted by Churchill against US opposition and led some to comment that the bid had been a bold blunder, not unlike his support of the Gallipoli disaster in World War I. This is too sweeping and harsh a conclusion, but whatever the background the abortive campaign, which lasted from early September to late November 1943, was lost to superior German air power, and at great cost, especially in terms of British ships and civilian lives. To write that the Germans then 'held control' of the islands until the end of the war may be correct in terms of colouring on a map but leaves out of account that soon after the British withdrawal, the SBS and others began again to harass the Germans, run arms to the Greeks and suborn the remaining Italians. Meanwhile Beaufighters strafed German shipping and British submarines blockaded their major ports, stretching German resources and nerves to the limit. Lodwick writes of parachute drills in Palestine (a follow-up to his SOE training at Ringway) and was briefed in Mersa Matruh, on the Egyptian coast, on his next perilous mission. Somewhere in this period he celebrated Sheila's birthday by knocking back some 'very bad brandy' in Tobruk.

In retelling Lodwick's 'post-brandial' story we will stick with the highlights of his official report; the images and anecdotes in his published books about life, often 'nasty, brutish and short', in the various jails through which he passed, along with his other adventures, are there for the reader to consult at leisure. They are worth a look. We will also weave in the account of Bombardier Nixon, his SBS partner both in battle and through the later adventures, which generally tracks Lodwick's, though it adds some points of detail and omits one bloody encounter. All in all, it shows him to have been a tough, observant and resilient soldier, of whom Lodwick and the SBS could be proud. Lodwick himself calls Nixon 'a real comrade'. The headlines are taken from Lodwick's cover page and are an abbreviated version of a story pockmarked with perils, in which Lodwick, to drag out an overused modern phrase, was very much 'in harm's way'.

Lodwick wrote his report as a serving officer in the immediate aftermath of his adventures, while everything – the attacks, the prisons, the German questioning and threats of a 7.62 mm Mauser bullet in the head, the sudden moves from one dangerous hotspot to the next – was painfully fresh in his mind. In two of his books he tells the same basic story but with the addition of many other memories and patches of colour, much like an artist going back to an early minimalist canvas and refreshing it from a new palette. 'Wrote' is not quite right since what we have is a dozen or so single-spaced typed foolscap pages. There are no evident errors or corrections (unlike the tatty manuscripts with which he later bombarded his London publishers) and, rather amazingly, it was prepared just four days after Lodwick was freed in Bulgaria. Whether he typed the material himself or had the services of a clerk, we do not know. We do know he liked to write his books by hand, but he could also use a typewriter.

Several of the SBS leading lights contributed to the Sound Archives at the Imperial War Museum, which also holds many evocative photographs. But to mine that mother lode would have turned this project into a new mini-history of SBS, something which may be overdue but which would overload us here. So we shall stay mainly with the story as he saw it at the time.

There is one curious gap. Like the dog that famously didn't bark in the night in the Sherlock Holmes story 'The Silver Blaze', nowhere in the report nor in his other writings does Lodwick mention that it was in the seas to the south of Crete that Max Valentiner's sneak torpedo had sunk the *Persia* all those years ago, taking with it to the seabed Captain Lodwick and so many others. Maybe a psychiatrist could make something of this. We can't.

If BOOKMAKER and its aftermath had been an adrenalin-pumping brush with danger, Lodwick's time in the SBS would test his courage beyond the worst fears of even case-hardened warriors, let alone sedentary authors and armchair readers.

13

Killing Them Loudly

The opening page of Lodwick's official report is succinct.

JULY 23RD 1944
Taken prisoner at Alikianos, Crete. Lodged in Rural Prison, Chanea

AUGUST 23RD 1944
Transferred by sea to Athens Political Prison

SEPTEMBER 1ST 1944
Transferred to Salonika Political Prison

OCTOBER 7TH 1944
Entrained for Germany

OCTOBER 9TH–NOVEMBER 5TH 1944
POW Camp at Mitrovitsa, Serbia

NOVEMBER 7TH 1944–NOVEMBER 24TH 1944
Operating with Chetnik Forces

NOVEMBER 25TH 1944
Contacted Bulgarian Forces

NOVEMBER 28TH 1944
Taken to Bulgaria

We will look at each in turn; background first. A good source is the reporting by three seasoned and sophisticated Greek-speaking officers parachuted separately into the country by SOE Cairo in 1943 and 1944 (their reports, variously stamped Secret/Most Secret/Officer Only, also went to London and were copied to Washington.)[1] Their aim was to try to understand the fight against the Axis and how British support could best be given. The picture they found was far from clear cut, in which the Germans may have been the main adversary but not the only one.

The Germans preach that it is the duty of Greeks to become the servants and workmen of the Greater Reich. The Bulgarians treat them as an unwanted minority in Greater Bulgaria. The Italians, their pride wounded by constant Greek reminders of the Abyssinian War, and their appetite stimulated by short army rations, sate themselves by wanton looting, beatings, destruction of life and property.[2]

And when it came to orchestrating resistance and British support, the unfathomable complications of Greek politics, the internecine intrigue and strife between Royalists, Communists and others, created shifting loyalties and sometimes insurmountable obstacles as the factions wrestled with each other and with the British to emerge in control of the country once the war was over. Wrapping up a gruelling and dangerous three-month mission, John Stevens wrote sadly: 'If the tone of my report is somewhat depressing, it is because it is a sorry sight to see great patriotism, courage and self-sacrifice stunted and rendered sterile by political chicanery and above all lack of leadership.'

There is nothing to suggest that any of these views would have been shared with Lodwick and his sunburned fellow gunslingers – the judgements were, in modern jargon, 'above their pay grade' – though he might have drawn parallels between Greece, his and John Collins' memories of Ireland and the even bloodier settling of scores in Spain.

Nor would their briefing have given much weight to the inevitable German reaction to raids like theirs; it might have blunted the edge of even the hardest of them. The much-decorated German commander, Kurt Student, mastermind of the original mass parachute drop which overran Crete,[3] was merely following the standard Wehrmacht terror playbook for occupied countries when he ordered that attacks on his troops would be met by 'reprisals and punitive expeditions which must be carried through with exemplary terror', including 'shooting, fines, total destruction of villages by burning [and] extermination of the male population of the territory'.[4]

It was one of the unforeseen complexities of terror that, because of the inevitable Nazi retaliation, Cretans might, and often did, oppose actions such as Lodwick's operation and earlier SBS raids. Retribution for the actions of Cretans might be an inescapable price, 'but reprisals for the actions of others were intolerable'.

Free of such distracting musings, Lodwick and a handpicked group of SBS NCOs and 'other ranks' – like today's SAS, the Service was unmilitarily insensitive to badges and stripes – had parachuted into Crete, their mission to destroy a German fuel dump near Alikianos (the village itself had been the site of an earlier German reprisal in which 200 young men had been shot and pushed into graves they had been forced to dig themselves).

They dropped in three weeks before the attack to reconnoitre, a period his report does not describe but which would have meant lying up by day, sleeping in caves or goat sheds, or under bushes, on edge every minute for a random German patrol, a betrayal or a clumsy mistake, and 'living off the land', a euphemism for scrounging and charity, hastily snatched fruit and a background of dirt and fleas. One SBS officer, perhaps an entomologist – they were men from extraordinarily varied backgrounds – had learned the hard way to identify edible grubs and insects (mealworms and grasshoppers among them), and munched them with gusto; the otherwise hard-boiled men under his command preferred to go hungry. Teams from SIS and SOE were already busy on Crete at their own secret tasks, and though we have no idea how much advance coordination there had been, we know from the report that in that period of reconnaissance Lodwick had more than one briefing meeting with an unnamed SOE officer. Given the fragile communications between London, SOE's Cairo base and Crete it is doubtful that the officer knew of Lodwick's stormy falling out with his organisation after BOOKMAKER. Or that Lodwick would have told him.

Back to the night when it all went up in flames. Warning them about the risk of their shadows being spotted in the moonlight, Lodwick divided his men – three NCOS and two Greek 'irregulars' – to attack opposite sides of the dump, an area some 200 yards long and 100 wide. In a guard hut at the entrance ten sentries – two others were always out on patrol, their Alsatian dogs' ears permanently cocked for danger – lounged, turned half an ear to propaganda and 'Lili Marlene' on the *Soldatensender* radio, and flicked through weeks-old German newspapers. The site was protected by barbed wire and deadly 'S' mines. Buried under a thin covering layer of earth or leaves, when an unwary intruder trod on them, the mines would leap three feet into the air and explode, spraying a hail of steel ball-bearings far and wide for maximum lethal effect; a killer jack-in-the-box. Its nickname among Allied troops, the 'Bouncing Betty', is deceptively homely for a death-dealer considered one of the definitive weapons of World War II.

Using a folding ladder, a contraption of rope and wooden slats improvised by Lodwick, he and Nixon manoeuvred sweatily, pulses racing, over the barbed wire and across the minefield. Lodwick had time to lay 22 of his 30 charges of '808' plastic explosive with delayed-action fuses, before a single shot alerted them that the other party had run into trouble. We hear more about that from a laconic report, found later buried in Lodwick's family papers, and written by a Private Stewart, one of those in the second party. He recorded what happened in a schoolboy prose that flattens the fear, noise and bloodshed, the 'kill or be killed' mayhem. Surprised by a sentry,

> I sprung forward and held his rifle with my left hand and shot him five times in the stomach with my carbine… I fired and hit another sentry that was running away from me… While this was going on Sgt. ASBERY was firing at the other sentries, which scuttled.

Scrambling out of the dump, he was grabbed by a bellowing German.

> We struggled for some time, and after a while I managed to draw my knife and put it into his stomach and he fell to the ground still shouting. The knife I used was a Greek one given to me by Lt. LODWICK who instructed me to use it if possible instead of a gun.

Hastily burying the rest of the explosives in a single pit, Lodwick and Nixon made it back via the flimsy ladder to the scrublands outside. The dump burst into flames just before midnight and the roar of truck and motor cycle engines, along with the bellowing of reports by German officers as if the telephone lines they were using did not exist, left no illusions that though the operation had been a success, Lodwick and his fellow 'doctors' were in acute danger. Hiding or running among the trees and bushes was useless. The red and yellow flames of the blazing fuel turned the moonlit sky to blinding daylight. The two men hid for four hours in a leaf-filled ditch under a camouflage net, thirstily husbanding the last tepid mouthfuls in their water bottles. Just as they were beginning to hope they might have got away with it, the baying of a guard dog led the Germans to begin to prod and scrape along the ditch with sticks and bayonet-tipped rifles. When they were just a few yards away the two men took deep breaths and clambered to their feet, their hands up in grudging surrender. They had run a terrible risk, but as Antony Beevor's definitive study of World War II Crete tells us, they had struck a major blow: 15 German soldiers dead (presumably the entire guard crew, plus others rushed in for a Canute-like attempt to beat back the flames) and 165,000 gallons of fuel consumed in flames and greasy smoke.[5] Ahead lay even more risk: not least being shot out of hand, tortured or at best left to rot in jail, an unrecorded, unlamented (except maybe by Sheila and his mother) disappearance in the fog and confusion of war.

14

Jailhouse Blues

Lodwick might give a wry smile to know that Chanea Prison, once an Ottoman stronghold, and where he was then held and interrogated, is still in use today as a jail, and a rather nasty one at that. Conditions at Chanea were still so bad just a few years ago that the prisoners staged a 'sit in' to protest about its overcrowding, harshness and brutality. He would be amused too to see the image Chania (as it is now spelled) presents to the twenty-first-century tourist – pristine beaches, a harbourfront lined with cafes and bars, fishermen selling fresh squid and other delights, all against a backdrop of snow-dusted mountains. About 3 km outside the town stands, or rather crumbles, what is left of a memorial erected by the Germans in 1942 to commemorate their parachutists who died in the Battle of Crete in May 1941. Called the Fallschirmjäger memorial, it is apparently known locally as 'The German Bird', or 'The Evil Bird'.

Lodwick, who was manacled but not ill-treated, decided early on to take a typically Lodwickian tack of bravado, opting for what Germans would call *ein Flucht nach vorne*, which literally means 'a flight forwards' but which conveys the sense of averting danger by challenging it head-on; we might say 'taking a bull by the horns'. Claiming, to add credibility, that he was a captain and Nixon a sergeant (each actually had a rank one notch lower), he told the Germans they were not really commandos, but had been sent by a higher authority. From encounters with undercover SOE officers during his three weeks on the island,

> I knew the German position to be most unenviable (not to say untenable) and it therefore occurred to me that if I pretended to be other than I was from the very first it would not be impossible to secure the capitulation of the island.

An ambitious plan, one might think, even mildly megalomaniacal, but rather in keeping with the élan, the 'nothing ventured, nothing gained' style which SBS delighted in improvising at times of trouble, and with Lodwick's instinct for grandstanding. He told his menacing interrogators the real aim of blowing up the dump had been to rub home to the Germans that they were in a hopeless position and needed to begin surrender negotiations urgently. He demanded to see the German commander in Crete. He didn't get that far, though a bevy of staff officers listened impassively to his story before taking him to see the burned-out dump and a sentry's crumpled corpse, a way of reminding him of the summary fate which awaited captured commandos: 'We can just shoot you.' It was a threat which hung over his captivity, sometimes unvoiced, sometimes bellowed, once even taken to the point of staging the preliminaries to a mock execution. Nixon was held separately and dealt with more robustly, but stuck to the 'name, rank and number' answer which was all POWs were obliged to say under the Geneva Convention – not a document to which the Nazis gave much weight. Messages passed to Nixon via a Polish orderly quickly gave him the gist of the yarn Lodwick was spinning, which he was then able to reinforce, to the point where the idea gained so much traction that there was apparently serious discussion with the Germans about sending Nixon to British Middle East HQ in Cairo with a German emissary, leaving Lodwick behind as a hostage. Who was playing whom? Why send Nixon rather than Lodwick? Were the Germans so scared that any chance of negotiating a surrender rather than fighting it out in flames and futility was something to jump at? Or were they trying to see how far they could go in unravelling secret British communications and transport lines, even perhaps identifying some of the other British clandestine operators of whose activities around the island they were nervously aware? But whatever the reasons, the half-belief that there might be something in the story, and Lodwick's constant reminders to the Germans that the Resistance were tracking his and Nixon's movements – and that if they were harmed, there would be reprisals – kept the two from being shot out of hand, as Hitler had decreed.[1]

Lodwick was at least right about the tracking. From up in the mountains an SIS officer passed word to the same Polish prison orderly that he could orchestrate an escape, but by the time the now cautious Lodwick had asked for verification and a detailed plan (he suspected a German trap), the orderly, who had the keys, had been transferred and nothing could be done.

On 23 August 1944 Lodwick and Nixon were taken by sea to Athens. They were bundled into the foetid hold of a tramp steamer, stopped for a day at Santorini and another at Syros, before rolling into Piraeus. They were taken to the Averoff Prison, in northern Athens, a name etched into the troubled history of modern Greece. Grilling Nixon, the Germans shifted their aim from the mission, now wanting to know what he could tell them about Lodwick's army career. He told them truthfully that he knew nothing, as they had not known each other long; they also tried to get the names of other SBS officers, but he would not answer, even though every refusal brought yet another threat to shoot him.

A little more than a week later, they were moved to Salonika (Thessaloniki), and another 'political prison'. Lodwick had at least seen some of it before when he shuffled and prevaricated through the questioning and the mindless routines and menaces of prisons in France and Spain. There was no boat for this leg, but a flight in a three-motored Junkers Ju 52, the sturdy transport 'workhorse' of the Wehrmacht, with an overnight stop at Mytilene. Lodwick does not tell us – it is doubtful whether he had any idea – that since the late 1400s, when the Ladino community had been expelled from Spain, Salonika had been a substantially Jewish city, most of them Sephardis. As World War II bore down on them, and despite growing local anti-Semitism, they had been able to escape the German extermination. But by October 1943 the noose had closed. The proclamations, the imperious hammering on the door, the connivance of local authorities and police, all the trappings painfully familiar to Jews elsewhere in the Nazi orbit saw them first herded into a ghetto, then deported to concentration camps, principally Auschwitz. Some 90 per cent of the city's prewar Jewish population are said to have died.

In contrast, the relatively 'kid glove' treatment Lodwick and Nixon were given there suggested, as did the tone of the next round of interrogation in 'a private and rather sinister building', that the 'high-level emissary' story was still being given some weight, and Lodwick sensed the plan was on the verge of working. But the bony finger of history soon poked into the plotline and, in his words, 'events made all further negotiations by Germans useless'. It was history whose fast-moving cross-currents a Gladstone or Bismarck would have understood, even enjoyed, though it was a period Lodwick and Nixon were lucky to survive. Romania, another minor but strategically well-placed player, had joined the Axis powers in November 1940, but threw in the towel in August 1944, allowing the Red Army to cross its territory to reach Bulgaria, an Axis lackey since March 1941. On 5 September the Soviet Union declared war on Bulgaria and its troops rolled in. Like their neighbours, the Bulgarians could recognise the new reality, especially when it stared at them down the barrel of a mud-spattered T-34 tank with a red star on the turret. On 8 September 1944 Bulgaria surrendered to the Russians. The next day saw the 'events' to which Lodwick refers, when the puppet government in Sofia was overthrown and the new ministers declared war on Germany and ordered their soldiers to push back the less than crack German units which had been occupying the country.

In Salonika the guards had two more problems on their hands: a British corporal and a private of the 'Raiding Support Regiment'. They were fortunate. Greek POWs from the Sacred Squadron had been dumped in the infamous Haidari concentration camp outside Athens. Greeks were expendable, but although the British group were less valuable now as pawns in a capitulation chess game, they could be useful 'bargaining chips' as things fell apart. It might have been easier to shoot them, but that was an option fraught with consequences. As Lodwick reminded them, reprisals could work both ways. So everyone would have to stay put until some other way emerged of getting out of the maze. The German scramble for places on trains going north to the Reich was intense, less one suspects for logistical reasons than because more and more of the occupiers were coming up with compelling operational needs to get places on departing trains before the British, the Russians or the Greek resistance got hold of them and took revenge rather than prisoners.

The Germans eventually found space on board for their captives: a cattle car, at one end of which they were crowded behind strings of barbed wire, guarded by itchy-fingered SS men with submachine guns, and cutting carefully measured slivers from the few tins of corned beef which were their only rations for the journey. It was supposed to end in Germany. It didn't. On 8 October the slow-moving train stopped at Skopje, a city which has known many overlords since its Roman heyday.

The next day the rail journey ended at Mitrovica. As the Germans dragged Lodwick and their other prisoners northwards through Greece, he would not have known, other than perhaps by rumour, that the Wehrmacht was being harassed by the rather imperially named POMPFORCE, led by his ubiquitous and adventurous chum George Jellicoe. The 'belted Earl' now commanded a fighting unit made up of a battalion of the Parachute Regiment, an artillery troop, men from the RAF Regiment (a rather feared unit of 'hard men' who usually had little to do with flying) and a team of Lodwick's cut-throat SBS comrades. A report to Whitehall from a British liaison mission called it 'an excellent force… one with which it was a pleasure to work'. In a wider Greek context the activities of POMPFORCE were 'a minor but agreeable episode' in the Allied effort.

Over the centuries, the last gasps of many military campaigns must have drifted dangerously and messily towards their conclusion in rather the same way as Lodwick's own war. Bunches of weary men, wandering an alien landscape, with guards who were probably just as hungry and bewildered, not knowing who was now friend or foe, and terrified of what lay over the next hill, waiting for a miracle rescue, or for someone in authority to say, 'It's over. You can go home now.' Trying to push their way through a torrent of refugee scarecrows wondering if their homes still existed. It was a terrain and experience surely familiar to Lodwick from the French debacle, but that cannot have made it any more comfortable. There was more danger and discomfort to come. Lodwick may have consoled himself with the occasional Hemingwayesque thought that it was all future grist to his writer's mill, but that would have been cold comfort when, for all his undoubted bravado, he knew every day might be his last. But it wasn't over just yet.

15

Guerrilla War

At Mitrovica, where the train puffed and squealed slowly in on 9 October, word quickly reached the passengers that this was the end of the line; somewhere ahead of them the advancing Red Army had blocked the railway. The group spent eight days in their cattle truck, until the order came from who knows where that they were to be marched to a nearby prison camp, still run by Italians who had remained loyal to Mussolini's Fascist State despite the 1943 surrender. There the prisoners' numbers – and the guards' problems – increased again when they were joined by 11 downed US aircrew along with an SOE officer who had been captured in Crete in civilian clothes, and, like Lodwick and Nixon, was lucky not to have been shot. On 7 November the motley band, their number swollen even more by 'assorted Russians and Bulgarians' rounded up in the confusion by the Germans, stumbled off, guarded by a gaggle of Wehrmacht soldiers and Italians and two police dogs. Germany lay too far away; we must assume the Germans were hoping to run into another Wehrmacht unit and maybe its transport. They had no such luck. Lodwick's plan to use a stolen Italian grenade hurled into the woods as the spur for a mass break for freedom was overtaken when Yugoslav Chetnik guerrillas – bearded, no-nonsense, gun-toting thugs – suddenly appeared out of the pine trees and took control. The POWs were now on their side.

What being 'on their side' meant was, for the moment, a finely balanced fate determined by timing and politics. The ambivalence and equivocation of the Chetniks and their leader, the Royalist General Draža Mihailović, had long since led the British to switch their material and political support to Tito's Communist Partisans. Mihailović often seemed keener to fight the Partisans, their rivals for the future control of what was then Yugoslavia, than take on the Germans, and there were well-documented instances of outright Chetnik collaboration with the

Wehrmacht. The shift had probably passed Lodwick by as he spun from one SBS action to the next. He would certainly not have known of the key part in that policy switch played by SOE's Yugoslav expert in Cairo, James Klugmann, an unalloyed and overt Communist sympathiser.

Ambivalent the Chetniks may well have been, but bloody and vengeful they certainly were, and before taking the POWs off to shelter in their mountain camp, the German and Italian guards were, in Lodwick's rather biblical phrase, 'put to the knife'. Whether out of delicacy, or a sensible desire not to be involved in any further enquiry, it is an incident which Nixon's account does not mention.

Lodwick and Nixon were uncomfortable, half-frozen bedfellows with the Chetnik guerrillas from 7 to 24 November, camped high up between the ancient settlements of Raška and Novi Pazar, and as Lodwick recalled, they were treated rather well. Not for the first time we wonder just what *lingua franca* this polyglot party used, but it was efficient enough for Lodwick, when he discovered that the Chetniks held a sizeable arsenal of British explosives and detonators, to persuade them to let him and Nixon try their hands at sabotaging the nearby rail line. He argued that dead Germans were dead Germans, whether in Crete or the mountains of Serbia. But it was not that easy. Lodwick found the Chetniks 'very lethargic' about action, perhaps because hour by hour their commander wavered, not sure which side would win and what the consequences would be, making inaction seem the 'least worst' option. He would also have been apprehensive about Wehrmacht reprisals against the local people. Rightly so; we have seen how they behaved in Greece, and when the 111th Battalion of the 749th Infantry Division was ordered take reprisals near Kragujevac, they returned with thousands of hostages and 'severe measures' followed, a euphemism for shooting over 2,000 of them. All the settlements in the area were 'depopulated'.[1]

After more dithering, the Chetnik commander finally gave his permission for Lodwick and Nixon to scramble down the mountain and pull out a stretch of rail, a quiet action which had loud consequences in the derailing of a locomotive and of six carriages, with ten Germans killed. 'It was the first time the Chetniks had attacked the railway, to my certain knowledge, for over eight months,' Lodwick reported.

A few days later the Chetnik Major gave the go-ahead for a 'major demolition' on the railway line. Either he briefed the Englishmen badly or they did not do enough reconnaissance but the supposed weak spots – drainage channels in the stonework embankment – did not exist so *faute de mieux* they laid delayed charges in a culvert, collapsing it and undermining the embankment anyway. Lodwick retained in his papers, evidently taken from SBS files, a 1944 British 'Memorandum on Railway Demolition', closely typed and with several informative illustrations for the would-be saboteur. Explosives were the surest way to cause maximum damage but if these were unavailable sabotage parties should at a minimum carry four crowbars, three picks, two shovels, four wire cutters, two sledgehammers, two adjustable spanners, four pairs of pliers and four screwdrivers. Compiled principally from reports by two officers of the Royal Electrical and Mechanical Engineers, it is a masterclass on the subject, which if posted on the internet today would generate much suspicious interest.

But the war rolled on, loyalties shifted like the rumblings of the San Andreas Fault, and on 19 November the POWs heard that the Chetniks and Germans were fighting each other on the road down in the gorge. Lodwick was by instinct and training keen to join in the melee; Nixon could not as, hardly surprisingly, 'his boots had given out completely', so Lodwick scrambled down by himself and helped carry the Chetnik wounded. Of the 200 Germans embroiled in the skirmish 140 were killed or captured; what the captives' fate would be is not hard to guess. He noted: 'Very large quantities of booty were taken, particularly chocolate', a nice human note to round off yet another foray into inhumanity.

One bone-chilling, drizzly minute the Chetniks were fighting the Germans. The next, with the POWs in tow, they were tramping through an apparent no man's land to negotiate with the advancing Bulgarian troops. The POWs were not quite out of the woods yet, literally or metaphorically.

Wearily they retraced their steps to Mitrovica, guns cocked, eyes and ears watchful, then by truck to Slivnitsa, just inside the Bulgarian border with Serbia. Although by now there was a British military presence there, Lodwick and Nixon had to get the Red Army's permission to travel on to Sofia and report to the British Mission. Lodwick tells us elsewhere that though they had left the Chetniks behind and to their fate, they had surreptitiously absorbed into their group an English-speaking Yugoslav naval officer, who they hoped might pass unnoticed among so many Americans and somehow get out with them to freedom. They had not counted on the sharp eyes of Russian 'military attachés' – probably the NKVD political commissars embedded in every unit – who insisted on pulling the man out as a presumed Chetnik. As a wheezing bus drove the POWs away to Sofia they saw him 'quite alone, behind us', his fate certainly to crumple by the roadside with a bullet in the back of the head as soon as they were out of sight.

It was in Slivnitsa that Lodwick and Nixon drew up their reports. For once, and quite excusably in the circumstances, Lodwick missed the local military and literary connections. In his day the town was a huddle of damaged buildings, burned-out vehicles littering the streets and tired men from several armies, armed to the teeth, roaming around, looking for drink, girls and trouble. In the twenty-first century it is neat and tidy, and is still proudly remembered as the site of a major victory by the Bulgarians over the Serbs in 1885. Whether George Bernard Shaw had ever been there, we can doubt, but that did not stop him using it as the fictional background to his comedy about the futility of war, first produced in London to great acclaim in 1894.[2] Its title, *Arms and the Man*, would also have appealed to Lodwick's feel for the classical – it is taken from the opening line of Virgil's *Aeneid*. Lodwick may not have picked up any other literary background but the Chetnik experiences churned in his mind and coalesced into his novel, *Twenty East of Greenwich*, judged by the *Illustrated London News* as

a queer variety of light entertainment... Throat cutting and torture are the commonplaces of this adventure, and yet it is all very gay, cynical and casual with sprightly backchat and a constant run of surprises. Moreover one can see that it is well-informed.

From Sofia Lodwick and Nixon were flown out to the Italian port of Bari, some 230 km across the Adriatic from Albania. World War II had transformed its ancient harbour into a major Allied supply hub, a base for US and RAF fighters and bombers, and an intelligence and subversion epicentre for the Balkans through which almost every baron of the secret world mentioned in this book had passed or was passing, Julian Amery among them. It was Amery, whose strong presence slid across the background of many adventures in the secret world, who shared with one of the present author's friends an anecdote about that shift in support from the Chetniks, so important for the war and so pivotal in determining the future of Yugoslavia. Puzzled about the reasons, since at heart he was a romantic who supported Mihailović and the Royalists, Amery had sufficient influence through his politically prominent family to find a seat on a plane from the Adriatic to London and ask. A Labour MP arranged for him to be put in the picture by a young officer in civilian clothes in the War Office.

'It was a damn fine briefing,' Amery remembered.

As he left, satisfied with the explanation, the young officer added: 'Just one more thing, Mr Amery. Never trust a Commie.'

'Thank you, Mr Philby,' a grateful Amery replied.

The SBS Diary shows Lodwick officially re-entered on the Officers' Roll on 31 December 1944, as a 'Returned POW', and George Jellicoe ('Captain/Acting Lt Colonel') still in command. 'You took your time about it,' he is said, perhaps apocryphally, to have greeted him. The Diary's only and somewhat anti-climactic mention of Lodwick's subsequent involvement is that on 25 May 1945 'Captain Lodwick and 50 Other Ranks take over Guard duties at stockade in BARI area containing mutinous LEBANESE'. Though he had plenty of experience himself 'on the inside', we can imagine that he gave the 'mutineers' short shrift, but the Diary adds no colour, merely leading us to the disbanding of the SBS in August 1945, and Lodwick's return to the UK as an officer on the 'General List'.

Three officers in the same entry are designated PYTHON. It is tempting to relate this to a clandestine operation of that name then being run in North Borneo, but the answer is again rather a let-down: PYTHON was the War Office coding for a rule that any officer who had served abroad for more than four years was liable only for 'home' postings. For many thousands of men (and their families) the process of postwar release was a frustrating one, flawed by political and bureaucratic shilly-shallying over categories, priorities and timing. Lodwick seems to have had a relatively smooth passage, although some faded papers on the SOE file suggest that, true to form, he was chivvying them and MI5 for some special treatment – a gratuity, a pension, a rapid release, who knows? – in 1945 but was told 'no go'. When SOE's important but controversial Cairo HQ was closed down as SOE began its own liquidation, one local wag picked up on the organisation's rather crude designation of men in the Lodwick mould to lament: 'We've hundreds of mugs who've been trained as thugs, and now they're at the mercy of the Greeks and the Jugs.'

One of the papers Lodwick tucked away is the record of his final cheque from the army's Paymaster General, in December 1945. It was for just short of £40, with the intriguing note – shades of the extravagant late Captain Lodwick – that it included £3 and two shillings 'For Servant'. An SOE Form of 18 December 1945 compiled as part of its 'funeral rites' gives Lodwick's address as St Mawes, on the coast of Cornwall, a 35-mile drive from Sheila's birthplace in St Ives. A letter from Sheila to her Surrealist friend David Sylvester tells us their waystation there (several more significant moves were to follow) was a cottage called 'We Two': 'Don't let the whimsy address put you off – we didn't christen this cottage!'

'Relatively smooth.' How hard must it have been to adjust from dodging high-powered German gunboats in a camouflaged caïque, Sten guns cocked, to a cute cottage and hastily repatched domesticity, the only knock at the door the local milkman rather than a German rifle-butt? For most who served, coming home was a relief. For some it involved facing families damaged physically by the war or psychologically by the strains of years of separation. According to one study, in 1947 alone the courts heard 60,000 divorce petitions, a sad total not reached again until the 1960s.[3] All had to recalibrate, find a job, understand the grey, grinding realities of civilian life. For Lodwick and so many others who had been 'at the sharp end' – risking their lives, taking others without compunction, living largely by their own rules – downshifting to a lower gear must have been especially difficult, both for them and for those who loved them.

Amid the hurly-burly of resettlement, rebuilding lives and finding new directions, we catch another glimpse of the ubiquitous Georges Kopp. He had reached London in 1943, but under whose auspices is unclear; his biographer comments that 'The MI5 file remains a source of wonder.'[4]

Lodwick wrote to him in 1946, and though we don't have that letter, Kopp's reply put a brave face on what we now know from his biographer was failing health along with precarious business prospects. He was about to move into a house named *Toftcombs* – a grey and draughty merchant's manor rather than an antler-hung baronial pile – on a large estate some 30 miles outside Edinburgh. Its transformation in recent years into an upscale hotel, offering the now obligatory wedding and conference venues, would have appealed to Kopp's entrepreneurial spirit. The opening comment in his reply suggests his view of Lodwick, when, in a distant echo of Maurice Buckmaster's less kind remarks, he writes, 'I sort of had the feeling that you must have been killed or something… I must say that your exploits justify either a coffin or a VC – and they didn't give you neither [*sic*].' Kopp had evidently stayed in touch with George Orwell, who had taken a house in the remote Hebrides around the time of this exchange, and with the writer's first wife Eileen, who had died the previous year, and he had enjoyed *Animal Farm* – 'it was more than inspired by Eileen'.[5] When Lodwick met Orwell himself during the war, an encounter on which he sadly does not elaborate, he remembered that Orwell could talk of little else other than Kopp, for whom he had 'almost a veneration'.

Showing a touch less admiration, Kopp wrote to Lodwick: 'George now goes in for journalism and writes platitudes in the *Observer*, the *Evening Standard* and innumerable American reviews which have plenty of money and no readers this side of the Atlantic. George certainly lost a lot when Eileen died.' Given the gruelling discomfort of British rail travel in the 1940s, it is unlikely that Lodwick took up Kopp's elegant invitation to Lodwick to repeat his World War II slog up to Scotland, and jolt all the way from Cornwall to help pull him out of 'that type of morbid languor which can only be cured by drinking neat whisky with an ex-commando of Irish descent.' Kopp had married a relative of Eileen's, and somewhere along his and Lodwick's complicated life paths had met the latter's mother Kitty, since he closes his letter by asking to be remembered to her.

But whether it came in bad dreams, other men's memoirs, tricky acquaintances from the past or even in bank statements, the war could not be left behind. Writing of his experiences in German jails, Lodwick mentions that in return for favours or food he used to give German guards post-dated cheques scribbled on scraps of lavatory paper, to be redeemed in London when peace came. As he remarks sardonically in his war memoirs, 'Almost all of these documents were duly presented in the first few months after the war.' Other notes were given to 'trusties' working for the Germans and meant as evidence of goodwill to be shown to any Allied forces into whose hands the 'trusty' might fall. Offhand references like these can make one pause momentarily, wondering if they are hard fact or a stitch of nostalgic embroidery. So it was a pleasant surprise to find one of these 'chits' tucked amongst his papers. It is in ink, in Lodwick's now familiar hand, on a leaf ripped from a 1942 French pocket diary. The leaf has been stuck on yet another slip of paper, this one cut rather than torn from a British passport. The note, clearly related to his Cretan misadventures, reads:

> This man is a Pole, conscripted into the German army. He has done everything possible for us at great risk to himself. Please treat him well. We are being moved

to Greece. Please inform our families that we are prisoners of war. We had a devil of a time during our interrogation but managed to stand firm and eventually they gave up threatening to shoot us. We shall try to escape in Greece. Four petrol pits on our target went up, making 9,500 gallons.

The note is signed by Lodwick and, in the same hand, 'Corporal Nixon'. Under what circumstances it came back into Lodwick's hands we do not know; maybe when he eventually returned to the SBS, whom it reached after the unknown recipient handed it over to prove he was a 'goody' as well as a 'trusty'.

Another postwar loose end not mentioned by Lodwick, though it can hardly have escaped his attention, was the fate of General Student, who had orchestrated the successful German capture of Crete through a mammoth parachute drop. In May 1946 a British Military Court sitting in Lüneburg convicted Student, who had pleaded not guilty, on three out of eight war crimes charges, including bombing Red Cross installations, disguising German soldiers in Allied uniforms and killing British POWs either directly or by deliberately driving them towards fire from their own troops. After a trial, the summary record of whose judgement seems in the circumstances painfully, almost excruciatingly fair, he was sentenced to five years in jail. However, the Allied 'High Authority', a US General who had the final call on sentencing, declined to confirm it, because according to the then *Manchester Guardian*, 'Allied officers… testified that the charges were unfounded and that he fought fairly'.[6] Student was released on health grounds in 1948. Any twenty-first-century internet viewer of even a handful of images of the later massacres carried out by the German firing squads would dispute the phrase 'fought fairly', as would Lodwick and every last man in the SOE and SBS teams caught up in the raids and reprisals. How could that happen? Only when we turn to the trial summary[7] does it become clear that the charges were entirely directed to the behaviour of the parachute forces under Student's command in the initial German invasion of Crete, and not his later role as governor of most of the conquered island. A Greek request for his extradition, no doubt to try him for those later horrors, was refused on the grounds that the long journey would aggravate the effects of a bullet wound in the brain Student had suffered in Holland earlier in the war; ironically one account claims it was 'friendly fire', a stray potshot by an SS sniper. At this distance in time it is impossible to assess the rights and wrongs, or any other factors which might have been at play in the initial charges, the judgements and the High Authority's later view. All we know is that Student, nicknamed 'Papa' by his men, lived until he was 80. Unlike the unmarked mass graves into which so many Cretans were tumbled, his death in 1978 is commemorated by a neat stone headstone in the little spa town of Bad Salzuflen.

Lodwick's mother, whom he named as his next of kin as he left SOE – 'wife' has been crossed out – was then living in Liss in Hampshire, where Selwyn Jepson was one of her neighbours. Like so many others, Jepson had ended World War II an almost broken man, his strength sapped by the feeling that, however cool and objective he may have been, however good he was at his job, his SOE recruiting work was in effect asking the men and women he selected to choose between life and death, and too often the latter.

In a revealing 1986 interview Jepson (who would have met Lodwick as editor of the *London Magazine* in the 1930s when the latter was trying his hand at short stories) said that as he recruited for the French Section, after an interview process he remembered as being 'like the confessional', he rejected many, chose a select few for undercover service in enemy territory, but also had a third category.[8] These were fearless (and, to put it bluntly, expendable) men who could be sent on *coup de main* operations and then try to scramble back home again via Spain, but whose accented or less than fluent French, or something in their personality, made them unsuitable as long-term clandestine operators. Lodwick, he remembered, was 'one of the best' of these. Many of his SOE agent recruits were women, a practice originally frowned upon by Whitehall as contrary to the Geneva Convention until Jepson, who knew Churchill, convinced the prime minister that it was not only acceptable but made good operational sense. Jepson thought women made better agents than men. 'They have a greater capacity for cool and lonely courage, and can work well without a mate. Men don't like working alone.'[9]

That closing SOE form may have been drawn up by a harried clerk with half an eye on what was left of the files, since it links Lodwick not with BOOKMAKER but with a much later and unsuccessful SOE circuit, SURVEYOR, which was penetrated and broken in the Abwehr's successful counter-espionage 'radio game'. There is no evidence, but to see the circuit cited in a Lodwick context suggests the arrest of the unfortunate Nadia may have been part of the collateral damage.

Like a headmaster's closing words on a school report, its final section provides a box for F Section's 'Evaluation of officer and suggestion for possible further employment'. This contains another atrabilious but unsigned outburst along earlier lines and seems all the more unfair, since it was written several years after their last encounter and takes no account of Lodwick's subsequent bold SBS service; it may actually have been a hurried secretarial précis of those earlier remarks. But in any event, SOE was going out of business, and even without the condemnatory file entries Lodwick's opportunity for further employment in skulduggery would have been limited; there were more swashbuckling supplicants than there were bucklers to swash.

Lodwick was lucky. He knew he wanted to be a writer and came home from the war with a mental kitbag stuffed with experiences and memories which he could turn into words, one of the motives he said had driven him to swagger up to the Legion recruiting desk and sign his fate over to France in the first place.

16

South of the Border

Had he been wounded on active service Lodwick could have claimed the automatic right to French citizenship – deemed *Français par le sang versé* – available to legionnaires from other countries. He wasn't, and even if he had been the process was no doubt too complicated in the postwar chaos, especially for a man with an equally complicated Legion record. Nevertheless, he still chose France as his next home. Though one of his letters in 1946 was written from what was then a little fishing village in Brittany, now swallowed by the larger St Malo, it was not long before he was back down south. He subsequently moved to Spain, the country he would call home for what was left of his life and which fed his author's gnawing appetite for new places, new people and new ways of life, not least the seedier fascinations and submerged secrets of the expatriate communities. They were not easy years professionally or personally but at least he could relive some of his experiences, if not as *la dolce vita* then at least in sun and relative comfort.

Two questions arise. The first – why live abroad? – is understandable for anyone with memories of grey, rationed, cold and power-cut-afflicted England, shuffling dejectedly into supposed victory in the late 1940s and without (literally) any of its fruits. Bananas were tantalising memories glimpsed only in prewar advertising cutouts in greengrocers' windows, oranges a black-market mystery, and shredded turnips were advocated as a quasi-salad to keep up the vitamin levels. Whale and horse meat and *snoek*, a bony and unappetising variant of mackerel, were unapologetically offered as alternatives to beef and lamb. Like any artist, Lodwick's professional skills as a writer could be deployed anywhere, and the sounds, smells, colours – and the colourful people 'abroad' – could do more for a writer's imagination than an evening drinking in Fitzrovia or Soho.

And like every other British–Indian family, exile, 'abroad' and separation were in the family genes; England may have been the 'Mother Country' and Cheltenham its *de facto* capital, but to the many generations of passengers on the Exiles' Line it wasn't necessarily 'home'. Nor, sadly, was India, about to be let loose from the Imperial yoke. So the second question is: why France and then Spain? He might have chosen the genial dampness of Ireland, or even one of those distant British dependencies rather unfairly dismissed as 'sunny places for shady people', much as the suspicious stranger on the French train had been seeking in Bermuda. Even though Lodwick was fonder of red wine than many, Keats' 'Provencal song and sunburnt mirth… a beaker full of the warm South' had less to do with it than more immediate memories, good French and the connections of friends and family. Centuries earlier General Peter Lodwick had retired to Bagnères-de-Bigorre, then best known as a spa town – like Cheltenham – in the Haut-Pyrenees, and in his *Who's Who* entry John Lodwick's maternal grandfather, the veteran 'India hand' Sir Henry Ashbrooke Crump, listed his retirement address as 'Villa Francesca, Alassio' on the Italian Riviera, about 50 miles from the French frontier; he died in Paris. Alassio was one of the then unspoiled small towns favoured by those who had 'done their time' in India and preferred the sun, and the far lower cost of living, overlooking the sparkling Mediterranean, to the rain, rapidly shrinking greenery and diminishing pleasures of the old country. Selwyn Jepson of SOE, who after his schooldays at St Paul's had studied French and Italian at the Sorbonne, had spent several lotus-eating prewar years on Capri and then in Alassio.

Sterling might have been weak, but the franc and the peseta were weaker still; fruit, vegetables, fresh fish and wine overflowed the market stalls and little shops. Lodwick had already spent much of his life in and around the Mediterranean coast, and Sheila was no stranger to it either. He spoke French well, and she could certainly get by. They were edging closer to Spain, though she would not in the end make it. Cassis, where they lived for a time, is not far from Marseilles, and Banyuls-sur-Mer is virtually on the Spanish frontier, where the foothills of the Pyrenees slide into the Mediterranean. Back then, both would have been charming, undeveloped and unspoiled, and familiar to Lodwick from his World War II adventures, the bars and cafes sprinkled with expatriates who might have found Cheltenham too strait-laced. Judging by his books, Lodwick liked to lounge around with the louche, and he derived much material from watching bad behaviour and behaving rather badly himself. The name he gave to his home in Cassis, where he wrote *The Cradle of Neptune*, can be translated as 'I Escaped'. Maybe it was the owner's invention. If Lodwick thought it up it would be a neat reflection of his errant spirit.

According to the history of his publisher, Heinemann, when World War II ended Lodwick 'became involved with smuggling rackets'.[1] He listed 'smuggling' as a hobby in his *Who's Who* entry, but this may have been one of his whimsicalities, something he boasted about to wide-eyed London editors. He did write knowledgeably about one smuggling scheme in *Somewhere a Voice is Calling*, though there is no evidence he was ever involved directly, perhaps beyond the cross-border trading of American cigarettes. That said, his portrait in the book of Barry Keating, the raffish former commando, now running guns and drugs in the Mediterranean, suggests that behind the fiction lay a real-life wartime boon companion and a close knowledge of his murky and dangerous lifestyle.

The book, its cover and that marble plaque in Banyuls-sur-Mer take us to what has to be a lightly fictionalised account of Sheila's last days. She is 'Gloria'; he is 'Thornton' (that memory-laden name again), a career-challenged consular official driven to murder by fears that he has been cuckolded.

Who can really know about the last solo walk down the dimly lit one-way street of someone else's death, its preliminary rituals, tutting nurses fussing with enamel bowls, thermometers, pills, bedpans and a spider's web of wires and tubes? 'Merciful release' and 'a long illness bravely borne' are comforting clichés but the description Lodwick gives of the death of Sheila/Gloria tell us plainly of her suffering and, at one remove and impotently, his own.

In his wartime memoirs Lodwick gives his version of how he and Sheila met. In the novel he tells us a bit more: that despite SOE's efforts to 'prise them apart', she followed Lodwick on at least part of his commando training in Scotland – 'I liked watching you play at soldiers' – had a service flat in St James's, and that she too drank rather more than modern doctors would reckon prudent.

Taking his narrative at face value, each of them loved the other, even though both fought shy of saying so explicitly. Ill and self-abusive she may have been, and given to wandering out into the town to drink in its tiny bars ('Thornton' locks away her passport to stop her roaming even further afield), but despite the lightning strikes of pain which were forcing her body to surrender, her mind stayed sharp. In the two years before she died she had got to grips with Portuguese, Serbo-Croat and Catalan, wrote poems, and ticked through *The Times* crossword with alacrity.

She had tried her hand at several novels but abandoned them. Living with someone who felt he was a master of the art cannot have made it easier. Indeed, in the 'Thornton' version – that 'she could see that although many people wrote worse, quite a number wrote much better than she could ever hope to do' – there may even be distant echoes of that Lodwickian arrogance picked up by his SOE trainers all those years ago.

We knew from her father Laddie's obituary that hers was a Scottish family; Gascoyne told us she had modelled for Man Ray, and Lodwick in his fiction – it is hard to differentiate this from what we know of the facts – says she had more money than him, though this was a life interest in a share of her mother's money which she did not or could not deal with in her will, and which reverted back to the family.

'I possess nothing. I am supposed to be well off but I haven't even a diamond, much less a mink. I have nothing at all,' he quotes her as saying, as we again tread warily though the no man's land between fact and fiction. Even at what she knew would be her last Christmas – she had not eaten properly since September and was in great pain – she sang 'Over The Sea to Skye' and other Scottish songs to their landlady's granddaughters, and taught them to play Postman's Knock. It was cold outside, and down in the small fishing port the locals marvelled at the freakish sight of a crusting of ice around the harbour's inner walls.

The small rented house too was cold, the chill of an ebbing life challenging the glow of the electric fire in the bedroom. Downstairs the maid is clattering the pots and pans. Along the corridors a child is sleeping and dreaming of Christmas.

'Thornton' and 'Gloria' – Lodwick and Sheila – are talking. Half laughing, half grimacing, her head deep in the pillows, sweat glistening despite the cold, she asks for water.

The pain is peculiar. I've been timing it. Every two and a half minutes it comes in waves. Three waves. And the third is a real thunderclap and accompanied, believe it or not, by a clashing of cymbals. Perhaps they aren't cymbals, but something metallic anyway. That's another thing that makes it feel like childbirth. I'm going to die… I can't feel my toes.

'You're not going to die, you're to stay in bed and in two weeks when you feel better you'll go to Le Boulou' (a small town in the hills), Thornton says, unconvincingly.

Gloria, a little later:

> I honestly believe I shall faint if this pain goes on much longer. Tomorrow you must make [the doctor] give me a morphine suppository. Make him do it. Tell him I drink but don't drug… the funny thing is that so many people like me. I really don't know why. I suppose it's in contrast to you. Not many people like you.

'No, very few,' he agrees.

'It must be because of your violence; one always feels it is there, like Etna or something. Thank God you don't drink as much as I do. It would be like living with a mad boy.' She pauses. 'Is it true that when I've been drunk I've gone about the town saying you beat me?'

'I don't know. I think perhaps you said you were afraid to go home and people made up the rest for themselves.'

In a low moment, Gloria/Sheila tells their maid that she wanted to live past the anniversary of the January day she and Thornton/Lodwick first met in France. In that she succeeded, dying on 12 March 1949 from pleurisy, a liver problem and a raft of attendant complications. Poor soul. Poor souls. He had been born without a father. He had seen his Grandpapa on his deathbed. When Gloria/Sheila died he smashed his fist into a radiator in impotent grief, whether consciously or unconsciously the same futilely painful gesture he had made when death came calling for Grandpapa at Ashley Lodge and years before when a fellow pupil had died at school.

She had often visited the local cemetery to read, and had once carved her initials on one of the benches, inside a heart. To spite his relatives by denying them the opportunity, a local vineyard owner had offered the weeping Thornton/Lodwick a niche for Gloria/Sheila, and another for him 'when your time comes', in his 12-foot-square family vault, a stylised image of which appears on the book's dust jacket. There she was laid to rest.

Here truth merges with fiction, rather like the moment when the optician adjusts the test lenses in the frames and a blurred double image on the chart suddenly becomes a single clarity. We began with a plaque in India. We are not at the end of our story but we are close to the end of Sheila's part in it, and the reading of another plaque mists our spectacles.

Telling the story in the novel, when he is asked to suggest wording for a marble plaque for Sheila's grave, Thornton/Lodwick's first attempt, 'Deeply loved and Regretted – RIP', is rejected by his local friends as 'too terse'. Many English tourists visited the cemetery in the summer and would want to know more about her. The fuller version Thornton/Lodwick then produces – in the novel the local mason is credited with the proud professional view that the inscription 'would last a hundred years, maybe two if it's scrubbed now and then' – is remembered by Thornton/Lodwick as

> Dying far from her native land,
>
> She found here a sure resting place
>
> Through the generosity of the owner of this tomb.

In the book, his friend Damien tells him the wording is 'admirable' and that there is also room to add the same words in French. When we look at a photograph of the worn plaque in the cemetery of Banyuls-sur-Mer we find the sad reality in French and in English. In this author's translation, the French epigraph tells those who chance to find it (it is mounted on a wall on the side of a vault which may or may not be the one in which she is interred):

> Here lies Sheila Lodwick (1911–1949)
>
> The beloved wife of John Lodwick.
>
> Let foreigners and summer visitors remember
>
> Her death so far from her homeland.
>
> She lies in this tomb
>
> Thanks to the spontaneous gesture of a Catalan.

The English version tells us:

> Dying far from her native Scotland
>
> She received sure shelter here
>
> By the kind and spontaneous gesture of a Catalan.

The wording is so clearly Lodwick's, almost identical in fact to the inscription he recalled in fiction. So who was the Catalan? Perhaps his friend Damien, living in France to escape the wrath of Franco after the Civil War, the vineyard owner he remembers as 'Peytavi', or maybe his friend and publisher Janés? With Sheila gone, so young, and so far from her roots and her younger years of excitement, the Roundabout turns yet again. It will restart in the South of France; but, like Ophuls' film, with some new players.

17

Riviera Glimpses

Sheila has died and Lodwick has remarried; given what he is 'novelised' by Georges Belmont as saying about the religious permanence of his marriage to Dorothy, it is beyond our scope to know what 'marriage' meant to him, and what he told French and Spanish registrars. Likewise, how he and Sheila's successor met, how they lived and how they parted are stories for her to tell, not us. It is late 1949 or 1950; as tends to happen with the Lodwick chronology, dates get blurred. It was a long time ago. But we have moved out of the realm of fiction and are back in the real world, if the Riviera can ever be characterised that way.

W.S. Merwin, later a much admired poet – US Poet Laureate, among many other accolades – was then in his twenties, newly married, freshly graduated from Princeton, and pleasantly and none too arduously engaged as tutor and companion to the son of a rich American with a villa in St-Jean-Cap Ferrat and a drink problem. It was a long way geographically, climatically and atmospherically from Merwin's hometown of Scranton, Pennsylvania, and his life as the son of a Protestant pastor.[1]

The Hollywood image of life on the Riviera before and after World War II is of striped blazers and white shoes, girls with fluttering silk headscarves, Bugattis burbling along sandy, traffic-free roads through the pine woods to balls at grand villas with manicured gardens along whose gravel paths portly butlers and pert maids glide discreetly with silver trays of cocktails. But there was another South, where writers and artists could rent cheap cottages for the summer, enjoying the sun, the jasmine, wisteria and bougainvillea, and the fruits and fish on offer in the bustling local markets. They could sip pastis and *vin de pays* in local, untouristy bars, and if they could afford the occasional treat, an upgrade from the wheezy local bus for the lure of more exciting shopping in a nearby town, the farmer who doubled as a taxi driver would ferry them at half the rate charged to unknowing 'foreigners'.

Merwin was a wide-eyed guest in the first world. Lodwick, and the middle-aged littérateur who introduced them, were sun-seeking transients in the second. He was the writer and translator Georges Belmont, whom we last saw as Georges Pelorson at Trinity College, Dublin in the 1930s as a popular lecturer, tennis buff, close friend of Samuel Beckett, poet and actor. He is one of those friends of Lodwick whom it is easy to judge harshly, but whose correspondence shows a human side which, while not entirely exculpatory, does give a sense of balance. Why he was in the South of France that summer is almost a novel in itself, and we need to explain it before we get to Merwin and Lodwick.

Like Lodwick's other much analysed friend, Francis Stuart, Pelorson had gone astray in World War II. Now calling himself Georges Belmont (the name borrowed from a hamlet in the Jura *département* of which he claimed to have happy childhood memories) he was on his way to becoming a serious and well-respected translator of foreign literature, and the occasional author of less respected novels, one of which touches our own narrative since it purports to give 'the facts' about the Dublin marriage and to give a glimpse of John and his family in the South of France. Belmont's own backstory shows that from his high school days in France he had demonstrated literary and linguistic talent, coupled as we saw in Dublin with a taste for the dramatic. He was also ambitious and had strong political convictions. In the 1930s these had developed into a hankering for a Trotskyite revolution which would shape a new France, even though he was an anti-Communist. This somewhat contradictory hankering led to a willingness to serve, and serve with enthusiasm, as a leading light in coordinating the proto-Fascist Vichy government's disparate youth movements, his declared aim to provide 'the political and revolutionary formation necessary for the New French State'. Like Stuart's Berlin broadcasts his service was a 'questionable moral choice', even though his daughter later claimed her father had been slandered all his life. Also like Stuart's, that life has been much studied and scrutinised in a search for explanations of its evident contradictions. And again like Stuart, the truth remains elusive, because Belmont wanted it that way.

Even if he hadn't, the background – France defeated, the Vichy government and 'collaboration', France resisting, France free again – is terrain, like Irish history, onto which an amateur commentator ventures with the same risk as Lodwick crossing the S-mined perimeter of that German fuel depot. The film *Le Chagrin et la Pitié*, not least the interview with Pierre Mendès France, is evidence enough of the problems; released in 1969, it was not shown on French TV until 1981.[2] Vincent Giroud's paper[3] is the most detailed study of Pelorson's intellectual and political trajectory before World War II, his friendship with Samuel Beckett and his spell at Vichy from 1941 as a stridently Pétainist and nationalist 'Head of Youth Propaganda' in the Occupied Zone within the *Secrétariat général à la jeunesse*. We have a glimpse of one happy moment in an August 1942 photograph (see Plate 27) showing him high up in the mountains of the Valloire, doing his awkwardly lounge-suited best to join in a folk dancing session with a cheery group of 30 young men and women about to set off on a 400-kilometre hike. Quite apart from the need to listen very carefully to every beat of the German pulse, Vichy was riven by internal politics and rivalry and in 1943 he was moved downwards and sideways to run *Les Amis du Maréchal*, a post he held till the new regime arrested him, along with thousands of others, in the postwar frenzy. Some have argued in his defence that in working for Vichy he was trying to bring focus and a sense of order to the young people of a defeated and dispirited nation, many of whose fathers were dead, missing or imprisoned in Germany as POW or forced labourers. If so, his reported rhetoric went far beyond that public-spirited end. Another commentator concluded that Belmont had a split personality.[4] One side was sincere and kindly, a revolutionary intellectual, sympathetic to the 'heart-rending situation' of his fellow countrymen; the other was a man of ambition who sought power to be able to put his theories about French identity and French 'soil' into practice.

Whether his evident enthusiasm for moulding a new generation of French youth justified throwing in his lot with the Vichy administration, so many of whose adherents and time-servers saw the future in collaboration with Germany and were convinced that Jews were 'an unassimilable blood group', is debatable. But those were torn and troubled times; the regime initially had strong public support and many from France's elite joined its ranks. Be that as it may, the price Belmont paid in the wave of *épuration* (purges) which swept France after the Liberation – five months in an overcrowded, makeshift jail, blacklisting by the Writers' Union, ten years' loss of his civil rights and a quiet suggestion that he should stay clear of Paris for a while – was far less than that of many more rabid collaborators, several of whom he had known since childhood. The most obvious reason for letting him down lightly was that, however virulent his speechifying and race-baiting, he was not in Vichy's top echelon, and there were bigger fish to fry (or, as the unsentimental French phrase has it, 'other cats to flog'); and many others who served Vichy, those 'transient and embarrassed phantoms', to borrow the phrase of an English historian of another era, found new careers after 1945, untrammelled by their past.[5] Perhaps he was helped by his friendship with Samuel Beckett, who lived in France and joined the Resistance in 1939. Among Giroud's many perceptive comments is that Beckett had a 'profoundly forgiving nature'. When the network with which he was connected was betrayed to the Germans in 1942, Beckett and his wife scrambled through France in Lodwick style to a remote countryside hideout, where they lived until 1945 in great discomfort and constant trepidation, including more than one grilling by the Vichy gendarmes.[6]

The past firmly behind him, Belmont became a sought-after literary translator and author, an editor at *Paris Match* and editor-in-chief of Marcel Dassault's glossy *Jours de France*, launched in 1949 after its proprietor Jean Prouvost had himself shaken off allegations of collaboration. (Dassault, by contrast, was Jewish, refused to work for the Germans and Vichy, and survived Buchenwald to build an unrivalled aircraft manufacturing company.) Belmont was a close friend of Henry Miller, whose books he translated, as well as those of Greene, Waugh, Burgess and many others. As editor-in-chief of another women's magazine, *Marie Claire*, in 1960 he interviewed Marilyn Monroe. For all his hard work Belmont goes unmentioned in a recent survey of French literature[7] and translation as a subject is given rather short shrift, at least in a twentieth-century context, on the grounds that 'the most celebrated modern translations... are famous largely because they are the work of authors known for their original writings'. He also published several novels. One, *Le Grand Pressoir* ('The Big Wine-Press') is dismissed by Giroud as 'deeply dishonest' and 'conveniently selective... Racial persecutions are not even hinted at. Based on this account it would seem that the gravest crime Pelorson would let himself be accountable for was political naïveté.' Another was Gallically dismissed by a French reviewer as 'like Beckett reciting Racine on a set designed by Piranesi'.[8]

Of more relevance to us is Belmont's 1966 novel *Un homme au crépuscule*. As we pointed out earlier, the title mirrors, hardly coincidentally, Lodwick's 1949 book *Just a Song at Twilight*. The latter's main character, Thornton again, is obsessed by the supposed infidelities of his first wife Gloria (Sheila) and his second, named Dominique, and his plan to take deadly revenge on the man who he suspects cuckolded him. In Belmont's novel, the same dark, triangular themes emerge. The narrator is French, and though its main character, John, is a painter rather than a writer, he clearly represents much of what Belmont remembered, or thought he remembered, about Lodwick. Its settings – Dublin, the rain-swept west coast of Ireland and the Riviera – are Lodwick territory and lead us into what we know of the Merwin encounter. On the other hand the portrayal of John's English girlfriend and her curious past, and the hints at an evolving *ménage a trois* reminiscent of Patricia Highsmith, all suggest an overheated authorial overlay, with a climactic scene that owes more to Balthus than Balzac.

The book, and the fact that it is based on direct memory, however distant, even distorted, give us a line of sight into Lodwick's life at the time. Belmont had taken up that 'quiet suggestion' that he put some distance between himself and postwar Paris and was in the South of France, renting 'a nasty concrete pillbox' and still working at a novel. 'John', i.e. Lodwick, and his two small children and a series of girlfriends lived in a nicer villa up the street and Belmont the novelist describes watching the Lodwick trio on their daily strolls to the beach, around six in the afternoon, when the heat had begun to ease. There, after they had played, paddled and trailed their little nets in the rockpools, Lodwick would suddenly uncoil himself and plunge into the sea, sometimes swimming quite a long way, the kids standing rather scared on the beach. (Lodwick is remembered by one of his children as a swimmer whose wartime training allowed him to leave 'hardly a ripple in the water'.) And there is the then sandy-haired, thickset Lodwick on his daily shopping rounds, with a bachelor's disregard for money (and perhaps buoyed by that wartime book prize) cramming his raffia basket with enough each day to keep a family fed for a week; the campers who were spending a lazy summer in their beach tents would scramble up before dawn and before the dogs began to prowl, to mine the succulent leftovers from his dustbins. Lodwick grieving over his dead wife, here called 'Norah', but comforted by several pliant mistresses until he settles into a longer if troubled liaison with the raven-haired Victoria, a girl with an ambivalent past. Here again we remind ourselves that though John is undoubtedly Lodwick, Belmont's book is a novel, and he is thus allowed poetic licence. Nonetheless, there are clear echoes of the real man in John, 'a tough

Englishman but with a touch of half-Irish', drinking too much, philosophising, quoting Balzac – 'only the Devil can help you walk alone surrounded by these bottomless pits' or 'In Hell, I know where I'm going. I am suspicious of paradise.' Lodwick pontificating on the virtues of an English schooling: 'The iron fist in the iron glove – a little of it does no harm.'

Belmont also gives us a stretched version of Lodwick's military career in World War II. Whether he is trying and slightly failing to remember what he was told, whether he or Lodwick embroidered, or Lodwick was trying to brush over the failure of BOOKMAKER, we simply don't know; the record hardly needed any inflation. Contrary to what we know from the British files, Belmont quotes Lodwick as saying that as an officer of 'the Intelligence Service' he parachuted into Crete twice and France no fewer than eight times.

Belmont's book has rightly struck a sour note with those of the family who have bothered to read it; they regard it as a travesty. Quite why he wrote it remains a puzzle, like so much of his own history. Years later he told an interviewer that he wanted to try the novel form to see whether he could do it, as distinct from translating, however elegantly, the words of others. But to 'borrow' Lodwick and his story, however modified, has to have some deeper reason. Maybe it was simply something he felt he could turn into fiction without much effort at invention or imagination. Since it was published only in France and in French, and Lodwick was long dead, there was little risk of libel action. It can't have been professional jealousy since in his own sphere Belmont had become more of a name to be reckoned with than Lodwick ever had. Maybe he was settling some old Riviera score, some perceived slight, some offhand comment replayed like Chinese Whispers along the cocktail-fuelled South of France gossip circuit. Maybe the real woman behind the fictional Vicky had pushed him away. After the fictional John has died in an Irish bog the narrator resumes his former torrid affair with Vicky, but with the ghost of John still hovering between them. How to exorcise it? 'I sometimes wonder whether I oughtn't to make sure of it by killing her.' A *noir* ending of which Lodwick would have been proud!

We might easily have left the story there, had we not seen some of the letters exchanged by Lodwick and Belmont from the 1950s, long before the book was published. Belmont wrote mainly in French but with occasional jump cuts into English. These are the letters of friends, friends who – to judge from one aside by Belmont – had known each other since the 1930s, when they swapped views on 'the need for a modern-day Aristophanes'. Friends who told each other about their work in progress, their moods, their families, complained about the sloth of publishers; and who could stay friends even after what seems to have been a moan from Lodwick about Belmont's inability or unwillingness to translate some of his books and arrange for them to be published in Paris. Friends who had friends in common, including Francis Stuart, Heinemann's Alexander Frere and relatives of Henry Miller for whom Lodwick arranged a meticulous tour of Spain. It was a level of friendship which saw Lodwick, when he was moving to Spain, parcel up Sheila's books and diaries and send them for safekeeping to Belmont. Not, it turns out, a great idea. But though we can chart Belmont's career as a translator, first of 'Westerns', then of increasingly more serious novels, his fits and start at writing poetry and a novel, and his eventual emergence at the helm of *Paris Match*, he does not mention even in passing his war and immediate postwar experiences, save perhaps for a comment in October 1950 that 'Things seem to be clearing up a bit and begin to look slightly better – only slightly. There always seems to be a tiny bit of luck left somewhere for me.'

Belmont felt free to push Lodwick as an author, writing and underlining in April 1951, in another of those abrupt switches from French to English:

I'd like you to write something <u>big and black</u>... That's what you're here for, John. To blacken all those bastards... why don't you start writing that? Why don't you explode, John? You're full of it, just let it pour. Sometimes you give me the impression of being some sort of Cyclop [sic] playing darts, instead of tumbling huge boulders all over the place. Or am I wrong? Am I too ambitious for you? Come on! You're just as bloody ambitious as I.

Belmont's memoirs, though far longer than *The Asparagus Trench*, are just as unhelpful in shedding light on the real man.[9] No doubt because his wartime life was too painful to explain, too loaded with risk, they are full of colour but end before World War II, and were not surprisingly described by one reviewer as 'selectively amnesiac'. Like *The Asparagus Trench*, the cut-off point is premature, though Belmont did not have the excuse of a life cut short; he died in 2008, aged 99.

His grasp of English was superb but we might legitimately wonder whether even he would have grasped the well-meant sympathy of Lodwick's headmaster that it was a pity Grandpapa 'did not make his century'.

The second page – the first and thus the date have been lost – of a letter written by Lodwick some years later provides a coda of sorts to the Belmont relationship. As Lodwick's family have kindly identified, it is addressed to Sheila's discarded son by her first marriage, who was planning a trip to Paris and had asked about Sheila's diaries. It is a letter written, unusually for Lodwick, with sensitivity and sympathy, in which he allows himself the surely genuine observation that 'I had the great good fortune to live with your mother for one fifth of her life. And I need no other compensation.'

As to the diaries, he explains that Sheila also had 'an enormous number' of books which Lodwick had 'kept religiously for some years. But when I came to Spain it was not possible to bring everything.' So he had packed up all the books and sent them to Belmont, 'a friend of mine, once a very great friend but we have now grown apart'. Lodwick had in fact written to him a little earlier wanting to check one of the books himself, but received no reply. 'He is so honest that I am sure there is some misunderstanding,' he wrote, suggesting that a personal visit 'would be doing me a great favour if you were… to clear it up – because if only for sentimental reasons these books, many of them annotated by Sheila herself, must not be lost.' What lay beneath the cooling off might be traced in the letters he and Belmont exchanged; a recurring theme sees Belmont telling Lodwick that, despite the latter's chivvying, he has not been able to place any of Lodwick's books with any of the important French publishers with whom Belmont was in close contact.

Whether anything came of this, we don't know. Did the books include Sheila's diaries? Were the books retrieved and then junked by her son; were they sold, are they in some US library vault, or a bookseller's basement; all questions without answers, more sad gaps in the puzzle.

This leads us back to Merwin and, at one remove, the great German novelist Thomas Mann. He does not date his Lodwick encounters but we can make the assumption that, clever as they both were, even with a dictionary at hand neither would have found their way easily through the allusive linguistic thickets of the German original. So their strange *Doctor Faustus* conversation can be placed in 1948, when the Mann masterpiece was first published in English. Merwin was still able to remember the conversation clearly when he wrote about it many years later.[10] On the other hand, what he recalls of Lodwick's World War II service is not direct memory but a recycling of what Belmont told him, again at odds with what we know, since it depicts John as 'an Irish novelist who been in that part of France as a clandestine operator for the British armed forces'. He had parachuted in 'to maintain contact with the Resistance and to assist with sabotage against the Germans in the late stages of the occupation'. Again citing Belmont, Merwin tells us that in his World War II adventures John had met 'Jeanne', a

> beautiful but ravaged woman, who said little but obviously possessed a powerful character, and lived with deep rage which Lodwick ascribed to her experiences during the war, when she had been raped by the Germans and seen them murder several members of her family. He said she had been able to take it out on several of the Germans before they left, but that had scarcely soothed her, or reassured her about what life had to offer. He had fallen in love with her just the same, the moment they met in the Resistance, and had returned to her as soon as he could.

Was she the model for Belmont's 'Victoria' with her louche past? It doesn't sound like it, all the more as Belmont's Vicky is English. To compound the confusion, Merwin remembers just one child, a boy, *chez* Lodwick, whereas in the Belmont version, and in fact, the boy's sister was there too. Who are we to believe? Merwin, as an intellectually detached observer, Belmont, as an acute watcher but a self-serving conjuror with facts, and perhaps in some odd way *parti pris*, or is it Lodwick himself, despite his real achievements, retelling life through a Walter Mitty frame, or even trying out different versions of the facts to see which of them resonated as a publishable story? If we were Anton Walbrook we could simply cut the Gordian knot by scissoring the celluloid film and restarting at a later point. If only. We can't do that, so we have to let the narrative run.

One of Merwin's observations is that 'John liked his red wine at all hours of the day. Usually he did not show the effects of it until near sundown when he was apt to be preoccupied and irritable.' It is an observation also made by Belmont (and later by Lodwick's London publishers) when he related his memories of how drink triggered some manic depressive switch and turned Lodwick into something close to a boor. Again, that is Belmont's 'take', not necessarily fact. As Merwin remarks of the mixed-up Frenchman, somewhat opaquely: 'His mind, his perceptions, the language in which he expressed himself, were fine, authentic and judicious, but he seemed to live with an ultimate doubt of himself, to suspect that he was a shadow of others.'

Belmont and Lodwick had tossed around quotations from Balzac. When Merwin and Lodwick discussed *Doctor Faustus*, after a canter through Camus, they were talking about the allegory-laden life of a composer who hands over his soul to the Devil in exchange for the promise of 24 years of fulfilment as a genius. Whether it was the Devil himself who tempted him or the mood-swing effects of a self-inflicted and finally fatal dose of syphilis is a mystery left to the reader. Lodwick asked whether Merwin would have accepted such a compact 'in exchange for something I thought of as my soul'. A startled Merwin said that he would have difficulty in believing the Devil's offer and his authority for making it. He thought that if the talent, urge and character were there to begin with, the deal was meaningless. And if they were not, it could not help.

'John seemed troubled by my answer, and I could not tell why, but there was something about him that suggested a man possessed and struggling with forces he could not control.' Echoing Gloria/Sheila's perception of Lodwick's anger banked up 'like Etna', and Belmont's memories of a pent-up fury, Merwin thought the forces 'took the form of recurring violence, a theme of violence in his life and occasional glimpses of it in his demeanour and his expression, like the fin of a shark'.

He saw something out of kilter, too, in the stories Lodwick told, at all hours of the day. Many of them were about his wartime adventures, and most focused on escape and evasion rather than combat. One of them – as we know but Merwin would not have – was a revision of a murderous impulse towards a colleague which threatened to overwhelm Lodwick on his World War II escape to Spain, and about which he wrote in *Bid the Soldiers Shoot*. His account then was that he had held himself back and it had remained as no more than a nasty thought at a stressful time. He now retold the story to Merwin but with its ending as a real murder.

'So John said,' Merwin mused. 'I wondered, though, not always at the time but afterward, how many of John's dramatic stories, or what parts of them, were true, and how much of them he himself believed.' We have no idea whether John included his infant memory of the bloody leg-chopping in far-off Kashmir. If he did, Merwin might have asked himself the same question. As he did about the body of W.B. Yeats. The redoubtable poet died in Menton in 1939, another literary exile from repressive Ireland. He was first buried in the nearby cemetery at Roquebrune, but after considerable confusion what were believed to be his remains were eventually disinterred and returned to his homeland in 1948. Lodwick told the story to Merwin with so much apparently circumstantial detail that the latter was prompted to ask others better placed to know, and concluded that Lodwick had stitched on his own verbal appliqué to make an interesting anecdote even more compelling.

Plaiting together other strands from the past, around this time Francis Stuart, known to Belmont from Paris and to Lodwick from the Dublin days, and his mistress, Gertrude Meissner, who had also worked in the Nazis' foreign 'broadcasting' service, were trudging along the long, painful and poverty-pocked road from the ruins of a defeated Germany towards an equally long and painful bid for rehabilitation. In November 1945 they had surrendered to and been detained by the French, seemingly a canny choice they made themselves; had they fallen into British hands, some of Stuart's broadcast comments from Berlin, his anti-British tone and especially his call to troops in Northern Ireland to defect could have had serious consequences. His reputation did not deter the *Irish Times* from publishing a Stuart poem in 1944 or including him among the authors whose work was selected for its 1945 anthology, *Modern Irish Poetry*. What had he done? It was not Stuart's early links with the IRA which stained him; to have spent time in jail for minor-league gunrunning might be seen by many in Ireland as almost a badge of honour. But as World War II approached, allegations – what was behind them was never wholly substantiated – of Stuart's contacts with German diplomats in Dublin and with the IRA had brought him to the attention of the Irish Special Branch. But war had not yet come, Ireland was studiously avoiding entanglement and no official objections were raised when Stuart accepted an invitation to lecture in Germany in April 1939 and was subsequently appointed as Lecturer in English and Irish Literature at Berlin University, the term to start in 1940. It did, and so did he, war or no war, since Ireland was still, and would remain, neutral. His Special Branch file grew thicker when Iseult Stuart, formerly Gonne, 'whose husband is believed to be in Germany', faced a Special Military Court in Dublin in 1940, charged with 'actively assisting' an attempt to cover the tracks of Hermann Görtz, a key agent parachuted into Éire by the Abwehr and captured only after many months at large. Görtz, who had previous form as a spy in England, had met Stuart in Germany, where the maverick writer gave him Iseult's address. Görtz is also claimed to have told Stuart, who may have had other Abwehr contacts, about his mission, though he was at pains to stress to his Irish interrogators later that Stuart

> had nothing to do with the Abwehr; he was no politician, he had no contact with the IRA and not much knowledge about them. But he was a genuine Irish patriot and the prototype of those people who later became my friends in Ireland.

Though Iseult had sheltered him because Stuart asked her to, and even bought him new clothes at Switzer's in Grafton Street, the court found there was insufficient evidence to convict her and she was soon released. A fleeting reminder of the sensitivity of Irish attitudes to Germany and Britain in World War II can be seen in the fact that even today a biographical note on Iseult refers to Görtz euphemistically as 'a German liaison officer' rather than an Abwehr agent. In fact, as British files show, dropping by parachute with a wireless set and carrying US $20,000, he represented rather more than a 'liaison officer'; he was a serious German response to an approach by an IRA emissary to Berlin suggesting an armed uprising in Northern Ireland timed to coincide with German landings by sea and air. Görtz, no suave James Bond but a craggy-featured 50-year-old lawyer, dropped out of the clouds over County Meath faced with a delicate balancing act. On the one hand, Germany had other and more important initiatives up its sleeve and at that stage in the war did not want to be diverted by an Irish sideshow which would inevitably prove more complicated and involve a far greater commitment than the initial optimistic IRA approach promised. At the same time Berlin did not want to offend the IRA, and was keen to find out just how credible a force it was, to encourage them to think of the Nazis as potential partners and concentrate for the time being on sabotage in Northern Ireland.

Rather like BOOKMAKER, his landing was botched and until he eventually made contact with the IRA he wandered across the countryside in boots, breeches and jumper, clutching his black beret to use as a makeshift cup for dipping water and clinking in his pocket the German World War I medals he had brought with him for sentimental reasons. To judge from this and accounts of several British counter-intelligence experiences, 'Tradecraft' was clearly not something the Abwehr taught their hapless emissaries, a failing of which SOE was sometimes also accused. Nonetheless, as the British archive notes drily, that Görtz had spent time in a British jail for spying for the Germans 'was not, perhaps, a disqualification in dealing with Irish extremists'. He soon began to think that the IRA was likely to prove 'ineffective and untrustworthy' and that it had been penetrated, the latter suspicion reinforced when his main contact, and later many of the organisation's other leaders and sympathisers, were arrested. Görtz went on the run for 18 months. That did not stop him building up what British reports from Dublin described as 'a small circle of personal adherents among persons of anti-British sympathies both inside and outside the IRA'. He was 'principally assisted' in this networking process by two supporters, one of them 'Mrs Stuart', i.e. Iseult Gonne, who as we know gave him shelter and rushed off to buy him new clothes to replace the now tattered bits and pieces in which he had landed and trudged across country, and which would have marked him out as an oddball fugitive even in the most down-at-heel back alleys of Dublin.

Ireland was not Britain. Attitudes north and south of the border were shaped and stained by historic and recent septic memories. British diplomats' reports to Whitehall noted the local ambivalence. While a large section of Irish opinion was 'actively pro-Allied', another, though smaller, was potentially pro-German, all of which called for deft handling by the Irish government and its security services. Britain's campaign against the U-boats wreaking havoc on the vital Atlantic convoys was hampered because it no longer had access to Southern Irish ports, once part of its domain, now neutral territory. If things got worse, Dublin worried, might the British invade to take the ports back? If they did, how would the Germans respond? It was a harsh fact of geopolitical life that Ireland, neutral and feisty as it might be, simply lacked the forces to defend itself against either possible threat. Looking back on the political history – which Lodwick would not have done though Stuart might – the worries of the Dublin government were the mirror image of those in Whitehall. For the London mandarins, Éire's declaration of neutrality created 'grave problems', according to a postwar summing-up. Not only did it leave Northern Ireland, across a porous border, as part of a combatant state, but the position of the Treaty ports became 'a new factor in our naval strategy with startling suddenness'.

Although in later years Stuart put up various fuzzy defences about his decision to broadcast from Berlin, mainly on the grounds that he was an Irishman speaking to his fellow countrymen in a neutral state, that neutrality was a fragile plant. While most of what he said in his talks from Berlin has been dismissed as 'muddled, tedious and amateurish', it is hard not to agree with the judgement that it was at best a questionable moral choice. Whatever his views about the Partition of Ireland, the British Empire and the power of the 'money order', no one – especially someone with his sharp intellect and enquiring mind, as they drank at a Berlin bar with storm troopers strutting on the sidewalk, or as they read the newspapers or listened to the ranting on the radio – could be unaware of what lay at the dark heart of the Nazi regime, let alone, as Stuart once did, compare Hitler to Gandhi. His scripts – again the subject of much detailed attention by the British and Irish security services at the time and in later years by academics – were thought by many, then and now, to have 'underpinned the official German propaganda agenda'; he began by writing for William Joyce, though the latter soon began to compose his own much more unpleasant and seditious material. A statement made to a British interrogator in May 1945 by a German national from Cardiff who, like Stuart, had gone to Germany planning to lecture but ended up as a member of a broadcast team, claims that Stuart had left the unit 'last year' because he 'did not want anything more to do with propaganda. I think at heart he sympathised with the Communists and did not like the anti-Russian propaganda.' Joyce's case was different. Though many scoffed at 'Lord Haw-Haw', the unforgettable nickname coined for him by Jonah Barrington in the *Daily Express*, his sneering, anti-Semitic and defeatist ranting demanded vengeance, which was duly if rather swiftly delivered. In the view of the controversial historian A.J.P. Taylor, the charge against Joyce was 'trumped up', as he was legally an American and had made a false declaration to obtain his British passport, possession of which put him under allegiance to the Crown and was the legal hook by which he was technically and actually hanged.

Apprehensive and bewildered, Stuart and Gertrude were shut in a jail in Bregenz, transferred to a guarded villa in Freiburg the following May but released without charge in July 1946. What saved Stuart was his Irish passport and the fine legal point that as an Irish citizen he might not have been guilty of treason against Britain. It was not just a nicety of the sort that delights constitutional lawyers, but one which had politically sensitive aspects. Whether Irish nationals owed allegiance to the

British Crown as citizens of what would anomalously but legally remain 'part of His Majesty's Dominions' until the Republic of Ireland Act 1948 recognised the country as a Republic was not something Whitehall was anxious to see argued in court. And whatever the delicate issues Whitehall had to juggle about making a case in London, there was little prospect of pursuing Stuart in Dublin either, since language in the Irish Constitution, hand-crafted by Eamon de Valera himself primarily as a weapon against the IRA, defined 'treason' narrowly.[11] In layman's terms, it meant involvement in acts of war against the Irish State, or attempts to overthrow it, and Ireland had stayed resolutely neutral throughout World War II. An Irish prosecution of Stuart would have faced an uphill battle in court, let alone the court of public opinion.

Görtz had an unhappier end: he committed suicide in 1947 when faced with deportation to Germany, terrified that in the climate of the times that might simply be a waystation along the rail track to a Soviet Gulag.

Stuart wrote two books in Freiburg but it was not until the couple made their way to Paris that his work began to attract serious attention from French publishers as well as Victor Gollancz in London. Nor was racing neglected, with frequent outings to Longchamp and Auteuil. It was around this time that Lodwick wrote to Gollancz to express his enthusiasm for Stuart's work, and asked to be put in touch. The handful of correspondence which Lodwick retained – letters from Stuart, and copies of Lodwick's replies, running from 1951 to 1954, though there may have been more – can be read either as the start of a relationship which developed with warmth and mutual admiration, or as the rekindling of a lost Dublin connection. Supporting the latter and more probable interpretation, Stuart mentions that he had recently seen L.A.G. Strong and the 'old gang'. Strong, though celebrated in his time as an English writer, had been born to a half-Irish father and an Irish mother, and was a close friend of W.B. Yeats, as well as a director of Lodwick's first publishers, Methuen. Stuart also writes of meeting the Irish writer Liam O'Flaherty[12] in a context suggesting that Lodwick knew him too.

The first letter from Stuart which Lodwick retained was sent from Paris, dated 'Whit Monday 1951', and its 'Dear Lodwick' opening, later overtaken by 'Dear John' and a reciprocal 'Dear Francis… with all love' underlines their progressive mutual respect. As well as comments on each other's work in progress, and other authors, on a non-literary level Stuart's letters often underscore his passion for the Turf, with his visits to Longchamp and St Cloud, his hopes for the Two Thousand

Guineas and a plug for Tantième, 'the best horse in Europe'. They also reflect his indecision about where to spend the rest of his life, with South Africa a strong possibility until he and Gertrude finally decided on Ireland, where on a visit that year he had been struck by 'the same cold and wet and dereliction' as he remembered 'but also the peculiar ease and friendliness of life'. In a 1954 comment, he told Lodwick he had been offered a job by the British Council – where, he does not say – 'but these people are no good, better keep clear & all that'. Was this the hand of Walter Starkie, or the Irish old boy network? And why the doubts? Was it perhaps reputational concern over even a vestigial link with Whitehall?

That will-o'-the-wisp Irish connection flickers again, unexpectedly, in Stuart's letters in the ambiguous person of Georges Belmont, with whom Stuart ate and drank in Paris and whom he liked and admired. Maybe they were drawn together as outcasts, self-inflicted casualties of World War II, though Stuart's letters give no hint of this. Stuart wrote to Lodwick that he thought Belmont, who had recently shown him 'quite a remarkable poem', was spending all his energy on translating instead of writing. Maybe he lacked 'some of that toughness which is essential for the writer'. Yet again the strong implication in Stuart's letters is that the three men knew each other well. Lodwick had sent Stuart comments on the latter's 1949 novel *Redemption* and possibly also *Pillars of Cloud*, and in his turn the Irishman had given his views of two of Lodwick's own books, saying he preferred *Stamp Me Mortal*. It is for Stuart experts to ferret out in which of his books the character 'Ballard' appears but in a 1953 letter Lodwick told him that to have been taken as a model for one of Stuart's characters was 'as far as I know the first time anybody has put me in a novel, so I consider myself lucky to have got off so easily'.

Given his history it took many years for Stuart's *Black List, Section H*, seen by many as his most important book, to find a UK publisher. He began it in 1960, a year or so after Lodwick died, and dedicated it 'In memory of John Lodwick, dearest of friends', which also suggests an intimacy closer than that of a publisher's postwar introduction.

Because it throws light on Lodwick as a wide reader, we will dip later in more detail into a letter dated 6 September 1953 answering at some length an enquiry by an unidentified 'Mr Walker' who had asked for his opinion on other authors. We don't have the incoming letter but part of the reply is relevant here since, after a wide-ranging survey, Lodwick writes, 'Personally my greatest admiration is for the man to whom I dedicated my last book – Francis Stuart.' The dedication, 'To Francis Stuart in love and homage', appears in what is probably Lodwick's most personal novel, *Somewhere a Voice is Calling*, published that year, again suggesting a long-standing friendship. And an odd one in some respects. Had Lodwick forgotten Max Valentiner's torpedoing of his father, the role of the German Condor Legion in razing Guernica during the Spanish Civil War, his own skirmishes with the Germans while fighting with the Legion, his near-death experiences at their hands and the brutal reprisals by the Wehrmacht against the local people in Greece and the mountains of Yugoslavia? For here he was, even more than with the ambidextrous Belmont, befriending a man who had thrown in his lot with 'the other side', though admittedly in a different and a debatable context. This was the same Lodwick who, despite the other negative comments on his SOE record, had impressed his trainers that 'he undoubtedly loathes the Germans and all they stand for'. Maybe it was just literary admiration, seeing the writer as artist, disregarding his past. Perhaps he felt what Stuart had done and said had been exaggerated or misrepresented, or that because of his talents the World War II aberration should be forgiven, if not forgotten. Or perhaps it was simply another case of Lodwick the rebel, Lodwick as Roffey, taking the unpopular side of whatever the argument was, his ever-present 'agin'ness'.

The two were kindred spirits in another sense. Lodwick was much taken by the blacker and bleaker sides of life and Colm Tóibín's introduction to a 1995 reissue of *Black List, Section H* highlights the thinly disguised narrator's delight 'in hearing of riots, no matter where, in civil disturbances, even in bank robberies; also in assassinations and anything that diminished or threw doubt on authority'. A second and deeper pointer may be what an earlier reviewer, also cited by Tóibín, called 'the secret journey to the father', in Stuart's case the bankrupt suicide, and in Lodwick's a yellowing portrait and the enamelled gold-trimmed DSO medal and fading ribbon of a hero who had died before he was born.

Paris eventually palled for the restless and domestically challenged Stuart and after surmounting the immigration bureaucracy he and Madeleine – the Christian name Gertrude had now adopted – moved to London, where they spent several hardscrabble years, first in a flat in the down-at-heel bedsitter land of Shepherd's Bush, described by Stuart to Lodwick as a 'residential twilight'. They then moved to East London, into a decidedly working-class area then bustling with life behind high walls, ships' funnels and bobbing cranes as the real Docklands, long before high finance took over. Inviting Lodwick to visit, which from the record he never did, Stuart fretted, in a phrase which would have resonated with both of them, that 'there are so few rebellious spirits – everywhere there is tameness and conformity'. When Iseult died in 1954 he and Gertrude were free to marry; excusing himself for not having told Lodwick about it, Stuart explained in a letter that directly after the wedding bride and groom had taken the train to Newmarket to watch the Two Thousand Guineas, and hadn't had time to tell people about the marriage. It also leaves them free to move out of our story, but not the relentless Irish spotlight. His election in 1996 as a *Saoi* or 'wise man' by the Irish creative artists' association *Aosdána* drew considerable controversy, and when he died in 2000 an obituary in the *Guardian* summed him up as 'caught between the forces of Communism, nationalism, Protestantism and the Catholic church', as good a summary as any of his 98 complicated and turbulent years.

Another view of Lodwick comes from the prolific polyglot author Peter de Polnay,[13] who knew him quite well, and who wrote his autobiography, as stuffed with names as a Danish pastry is with currants, in 1978. He met Lodwick in Spain, where the author and his two children had moved after Sheila died.

De Polnay was yet another peripatetic writer who had spent happy times on the Riviera and knew Spain well. In his characteristic gossip-column style he wrote that he was introduced to Lodwick in Cadiz by 'Barry', a Canadian who had claimed to have once been secretary to the American actor John Barrymore. Lodwick had rented a house in Cadiz – 'as vast and as cold as an iceberg' – for the summer. Whether de Polnay knew the background, we have no idea. He does not mention it. It was only a recent chance riffle through some family papers which gave the context. Lodwick rented the house in Western Europe's oldest city from the summer of 1954 to January 1955. The inventory and rental agreement drawn up by the Spanish notary suggests it was well furnished, but it did not seem to merit a second glance until the name of the owner tugged at a remote memory. He was José María Pemán (1897–1981). It is an understatement to describe him as 'a distinguished Spanish man of letters'. He was indeed a writer, poet, novelist and scholar but also a right-wing intellectual who had Franco's ear, who guided Don Juan de Borbón through the tricky waters of negotiating the post-Franco reinstatement of the monarchy and was among those who advised on the schooling of the Duc's son, Juan Carlos, who became king when Franco decided to pass over his father. He was also a 'supernumerary' member of Opus Dei, the secretive Catholic body set up in Madrid in 1928, whose well-placed adherents around the world have wielded considerable influence; just how much and where are topics on which conspiracy theorists and film-makers speculate with profitable delight.

Seen on a contemporary photograph, both the house and the street itself have an art nouveau elegance. That an influential intellectual figure in the regime would rent his home out to Lodwick suggests that the latter was taken seriously as an author, that his reputation for being 'difficult' might have been overdone and that he may not have been quite as inimical to the Franco government as some of his London friends such as Mervyn Jones later speculated.[14]

It was clear to de Polnay from the first time he called at the house that Lodwick lived by his own rigid rules for working, eating, and sleeping, rules to which guests failed to adjust at the risk of going unfed, finding the main rooms in darkness or being snapped at brusquely. Though they were friends for years, his account of their relationship has the flavour of the ill-matched Felix and Oscar in Neil Simon's *The Odd Couple*, attributable in large part to Lodwick's irascibility but balanced by shared experiences. De Polnay was also an author, though not at Lodwick's level, and they had much in common. He too had a background of adventure and misadventure, having spent the World War II years in Paris, peddling pictures and producing Resistance broadsheets. He had escaped over the Pyrenees and spent time in Spanish detention camps on his long way back to England. His portrait of Lodwick is of a man who 'looked like the Naval officer he had intended to be before the war'. (He had obviously not read *The Cradle of Neptune*.) 'His head was large, and he was broad, though there was little fat on him.' He took his calling seriously and 'considered the writer to be far above the usual run of people, an anointed, privileged being... he considered it his duty to his talent to live a life above the rules and regulations laid down for others.' Though this sounds, and probably is, insufferable arrogance, Lodwick was far from the only writer to feel that way. In a 1935 letter Belmont's friend from Dublin days, Samuel Beckett, wrote:

For years I was unhappy, consciously and deliberately... so that I isolated myself more & more, undertook less & less and lent myself to a crescendo of disparagement of others and myself… misery & solitude & the sneers were the elements of an index of superiority & guaranteed the feeling of arrogant 'otherness'.

Lodwick did de Polnay the fruitful kindness of introducing him to his Spanish publisher, Josep Janés, who agreed to publish two of de Polnay's books in translation. In 1958 Lodwick rented a house for a fortnight in Camden Hill, London (one of the settings he used for 'the amorous and criminal adventures of… a number of shady middle-aged characters' in *The Moon Through a Dusty Window*). De Polnay caught the moment: 'Our friendship was at its climax and it was the last time I saw him… I mourn him and often find myself talking to him.'

That's his memory of the man. What attracted Lodwick the writer to Spain, what did his peers think of him – and what did Lodwick think of them?

18

On the Road Again

The spell in Cadiz apart, much of Lodwick's postwar work was written, often hurriedly, in Barcelona, in an apartment at 34 Principe de Asturias, a busy central street, with distant mountain views from its main windows.

Why Spain? After all, Lodwick lived most of his life as a rebel, or at least a reflexive challenger of any and all authority. He had seen Fascism in action at first hand. And in the wake of his failed SOE mission he had seen some rather bad and some good aspects of a Spain struggling with the combined social and economic effects of a terrible civil war, waged by both sides with a bloody mix of modern and medieval savagery, and with its awkward pariah position as an Axis–tilting 'neutral' in World War II. He must have had memories from Ireland of the pervasive and repressive power of the Church. So why choose to live in a country which, by one admittedly rather partisan account,[1] was a bastion of authority exercised through omnipresent, heavily armed police, informers, the grim reality of prison camps, clericalism still rooted in the Middle Ages, censorship and pervasive poverty? This was mainly rural but all too visible in the shanty towns and ad hoc camps thrown up on the fringes of the main cities as despairing peasants abandoned the increasingly meagre pickings of the land in search of depressingly scarce work. It was not entirely unlike eighteenth- and nineteenth-century Ireland. These were aspects of Spain the growing tourist trade did not see, though it was harder to avoid the press and radio glorification of Franco, 'el Caudillo', at decibel levels of hyperbole and hypocrisy recently accorded to Hitler and still at the time the norm in that other epitome of the authoritarian state, the USSR.

But all of that is for historians to wrangle over. The answer to the question of Lodwick's choice is simpler, in part at least. One element is indistinctly traceable back to Sheila and those helter-skelter prewar years. Hugh Lisney, a Leicestershire gentleman farmer, spent three years as a British regular officer, married in 1936, retired in 1940 because of ill health and went to live in Cadaqués, the easternmost point of the Spanish land mass. An unspoiled whitewashed fishing port on the coast some 30 miles south of the French border, it seems little changed today, except for prices. In the high season it has more French guests than Spanish and travel writers still enthuse over its narrow, steeply sloping streets and its 'perfect half-moon of a pebble beach', framed by whitewashed houses. A recent elegant, though emotionally stressed, story of love and loss in Cadaqués describes it as 'a remote place, isolated by mountains and accessible only by way of a hellish road where savage winds madden anyone who doesn't strictly deserve the beauty of its skies, the pinkish light of a summer sunset'.[2] There is even an older echo of nineteenth-century Essex and the Lodwick past, in the claim that Cadaqués too had witches, spotted by locals 'scrambling over the bell tower'. It began to develop in the 1930s as an artists' and writers' hideaway, where a social diarist might spot Thomas Mann, Pablo Picasso or Luis Buñuel.

Its 'artiness' escalated after World War II when Salvador Dalí made his home and studio there. We last saw Dalí choking in a Mayfair gallery, while we know from Gascoyne that Sheila Lodwick had gone to Paris in an unsuccessful bid to model for Man Ray, another Cadaqués habitué. The Lisneys' daughter Suzanne was once described as a 'muse' to Man Ray and Dalí and a later photograph of her, at a 'homage' to Dalí held, appropriately, in the local bullring, shows her with Man Ray and his wife Juliet, alongside Marcel Duchamp and his wife 'Teeny'. Given the Surrealist links it is reasonable to assume that, though she was much younger, she would have known either Lodwick or Sheila or both.

The Lisneys were staunch friends, as we shall see, and must have played a part when he was thinking about where to live. But there were surely deeper reasons. To a mind as inquisitive and questing as Lodwick's, always in search of raw material, colour and experiences, Spain must have been a fascinating country. For centuries it had been a colony of a Muslim empire and its mix of races – Visigoths, Moors, Romans, Greeks and Jews – and their cultural, architectural and linguistic traces must have been a source of endless fascination. No one is sure who first came up with the phrase, but 'Africa begins at the Pyrenees' gives a sense of how many felt and feel. Its diverse geography offered sights, sounds, smells, foods, castles, cathedrals, churches, mountains and weather patterns more varied even than France, and certainly more so than anywhere within easy reach of Earls Court. The price postwar expatriates paid was to turn a blind eye and a deaf ear to the politics, as well as the all-too-visible human and structural scars of the Civil War. Depending on whom they were talking to and where, they accepted different realities and different truths and it might have been possible – just – to blur visions of the ghastliness of the 1930s by trying to put them in the context of thousands of years of conflict, invasion and the shedding of blood, or metaphysical debates about how much worse it might have been had the Communists or even the anarchists taken power.

Living was even cheaper than in France, and as long as he kept clear of politics an Englishman would be left untroubled, especially one with a growing reputation as an author, hopefully bringing in some foreign exchange and foreign friends. It was George Orwell, whose memories of Spain cannot have been of unalloyed fun, who nevertheless wrote in *Homage to Catalonia* that 'I would sooner be a foreigner in Spain than in most countries. How easy it is to make friends in Spain.' Even so Lodwick would not have wanted to risk the annual renewal of his residence permit by the omniscient police. This meant rather more than not sticking up posters or writing critical articles in the foreign press. Though Lodwick spoke and wrote Spanish well, the self-censorship meant avoiding any chitchat about the regime or the state of the economy in a bar or at a wine-fuelled dinner party, even with close friends, and disciplining the children to equal reticence at school. Rather like occupied France, it also meant turning the wireless down to murmur level and moving it away from the wall if, fatigued by local programmes sympathetic to Franco, you wanted to listen to foreign broadcasts. Amongst Lodwick's papers is a stencilled sheet in Spanish giving the times, frequencies and topics of broadcasts from the then unrelentingly Communist Radio Prague. No comments either, even – or especially – if you were a Roman Catholic, about your dislike of the power and influence of the Church.

It can't have been easy to maintain the facade. Meryvn Jones, Lodwick's London friend, wrote after his death that,

> Along with this enormous zest for life, and his quick, generous sympathy, he
> was a rebel through and through. Humbug, pomposity and intolerance were his

enemies. He despised Franco, but made his home in Spain. I believe he liked living in a country where at any moment he might have a chance to hide a friend from the police.

There are echoes in this of the playwright David Storey's eulogy for Lindsay Anderson, the iconoclastic Cheltonian creator of *If....* He thought subversiveness was Anderson's trademark, and his satire, often mistakenly accused of mean-spiritedness, derived from genuine outrage. 'He had an appetite for a world nobler, more charitable and above all more gracious that the world in which he found himself.' We can't overlay that in its entirety on Lodwick but some of it rings true.

Family memories bear out at least Jones' comment about the Spanish leader. In private Lodwick called the General's Falangist followers *Matamoros*, a double- if not triple-edged reference, first to St James – Spain's patron saint, whose iconography is another complicated slice of Spanish history and belief, but who is generally known as 'the Moor Slayer' – and second, to Franco's campaigns against the Berbers in North Africa, one of the complicated preludes to the Civil War. *Matamoros* is also one of many Spanish words which can be translated with several shades of mean-ing: one of them is 'braggart'; another suggests 'swashbuckler'. Neither invested the General with the dignity he and his acolytes demanded.

The writer and critic V.S. Pritchett had first travelled across Spain in 1928.[3] He told a BBC radio audience in 1951 after another trip that 'conventionality, a sort of Victorian prudery, the fiercely anti-intellectual and the dull, have returned to Spain... Censorship has killed the arts and driven good intellectual minds into little safe corners.' But despite this he found himself 'among human beings' in a land where 'a kind of gifted incompetence keeps the bizarre, the comic, the dreadful, the simple human things before the traveller's eyes'. The danger of our Spanish snapshots in time is that they can mislead – in either direction. At the same time as Pritchett made his broadcast, a BBC special correspondent reported a black market in almost every commodity, and was struck by the 'bootblacks and beggars' in the street; many were disabled veterans who had fought on the (losing) Republican side. Franco had granted pensions to his Nationalist war-wounded, but refused them for his former opponents. The police and army were everywhere. While many of the buildings wrecked by the Civil War were being reconstructed, a photograph the correspondent took showed a high-rise block of flats in Madrid close to completion; the wide street outside is deserted except for – perhaps because of – a mounted patrol of six Moroccan Lancers trotting along, their spears held high. In June 1952 the last rationed items – coffee and sugar – were made freely available, and ministers said, in a counter-productive attempt to soothe, that bread supplies were assured until October. It was in 1952 that the Canadian-born writer Mavis Gallant[4] travelled wearily by train from Paris to Barcelona, where she pawned her typewriter and other bits and pieces to stay alive in a city of 'grey stone houses, trolley lines and dust. Like a bourgeois part of Paris, suddenly deserted, disappearing under grit and sand… a big city, dirty and gloomy.' The same flavour of grimness, compounded by vengeful reverberations of the Civil War terror, is well caught by Colm Tóibín in his story about a young woman trying to rebuild her life in the Caudillo's 1950s police state.[5] Franco's vain attempts at making the Spanish economy self-contained were floundering, and by one account even in the mid-1950s record inflation had reduced real wages to some 35 per cent of their pre-Civil War level.

But changes – slow, grudging, but inevitable – were on their way. A rapid run though the London press archives in the 1950s shows that Spain was working hard to shed some of its outcast status, opening up culturally, economically, internationally and as a tourist destination and taking a definitive turn for the better in 1953 when Cold War calculations led to a treaty allowing the US to build military bases on Spanish territory in exchange for financial aid. But even in 1957, after a fare hike led to a 15-day boycott of Barcelona's trams, a student protest at the university was smashed by police, 150 young people were arrested, and their identity cards were taken away 'for further investigation'. Professors who resigned in sympathy were given the stark choice of withdrawing their resignations or facing a military tribunal. The iron fist was still there.

Things were bound to change, though Lodwick did not live to see the transformation. Paradoxically the regime itself had created the material circumstances which enabled a new democratic society to emerge through 'an emphasis on stability which destroyed any chance of the regime's having a future'. That lay unimaginably ahead.

Meanwhile there were consolations. Barcelona's extraordinary architecture, the bustling market halls, the weather, the beach, the cultural life, and even then a vibrant economy made it an agreeably liveable city, whose Catalan identity and pride, much as Franco sought to stifle them, gave it the feeling of a city rather distinct from the grimness of 1950s Spain. An agreeable place in which to write, even to a schedule dictated by money, to take a drink with friends, to eat late and well even on a tight budget.

That's where he lived, wrote and worried. And read.

19

Reader and Writer

Many writers left their mark on Lodwick, writers whose books he found the time to read even when under pressure to produce. Take the letter Lodwick wrote from Barcelona to the otherwise unidentified 'Mr Walker' in September 1953, from which we have already quoted his comments on Francis Stuart. From the tone we can guess that Mr Walker, writing enthusiastically from an address in Chiswick, was an academic and a Lodwick fan. Lodwick told him, 'Among British contemporaries William Sansom and P.H. Newby are the most in intellectual favour. Both are excellent writers, and Sansom, I should say, is potentially a great one.'[1]

> If you have not read the two Germans, [Franz] Kafka and Jakob Wassermann, then you must certainly do so – particularly the latter.[2] With the French the choice is inexhaustible, but if you have not read him, read everything by André Malraux, and anything you can get hold of by a genius called Henri Bosco[3] who has, I think, been translated recently into English. There is also a Spaniard who is all the rage in England and America just now – though he has been dead a very long time – called Pérez Galdós.[4] I don't know the name they have given his book in England but you will be able to find out. Among Americans I am not on easy ground because I don't think much of most of them, but I am extremely fond of Scott Fitzgerald, and if you do not know him start with *The Great Gatsby* and then read *Tender is the Night*. Budd Schulberg's book about him *The Disenchanted* is also well worth your trouble.[5] They also have a young fellow who is my personal bet called Shelby Foote,[6] but I am not sure whether he has been published in England.

Lodwick would have been amused to know that Foote's novels and his important Civil War history remained, like the author, rather out of public focus until 1990 when he was commissioned to narrate a PBS documentary on the Civil War for US television. His folksy drawl and his deep knowledge made him 'the toast of Public TV' and kick-started sales of his history.

> The others – as indeed, so many others – are too well known for me to recite them to you. The only other book which you really must read is *Under the Volcano* by Malcolm Lowry: you will never forget it…
>
> If you want to know who I think are the greatest of all novelists then I will say that it seems to me a triple dead heat between Stendhal and Flaubert and Dostoevsky. When you've read them almost everything else inevitably seems dull.

But as we noted earlier, Lodwick reserves his final accolade for his friend and mentor: 'Personally my greatest admiration is for the man to whom I dedicated my last book – Francis Stuart.'

Walker replied, apologising for being a nuisance, and telling Lodwick that he had taken his advice and read both Bosco and Foote. He hoped Lodwick would visit England again soon. 'I should like to spend at least four hours with you whilst doing justice to some good Italian cooking.'

Lodwick, remember, was almost wholly self-taught, making it even more remarkable that such a broad range of writers, some now – like Lodwick himself – long forgotten, caught his attention in the south of France or in censored, introspective Spain. On the flimsy evidence of a letter found amongst his papers, many of his books came from Hatchards in Piccadilly, though he was not always timely about settling up. We know that he was stimulated by his Dublin circle, that some of those friends, like Belmont, overlapped with his life in France, and that through Walter Starkie, who now reappears on the scene as the Roundabout turns, and his publisher in Spain he was also close to Spanish and Catalan literary, musical and artistic circles.

Starkie had been appointed Professor of English Literature at the University of Madrid in 1947, after his Institute contract was renewed – he held the post until 1954 – and until the late 1950s he criss-crossed Spain, speaking, playing his violin and, in the words of the British Council memorial to him, 'hosted visits to Spain by a number of distinguished British speakers'.[7] This sounds a calm, almost idyllic intellectual lifestyle, despite the hardships in the tough world outside the front door of *el Inglés*. Some of Lodwick's visitors, as remembered by his family, overlapped with the literati drawn by Starkie's magnet. Lodwick's Barcelona friend and publisher Josep Janés was much in Starkie's orbit. Himself a poet and translator, Janés would have claimed – not too loudly in those days – that he was a Catalan first and a Spaniard second, a sentiment which landed him briefly in jail at the end of the Civil War, facing the capital charge of 'separatism'; intercession by important authors saved the day.

Like Lodwick, Janés is described in some biographies as 'an autodidact' who became a significant cultural figure, and was the publisher in translation of many of the major novels, plays, poems and autobiographies of the day, and indeed of times past, from Oscar Wilde to Tennessee Williams by way of Churchill, P.G. Wodehouse, Jerome K. Jerome, Kipling, Proust, Edith Wharton, Virginia Woolf and, needless to say, Somerset Maugham. At least three of Lodwick's novels were on his list in translation. It was an important venture whose focus and international connections blurred the vision of the Spanish censors. He had done well; a recent eulogy speaks of 'a splendid house' and 'half a dozen cars', though he had rough patches along the way, and is said to have quipped that he was 'less a man of letters than of Letters of Credit'. Peter de Polnay remembered him as a man of medium height, with long hair and a pale face, 'his voice filling any room. Ostentatious, even vulgar, yet he had charm and streaks of kindliness.'

Lodwick's visitors, at least those we know about, were an eclectic bunch. Somerset Maugham had long since fallen in love with Spain, had toured it before World War II, and his 1935 book *Don Fernando* displayed a deep understanding of its history and culture. Maugham came back to Spain in 1948, wealthy and aloof, to research the seventeenth-century painter Zurbarán, an artist he greatly admired. He also found time to sit on the jury for the *Premio Internacional de Primera Novela* ('International Prize for a First Novel'), an award sponsored by Janés. The prize went to Francisco González Ledesma, described in his obituary as a pioneer of the *noir* detective genre; a talent Lodwick would have applauded. A Maugham trip in 1949 was cut short by food poisoning but he returned in 1954 to enjoy the country and the Spaniards, 'the only polite people in Europe'. As we know, Maugham and

Lodwick shared the same publishers, Heinemann in London and Janés in Spain, though Maugham was a long-standing, high-value celebrity, whose manuscripts were often sent to the printers by Heinemann without editorial input. In contrast to Lodwick, his work sold on an enviably massive scale and had been the basis for several Hollywood epics.

Where and how did Lodwick meet Somerset Maugham? Alexander Frere, their mutual and canny friend and publisher at Heinemann, may have played a part in introducing them but most likely sage and acolyte would have run into each other in those halcyon postwar days on the Riviera, where Lodwick philosophised and spun war stories with W.S. Merwin and drank with Georges Belmont.

There are several letters from Maugham in the family papers. The first is dated August 1952, and unlike the others comes from the Hotel Beau Rivage in Lausanne. Maugham expresses mild concern to 'My dear Lodwick' that he is reading and re-reading Maugham's 1930 novel *Cakes and Ale*, 'because you are going to write a more or less similar book'. It would be better, he adds, for Lodwick to rely on his own 'talent, experience and originality'. In July 1953 Maugham thanks Lodwick, this time from his home in the Villa Mauresque at St-Jean-Cap-Ferrat, for his 'very nice letter' and an unnamed book, and applauds his (unfulfilled) intention to write a play, though he warns that 'English actors cannot speak long speeches and English audiences find it hard to listen to them.'

Two further letters have dates but no year, and are handwritten from the Villa Mauresque with a neatness and elegance distinctive in itself and exceptionally so for a man of around 80. They deal with Lodwick's contentious foray into writing the life of Calouste Gulbenkian.

When Lodwick set to work on *Gulbenkian*, described as an 'interpretation' of the oil magnate and art collector rather than a full-blown biography, and a collaboration with Gulbenkian's former confidential secretary D.H. Young, he anticipated a negative reaction with typical glee, telling his friend Mervyn Jones: 'I am writing a book about Gulbenkian… it is quite fun, and I promise you, extremely subversive… Rumours reach me that the disunited Gulbenkian family, goaded into retaliation, have commissioned somebody… to write an official biography.' He was right. On the one hand *Gulbenkian* was raked with grapeshot by the Foreign Office mandarin S.H. Longrigg,[8] who wrote in the *Journal of International Affairs*:

There may well be readers of this book, who, seeking solely entertainment, may find it diverting; the author is an experienced fiction writer, and with imagined dialogues, doubtfully authentic episodes, sprightly comment and cynical-facetious distortion of history does his best with the material, but there is nothing here for the serious student of history or international affairs or high finance or the oil industry or the Middle East.[9]

The book, he concluded, 'can scarcely be other than painful reading for the friends of the late Mr Gulbenkian', of whom we assume Longrigg was one.

On the other side of the Atlantic – and of the debate – George S. Gibb told readers of the *Harvard Business History Review*[10] that he had read both Gulbenkian books, noted that the family had 'taken an exceedingly dim view' of Lodwick's work, but observed that it seemed to be based on sources, principally Young's insider views, that were 'more valid and certainly more objective' than those used in the history the family had commissioned. That made Lodwick's work 'an incredible chronicle… and vastly more appealing.' Readers were warned that Lodwick did not know much about the US oil industry and had not brought to his work the discipline of a trained historian, who might have made more out of Young's insights. But he 'appears to have an intuitive grasp of broad developments that at times brings him close to Truth [*sic*] and lets him set it forth with considerably greater force and simplicity and clarity than is possible in a more conventional kind of historical appraisal'.

Contrary to the insouciant impression Lodwick had given Mervyn Jones about the book's reception he had obviously voiced a deeper concern to Maugham, to whom he had sent a copy, perhaps another example of his ability to express himself differently to different people depending on his mood and who they were. Replying *de haut en bas* from the pinnacle of authorial success and wealth, and ignoring the reality that reviewers were quite often men and women of considerable distinction, Maugham commented waspishly: 'Do you think [reviews] greatly matter? They are written by bored, tired journalists who want to earn a little money, and forgotten as soon as they are read.' In contrast, the late Sir Raymond Carr, distinguished Hispanic scholar and a prolific reviewer after he retired as Warden of St Antony's College, Oxford, once remarked that 'If some poor sod spends all this time writing a bloody book, you must find something good to say about it.'

Maugham found the Gulbenkian book to be 'extremely well written, as is everything you write… I wish you had been writing a novel rather than a biography.' Maugham obviously knew the background and may well have encountered Gulbenkian himself in Portugal or on the Riviera. He regretted that Lodwick's collaborator Young, who obviously knew so much, had not been 'more communicative'. As it was, the subject, 'the old Armenian, remains a terrible, strange, sinister figure in semidarkness. This, I take it, you could not help.' His comment was echoed in an *Irish Times* review which commented that 'Even a skilled novelist like Mr Lodwick cannot breathe life into stocks and shares, and without them Mr Five Per Cent was only mean and misanthropic.' The book did not sell well, and was soon being remaindered at four shillings a copy. An uncorrected proof copy stamped 'Not For Sale' was recently offered on eBay for a target £8, with no bids yet shown.

In another letter, undated and without a specific reference, but from its context clearly a response to *Bid the Soldiers Shoot*, Maugham praises the book as 'grand, in many ways the best thing you have done and of course admirably written… but, Lord, what a life you have led and what horrors you have had to endure! You must have great powers of resistance.' Unable to resist a mild dig, Maugham ends by asking to be remembered to Janés; 'and tell him that if he would like to send me some money it would be welcome'.

Quite what happened next has to be inferred from a handwritten letter of Frere's to 'My Dear John'. When he heard Maugham's comment Janés must have written to Frere, who took sharp exception to what he clearly interpreted as a suggestion that he was party to the withholding of Maugham's royalties. Janés 'should keep his thick Spanish nose out of my affairs and stop trying to make trouble between me and my octogenarian friend and me and you.' We find no other trace of this spat, which seems to have blown over, but it suggests that Lodwick was either tactless or taking an opportunity to make a little mischief. Or both.

In November 1954, Lodwick wrote to 'Dear Mr Maugham' enclosing a copy of an article he had written about Spain, first because he hoped Maugham would find it amusing, but also because Lodwick apparently mentions Maugham's books and the Spanish censorship, and thought he should get Maugham's prior approval. If it was ever published, the article cannot now be traced, nor can any reply.

Gulbenkian was not Lodwick's first brush with literary controversy though the earlier one seems to have been kept quiet and eventually smoothed over. As SOE had conjectured, and as indeed he told his French chums when he enlisted, war offered an experience that could be turned into books. He was right. He made good use of his short but complicated time with the Legion and his even briefer spell on BOOKMAKER and he mined at least two books from his SBS experiences. In 1947 he wrote about the Service as *The Filibusters*, and though it was not an official history other books on clandestine themes had so much trouble with the Whitehall censorship machine that one wonders how he slipped it through, especially since, as he admits, his book was based on 'dog-eared, yellowing operational reports and instructions… unit folklore and questioning survivors'. He also had access to the SBS War Diary, which eventually passed into the National Archives. Passed, we might surmise, reluctantly, since its front page is marked 'Closed until 2045', an embargo later over-stamped 'cancelled'. The book may have dodged the official bullet but it still managed to provoke a spat with senior ex-SBS colleagues, who claimed Lodwick had reneged on a written deal that royalties would be split 60/40 between the SBS Benevolent Fund and the author. Letters from former SBS officers escalated from polite nudging to stiff and then positively acrid – no doubt to Lodwick's secret enjoyment – condemning his rejection of 'a debt of honour, disgraceful and mean beyond words'. The amount involved cannot have been substantial but the affair would not have done much for Lodwick's reputation in White's Club or officers' messes. Ripples may even have reached Whitehall, since one of his fellow SBS officers, who was party to the correspondence, happened to be the brother of a senior World War II GCHQ officer who later became a Treasury 'mandarin'. The row must have been settled since the book was reissued in 1990[11] with a foreword by Lodwick's wartime commanding officer George Jellicoe, a coincidence that allows this author to include himself, albeit based on a 1970s working acquaintance, among the host of fans of the man Lodwick and his fellow freebooters knew as 'the belted Earl', 'Curly' or 'His Reverence'. Meeting Jellicoe when he came to the City as a globetrotting merchant banker, his colleagues knew none of the details of his military service, except that there had been real heroism wrapped in the cliché that 'he had had a good war'. But like everyone with whom he came into contact, they were hugely taken by his boundless charm, determination and the fact that he seemed to know everyone that mattered in Whitehall and the wider world. In 1973, acting under pressure, he 'did the decent thing' and retired from politics, hounded by the British press in the wake of what nowadays would be dismissed as a minor sexual indiscretion. Jellicoe was almost a folk hero in Crete and mainland Greece for his World War II exploits, and the London 'scandal' led one Athenian lady to comment: 'Ridiculous. Why shouldn't he? Look at Lord Byron!'

This is about Lodwick, not Jellicoe or Maugham, but as we will soon quote Rebecca West[12] at length on the former, we can round off with a brief look at her thoughts on the latter, voiced in a 1981 interview with Marina Warner for the *Paris Review*. West was then 89 and though she was less opaquely critical than she had been about Lodwick (as we shall see), her opinions had the trenchancy of old age and do not reflect the consensus view. Maugham, she said,

> couldn't write for toffee, bless his heart. He wrote conventional short stories much inferior to the work of other people. But they were much better than his plays, which were frightful. He was an extremely interesting man, not clever or cold or cynical. I know of many affectionate things he did. He had a great capacity for falling in love with the wrong people.

Though he could be bitchy, arrogant, and even icily unpleasant, Maugham would surely have been a more urbane and predictable visitor to the Lodwick household than the Irish poet, novelist and playwright Brendan Behan.[13] As a young lad growing up in a militant family, he had been an IRA 'hardman' and bomb maker who had spent serious time behind bars; as he became a literary lion, bars of a more hospitable kind embraced him and he once described himself, reversing the usual cliché, as 'a drunkard with a writing problem'. In another of our loops of coincidence, in Donleavy's Lodwick-evoking *The Ginger Man* Behan bursts into a basement booze-up thinly fictionalised as 'Barney Berry'.

Again we have no date for the visit, and the story that is put about of Behan's encounter with a Spanish immigration officer is likewise undated and almost certainly apocryphal. The well-informed Spanish police would have known of his reputation and his record, and he may have rolled off the plane well served by airline hospitality of a kind which is now only a fond memory. He was taken into a small, windowless room on one side of the arrivals hall and asked: 'Señor Behan, what is the purpose of your visit?'

'I'm here for General Franco's funeral.'

'But the Generalissimo isn't dead!'

'In that case I'll wait.'

Talented though he was, Behan, whose IRA backstory, let alone his writing, must have led his path to cross with Stuart's, was not a visitor who was likely to be invited back by even the most broad-minded host. He was particularly remembered in the Lodwick household for his 'smelly socks' and the need to try, at least, to keep him away from the drinks cabinet. He had also spent several postwar spells roistering in Paris. Stuart had spent time there before the war, but if their paths ever crossed in those later years, Behan would have found a very different Stuart, dependent on food handouts, cold-shouldered by the Irish Legation and terrified of arrest; hardly a congenial drinking buddy.

Certainly Behan's nationality and growing fame would have made him a natural target for Starkie, even though to have him as a guest speaker at a prim literary evening in Barcelona would have required an intriguing calibration of risk and reward. Maybe Behan was also hoping to find a publisher, but the only Spanish edition of his *Borstal Boy* we can find was published as recently as 2012. There may have been others which have disappeared from the radar.

A more direct link from the Lodwick past may have been Dylan Thomas, the Welsh poet and playwright, whose brilliance, like Behan's, was also bedevilled by booze. We last glimpsed Thomas with Sheila in a susurration of Surrealists at the London Exhibition. Family memories identify him as another Spanish visitor, though Thomas' most recent biographer, who did a thorough job tracking his travels, found no record of any trip to Spain.[14]

But the *La Ronde* effect, one story looping back to another, is seen again in 1948 when leading lights in the Spanish academic and literary establishment contributed to a volume of essays – a *Festschrift* as scholars are fond of calling these encomia – in Starkie's honour. It goes almost without saying that it was published by Janés, but it also included Catalan translations by Maria Manent and Janés himself of poems by Rupert Brooke and Dylan Thomas.

A non-literary character whose mangled English, heavy accent, bear-like build and complicated passport history must have given the Spanish immigration officers, let alone Lodwick's neighbours, plenty to gossip about was Russian-born Gregory Ratoff, Hollywood actor, producer and director.[15] Waving his trademark cigarette holder, Ratoff spoke gutturally and persuasively to Lodwick about his plans to film the James Bond novel *Casino Royale*, on which he had first an option and later full rights.

Ratoff was a friend and business associate of the symmetrically named writer and producer George St George, who also had Russian roots. He and St George had worked together on several movies now lost in time, from *The 300 Spartans* to *Abdullah's Harem*, the latter starring Kay Kendall and Sydney Chaplin. St George also got a partial script credit for *Orders to Kill*, a 1958 film which might have been prompted by some of Lodwick's memories; it deals with a US agent parachuted into World War II France to eliminate a suspected traitor in the Resistance. Anthony Asquith directed, and Eddie Albert played the lead, supported by a slightly improbable combination of Lillian Gish, Irene Worth and James Robertson Justice. Like so many adventures in the film business, the chronology and hard facts are almost impossible to sort out but we know that Ratoff, armed with the option rights, suggested Lodwick try his hand at a screenplay for *Casino Royale*. There was some collateral fun – trips to Paris, Portugal and London, meeting the comely Jill St John – but Lodwick was hardly the first writer to learn the disillusioning lesson of Hollywood's 'Boulevard of Broken Dreams', littered with abandoned ambitions, broken promises, shredded scripts and hastily vacated bungalows at The Beverley Hills Hotel.[16] In a homesick letter to Barcelona, written in Spanish from Paris where he was working on the project, Lodwick told his family that 'things are going well, but with Ratoff, badly. He is always in London and [despite] all his promises he has given me very little money.' In another letter he complains that the work is a nightmare. 'Ratoff is like a child – he is always asking for more-more-more.' At some point Ratoff dispatched St George to instil discipline into a wayward Lodwick. After some clearly fruitless encounters St George hand-wrote Lodwick a ten-page letter trying – to the untutored eye, rather well – to explain what writing a film script was all about, and explaining frankly that, while Lodwick had considerable talent, it was as a novelist, and he needed help in writing a screenplay, a very different skill set. Unless Lodwick cooperated, St George would leave town. The Hollywood studio moguls are

> people who know their business far too well not to know exactly what they want. They have experimented with unconventional film ideas for many years – one must give them that credit – and have discovered the only safe formula which brings money into the till. And that is the only reason why they are in this business.

And today more than ever before they are not in the mood to experiment with anything they are not absolutely sure of.

Words that are just as true in the twenty-first century.

Lodwick was not about to change his spots or his style, and in a later letter from New York St George apologised for 'a bit of harsh feeling based solely on misunderstanding of moves and motives and difference of opinion as to tactics of life.'

To round off the *Casino Royale* story, when Ratoff died his widow sold the rights to the flamboyant producer and 'super-agent' Charles Feldman. His film version, produced in 1967, was an almost unwatchable 'spoof' which failed at the box office even though, or perhaps because, its cast list was not just heavy but grossly overloaded with stars, no doubt many of them clients or chums of Feldman.

Its history has been well analysed by Jeremy Duns.[17] But the point of this exotic diversion is that when he first announced his plans in 1956, Ratoff told the media he was negotiating with a 'noted scenarist' to write the script. Lodwick certainly did produce one version, a copy of which remains in family hands, but how much of his material, or the contributions of Ben Hecht, the 'Shakespeare of Hollywood', made it into the Feldman version, is impossible to tell.[18] The industry database attributes the script to Wolf Mankowitz, John Law and Michael Sayers, with uncredited nods for contributions to Hecht, Joseph Heller, Woody Allen, Peter Sellers and Billy Wilder, among others; credit is given to no fewer than five directors.

Back in the real world, while visitors came and went Lodwick worked, to a strict schedule, sometimes all night, eating at unconventional hours, writing by hand and sending his manuscripts to London for typing. Though his first books were published by Methuen, the bulk of his work was issued under the Heinemann imprint, with a one-off diversion to Cassell when Heinemann turned down his book about a voyage to Spanish Morocco. 'Mr Lodwick's next book is about camels,' they sniffed, though *The Forbidden Coast* is actually a rather readable and well-informed travel story. How many copies it sold we do not know, but in a book about his own wanderings in South America, Evelyn Waugh had noted lugubriously:

Who in his senses will read, much less buy, a travel book of no scientific value about a place he has no intention of visiting?... One does not travel, any more than one falls in love, to collect material. It is simply part of one's life.[19]

Quite why Lodwick and Methuen parted company is lost in time, but a clue comes from a personal if stiff letter to 'Dear Lodwick' from a 'Literary Advisor' at Methuen, unidentified beyond the signature 'Lars'. It suggests Lodwick was complaining that Methuen had taken against him as they had not sold enough of his books. 'Honestly, this belief of yours about the firm's hostility to your work is all moonshine.' The real reason, he explains, was the acute postwar shortage of paper which meant all print runs were necessarily curtailed.

Lodwick must also have had an enterprising agent; to have had books published, been awarded a prize and reviewed in the *New York Times* in the middle of a world war suggests that someone was working uncommonly hard on his behalf. But this person too has proved impossible to track down.

We at least have the advantage of a ringside seat on the Heinemann relationship, and can see what they and press reviewers thought of his work. Most authors, except for those at Maugham's level who claimed to be above such things, regarded reviewers with a mix of fear and loathing, and their relationships with publishers often had the characteristics of an edgy marriage. Lodwick was not immune to criticism, but his books were taken seriously and handed to top-flight reviewers for comment. Whether one of his literary friends or an enterprising agent brought Lodwick and Heinemann together is lost in time. Like most of the proudly independent imprints of the era, the firm has long since been sliced and diced, and what remains is now an important element in a much larger group. In Lodwick's day Heinemann was a film-maker's vision of a British publisher, housed in an elegant Georgian building in Bedford Square, an antique grandfather clock ticking gently in the black and white tessellated entrance hall.

Lodwick the writer is another chapter. No killing, no jails, but in its own way just as precarious a life.

20

Publish and Be Damned

The official Heinemann history tells us that, of the hundreds of new novelists the firm took on between 1945 and 1961, Lodwick stood out not just because of his talent but also 'because of his extraordinary character and his love–hate relationship with the firm'.[1]

Two distinguished Heinemann editors, James Michie and Roland Gant,

admired his writing, which we felt was something special, though also remarkably careless. He never became a really important writer, maybe because of so many Spanish wine stains on the manuscript. He possessed overwhelming charm and rascality of the good sort.

A surviving letter from Michie to Lodwick shows the tact with which the firm approached an author who was known to be volatile, and the care they put into their side of the work. Tackling *The Moon Through a Dusty Window*, he complains gently about 'centrifugal digressions' and suggests that the book needs cutting: 'for you to take a long session with it with the knife in your hand'.[2] His colleague Anne Hill had given the same advice on *Bid the Soldiers Shoot*, advice which Lodwick had been reluctant to accept, but the resulting 'hard and finite shape' had led to it selling '1,000 more copies than any of your previous three books'. By cutting *The Moon*, Heinemann would 'be able to give you a new push forward into the shy arms of the British public'.

A.S. Frere (1892–1984), who had been with Heinemann since the 1920s, became Chairman in 1944 and stayed at the helm until 1961. It was a period which ended with one of those financially driven publishing takeovers which became a sad inevitability in a business that had tried hard to remain a genteel profession until financial and commercial pressures led to their being swallowed up by larger and sometimes distinctly non-gentlemanly players. Heinemann had built an enviable and eclectic list of authors, from Galsworthy to Graham Greene, J.B. Priestley, and Somerset Maugham via the controversial Walter Baxter (one of whose books landed Frere in court, happily with a successful outcome) to the Golons' unashamedly romantic French novel *Angelique*. And of course John Lodwick, with whom Frere's 'debonair, aristocratic presence'[3] might seem a clash, were it not that Frere felt as much at home drinking at the Dôme or Coupole in Paris as at London society parties, or as his biographer appealingly puts it, 'demonstrating his remarkable skill as a tap dancer'. Lodwick might also have enjoyed, as long as he was not the main topic, what another of Frere's colleagues privately described in a letter as his 'convoluted, acid-tinged, viper-tongued conversations'.

Though Lodwick guyed Frere in his supposedly fictional *The Butterfly Net*, his target was not annoyed. He probably enjoyed it. In a passage which surely recalls Frere as he was, Lodwick imagines his reaction as the latest draft thumps onto his desk, recoiling at another of 'those terrible manuscripts typed on what appears to have been a Boer War machine, covered with wine stains and private notes to myself'.

In the real world Lodwick wrote to Frere often and at length 'about his wives, his children, his moods, progress with his current novel, above all about his debts and his need for more money'. To help Lodwick out Heinemann paid him a lump sum for each book in monthly instalments, giving him rather more, as they later calculated, than he would have received from the conventional scale of royalties. Unaware of the shadow of the unseen father whose non-memory haunted Lodwick, his conflicts at school and at Dartmouth, and his unhappy parting of the ways with SOE, the Heinemann historian tells us that 'he seemed to be dependent on the firm almost as a parental institution'.

The mood swings can be seen in his letters. At one point he told Frere, 'I always think of you as my best friend, and you know very well that if you cut me off tomorrow I should still be your friend'. And in a letter to Jonathan Price, a Heinemann editor, Lodwick wrote:

> When I was in England last year nothing impressed me more than the charm, the general niceness of all the young people upstairs in Heinemann. Living abroad as I do, I felt as if I were coming into my club, and I felt very proud, but

also what is more natural to me, very humble. I want to be your writer. I don't like changing publishers. That is a dirty procedure.

Despite the switch from Methuen, we have to take that comment at face value. But he could also be irritable. In another letter to Frere, he spat:

> You once told me that were it not for my various children, you would have had no hesitation in casting me adrift. All right, God damn it, do it then. Do you really imagine that I am a less proud man than you, or any member upon your board?… Do you really want me to stop and write detective stories under various other names for one of your competitors? I remain loyal to the last, until people prove disloyal to me. You have always been damned decent to me, like the time you walked up the road on your hobbled leg. But I can take the bad news and make other dispositions too – if you don't want me any more.

Lodwick was hardly the only author with money worries. One of the many authoritative commentators on Francis Stuart's life notes that in the mid-1930s, 'Driven by the pressing need for money, which was due in part to his own incontinence, he was writing at a feverish pace.'[4] But to quote Evelyn Waugh's *Ninety-two Days* again,

> I have seldom met a male author who enjoyed doing his work, and never heard of one who gave it up and took to something more congenial… Though most of us would not write except for money, we would not write any differently for more money.

Although most of D.J. Taylor's data on writers' earnings relates to the pre-World War II years, it is clear that with some stellar exceptions the postwar life of most authors was the same hand-to-mouth 'pram in the hall' existence, advances and royalties scrappily augmented by journalism and reviews of books which could themselves be sold on to the local bookstore.[5] Waugh would have been one of those exceptions, though he rarely conceded it. Lodwick was one of the many left tirelessly tramping the Grub Street treadmill.

Though the firm's history suggests Heinemann not only liked *The Butterfly Net* but helped with some of the background and had no quarrel with the portrayals, the letter Lodwick wrote to the unidentified Mr Walker in September 1953, some time before the book appeared, gives a slightly different slant.

> My publisher is going on at me because I have written a satirical book about publishers and writers and literary London. He says I won't hold my public – whatever that is – with a book of that kind.

He went to the unusual lengths of sending Mr Walker a typescript and asking for his views.

> Please don't worry if you wish to be critical. I have been reared on criticism. My publisher's argument is that I am read because people know what to expect, but from my point of view that is precisely what I don't want them to know. A writer <u>must</u> experiment and change his skin from time to time.

Lodwick asked Walker to return the typescript, which we assume he did, though sadly we don't know what he made of it. For writers to part with manuscripts is unusual but maybe Lodwick was, as so often, different.

We do know what Angus Wilson thought.[6] Flushed with the success of his novel *Hemlock and After* he made it clear to readers of his *Observer* review that he did not like *The Butterfly Net* at all.

> The story is filled with a lot of booksy talk and worldly philosophising… [it is] less engaging to hear Mr Lodwick's views on various well-known publishers and the Authors' Society and hardly engaging at all to be treated to rollicking man-to-man talks about the true art of sexual love, life after death and the merits of Stendhal. The novel is, I imagine, a sort of *roman à clef*, if any reader should have leisure enough to devote himself to 'cracking' the cipher.

'Cipher' is a word which might have meant more to Wilson than most of his readers; he spent part of World War II cracking Italian codes at Bletchley Park, before a nervous breakdown sent him to the relative tranquillity of the British Museum. The comments strike a modern reader of the book as verging on the bitchy. Wilson gives no credit, for instance, to the sharply drawn portrait of the ubiquitous and charmingly sly Mr Mendoza. Part of that 'cipher' which irritated Wilson is the fun Lodwick pokes at the parsimonious, long-suffering and canny Frere; another is that its hero, another Dormant, is commissioned to turn into publishable material the memoirs of the deceased Lord Drawbridge, who like Grandpapa Lodwick was once a senior public servant in Imperial India and a product, like so many of them, of Haileybury.

In April 1954 Frere wrote in response to an unknown but clearly painful issue about which Lodwick had complained. Sent from Frere's stylish rooms in the exclusive Piccadilly enclave known as Albany it has the overall tone of the proverb that 'a soft answer turneth away wrath', an adage of which Lodwick so often lost sight. 'Why,' Frere asks, 'should I get angry with you because you tell me what nobody else would have the friendliness or affection to?'

He concludes: 'You are real: you are a man and can write like an angel when you are not whoring after your own inventions. You have my deep affection. And I thank you.'

There is another view from inside Heinemann's then gracious and spacious offices. It comes from Rebecca West, whose old-age views on Maugham we have quoted already. All the main publishers then employed, and often still do, freelance 'readers' to assess manuscripts they were seriously considering for publication. Working in that capacity for Heinemann, Rebecca West had met Lodwick and, according to the dust jacket for *Somewhere a Voice is Calling*, also read his earlier books. Though she took the work seriously it was something of a sideline since, always a busy writer herself, she was even more in demand in the wake of her coverage of the Nuremberg trials and the publication in 1949 of her highly acclaimed reports on the trials of William Joyce, some of whose early scripts were written by Francis Stuart and Julian Amery's deluded brother John.

When Rebecca West read the manuscript of *Somewhere a Voice is Calling* neither she nor the Heinemann editors could possibly have known how much of the highly readable novel is Lodwick writing about himself and his marriage. If some of the manuscripts delivered to Heinemann had wine splashes, it is not fanciful to imagine that the pages about 'Gloria' might have had tearstains too.

The cover image of a family burial vault beside a wine-dark sea hints at the story behind the story. So does the title, since Gloria/Sheila has been dead for perhaps three years, and 'Thornton', remarried to a French wife, is revisiting her burial vault, and wonders if she might speak to him from behind its grille. The storyline, involving jealousy over real or imagined infidelities on both sides, smuggling, the gratuitous killing of a cat, and climaxing in murder, is cleverer than this summary might make it sound. It is also inexpressibly sad when, as we recorded earlier, it replays Gloria/ Sheila's slow descent into darkness, an account which is too painful to be anything other than the memory of real dialogue. But first let's see what Rebecca West thought, with the introductory caveat that, although Heinemann correctly judged her to be 'percipient', when one re-reads the book in the light of her comments her more fantastical observations are hard to fathom and we have not reproduced them in full. It is possible that the editors tweaked the final manuscript to tone down or remove some of the elements which so troubled her. The reference to 'traitors' must be to Joyce and Amery. Despite strenuous efforts in Madrid by his brother to find documents which might have exonerated him by demonstrating he had acquired Spanish citizenship during the Civil War, John Amery pleaded guilty and was hanged.

Her report to the Heinemann editors conflated Lodwick and his book.

> This man is a distressing creature. He upset me when he came here, because he was so like one of my traitors: not that I suspect him of any treachery, it is the abstract treachery to candour, the mere doing of things furtively and against the common understanding of the world, which covers people with a Graham Greene mould. If you get rid of candour you disorient people, they go off to the wrong point of the compass with an air of infinite cunning and superiority to the people who are outside the frame, and it is spiritually nothing… God, I am worried about this book. It is so good in a sense. The reality of Thornton and Gloria.

All that off her chest, she comes to a positive conclusion, with words of praise adroitly lifted as a sales message for the book's dust jacket:

> How much more interesting than nearly all his contemporaries. How beautifully supple [altered by the publisher to 'subtle'] his writing, he folds a sentence round a fact or a thought as the girl in the shop ties a scarf round your neck and you can't do it at home in the same way, not ever.

But what good did it do him? How successful was he with the pen rather than the pistol?

21

Scorecard

How many books did Lodwick sell, and what did reviewers think of them? The two questions are interrelated and, in his day at least, a literary landscape without today's festivals, e-books or social media, the second actually drove the first. In our electronic age it is easy to find out how any book is doing. Essential too, since publishers are sometimes negotiated by shrewd intermediaries into paying eye-watering advances and can find themselves monitoring the sales figures with dyspeptic anxiety.

In Lodwick's day things were fuzzier. Charts only came into their own after bookstores began to install 'point of sale' machines in the 1980s so that sales could be verified and counted. Before that the metrics were compiled in various different ways, with some data from publishers and some from retailers such as W.H. Smith and panels of independent stores. As the industry evolved, the criteria and the data sources could change from year to year; in any event the end results did not give actual sales numbers, only rankings. Counting and comparing to other titles were not the done thing in those more genteel days.[1] And though we tried to dig deeper, both the firms who published Lodwick have changed hands several times and much of the network of booksellers that supported them has vanished, so that save for the Heinemann history, records and archives, or even 'the institutional folk memory' are nearly impossible to find.

Some of the early files of the once independent Victor Gollancz imprint, proud publishers of Francis Stuart amongst many others, were recently offered for sale piecemeal by a London dealer. It would be nice, but a stretch, to think that many of Lodwick's works matched the 18,225 copies sold (out of 23,118 printed) of his friend Orwell's illustrated essay *The English People*. Even that was placed only 61st among the 'Most Popular' books of 1947, but how those rankings were compiled we have no idea. In the top spot? James Fisher's *The Birds of Britain*, first published in 1942. *Sic transit*, Lodwick might murmur – copies of *The Birds* are now for sale on the internet for one dollar while what looks like a first, if well-worn, edition of *Bid the Soldiers Shoot* is on offer for a curiously precise £8.61 (plus postage).

What we do know is that Lodwick's books were well advertised, and that literary editors on important papers thought them worth assigning to serious reviewers. We promised to avoid pseudo-literary analysis of Lodwick's work. So how best to relay what those critics thought? We can't simply reprint each review; and anyway, by confining our search to the 'mainstream' British and US press there must be some reviews we have missed.

There is also the risk that by highlighting passages from an already rather random selection of them we might introduce some unconscious bias. Most authors – artists, actors and musicians too – cherish the secret hope that critics will try to follow the injunction in the song and 'Accentuate the positive', but in their hearts they know that reviewers' pens may often be dipped in acid, if only to make 'readable' copy. To be fair to most of those who gave serious attention to Lodwick's work, they did try to point out the good as well as what they felt were the bad and the ugly aspects, and Lodwick claimed that by and large he was unfazed. As he wrote to Mervyn Jones:

> Some of the critics really seem to hate me like poison; and this can't be personal because, not living in England, I've met hardly anyone in the literary world. Maybe in time I shall be considered as respectable as, say, C.P. Snow – but I hope not.

Reviewers were not the only people who might pronounce Lodwick less than respectable. We wrote earlier of his youthful dismissal of the power of the Irish Censors when he was a novice Dublin producer in the 1930s. He underestimated them, even though looking back today many of their judgements seem more laughable than prissy. Well into the 1950s the Censors must have felt they were doing the right thing to outlaw the bodice-ripper novels of Hank Janson or a magazine offering airbrushed glimpses of *Prairie Pranks*. And it is relatively easy to understand, in the climate of the times, why they might have quailed at J.P. Donleavy's view of Ireland and marriage, though it is a lot harder to see quite what they found objectionable in Richard Gordon's light-hearted *Doctor in the House*.

The meticulous records of C.J. O'Reilly, a member of Ireland's Censorship of Publications Board between 1951 and 1955, show how seriously it took its task as it waded earnestly through many hundreds of books and magazines.[2] No surprise really, since it included a priest, a district judge, a solicitor and the Professor of Education at a Roman Catholic training college. What were they sniffing for? The triggers included scenes of passion, vulgarity, nudity, adultery, 'fornication', infidelity and the perennial Irish 'third rail' issues of abortion, contraception and 'slighting the Church or its clergy'. Given such a broad sweep, it is again no surprise that books blacklisted ranged widely, with Irish writers such as Samuel Beckett a major target, though individual books by Graham Greene, Aldous Huxley, Nicholas Monsarrat, Anthony Powell, Nevil Shute, Sartre, Proust, Steinbeck and many others were also given the thumbs down.

Lodwick did not escape their beady eye; his Dartmouth story, *The Cradle of Neptune*, was thought to have a hint of what O'Reilly often referred to as 'homosexualism' and was banned, followed later by an unexplained thumbs-down for *Love Bade Me Welcome*, *Somewhere a Voice is Calling* and *The Butterfly Net*. An illustration of the system's fatuity may be seen in the fact that though the last of these was among many titles banned in October 1945 it had been reasonably well reviewed in the *Irish Times* just a few weeks earlier. Stretching a point in order to be fair it could perhaps be said that had the Censors looked at the covers and dust jackets of some of Lodwick's novels, especially the paperback editions, they might well have reacted badly; several are rather closer to the whip-wielding virago on the cover of Janson's *Frails Can be So Tough* than the literary mainstream. But times change, even in Ireland. All the banned books have long since been reprieved, and the Board was dissolved in 1964, having arguably done more to boost banned authors' overseas royalties than defend Irish decency.[3]

There are caveats to what follows.

First, others reading his books through twenty-first century eyes – and with twenty-first-century tastes may come to different conclusions. Second, as with those negative views so freely bandied about in the Baker Street corridors of SOE, Lodwick is not here to speak for himself, and would most likely have a rather different take on why he wrote what he did, what actually happened, who the characters really were, perhaps even expressing himself with that 'certain tendency towards belligerence' which he claimed was a hallmark of Lodwick family communications.

Though strictly speaking it is not a book review, as good a starting point as any is to look at what Anthony Burgess had to say. An even more awkward and elusive character than Lodwick and another well-known writer who also fell foul of the Irish Censors, albeit at one remove when they banned the film of his dystopian novel *A Clockwork Orange*, he made the point in 1967 that a new generation of Heinemann editors had never heard of Lodwick.

But Burgess had heard of him. His extensive 1971 survey *The Novel Now* included a chapter on 'Exports and Imports', discussing authors who wrote about foreign countries either as expatriates or because the country they were writing about was their homeland.[4] Of Lodwick – who even then, he noted, was at risk of becoming a neglected author – Burgess wrote that he lived in Spain

and set some of his best work there. *Somewhere a Voice is Calling* and *The Starless Night* could not have been written by the casual literary tourist… They are a special kind of fiction, giving a violent English hero – one who could hardly survive for a day in suburban Britain – the only kind of release for his passionate talents… It is the 'European' quality of Lodwick's writing that repels some readers. He is not afraid of rhetoric, grandiloquence; his knowledge of foreign literature is wide; his irony is subtle; his mastery of the English language matches that of Evelyn Waugh.

Starting with *Running to Paradise*, taken from a poem by Yeats, Lodwick's book titles display his or his publisher's fondness for the literary, with phrases from Shakespeare, Coleridge, Tennyson, George Herbert, and even conceivably (in *The Butterfly Net*) from the deeply unpleasant black magician, Aleister Crowley. A couple of others give peat-scented hints of the Emerald Isle. *Just a Song at Twilight* and *Somewhere a Voice is Calling* are ballads made hugely popular by the celebrated Irish tenor John McCormack (1884–1945). In those far-off days before electronics turned family life on its head, his 78 rpm records were a staple in almost every genteel Dublin drawing room, so Lodwick would certainly have known the melodies. He might even have seen the great man in person when McCormack made a 'Farewell Tour' across England and Ireland in October and November 1938.

For specific reviews, we can start with C.P. Snow, an acute if occasionally heavy-footed observer of English life and behaviour, and now, like Lodwick himself, rather out of fashion.[5] He first looked at Lodwick's work in the *Sunday Times* in June 1949. Taking aim at *Just a Song at Twilight*, he accentuated the positive by introducing him as 'a natural story teller of considerable gifts', and the book as 'consistently readable'. But Lodwick had

> one great disadvantage. The flavour of this book is most unpleasant – a flavour of decay, of petulant complaint against life. This may not hold him back in the short run. It may even be an attraction. But in the long run it will do him much harm.

Snow refilled his pen 18 months later when he was asked to review *First Steps Inside the Zoo*. He summed it up in one paragraph:

> John Lodwick… is his peculiar self. It is a kind of spy story set in the Riviera among a menagerie of characters of preposterous seediness. The flavour of the book, as is customary with Mr Lodwick, is nasty. But I have to admit it is mad-deningly readable.

Writing for the *Listener*,[6] David Paul began by criticising the title itself.

> The precise meaning of… *First Steps Inside the Zoo* escapes me. There is nothing preliminary in it in subject or treatment… The simplicity of the plot is eked out in the midst of a bewilderment of characters. The result is certainly readable and at times amusing enough, though the situations often promise more amusement than they provide. As satire it could have been more callous and more cruel if the author had used a little more discrimination.

Discussing *The Cradle of Neptune* in *The Times Literary Review*, Anthony Powell,[7] another heavyweight commentator, wrote that

> To deduce that… Lodwick found the discipline of The Royal Naval College, Dartmouth at times somewhat uncongenial would perhaps not be unreasonable, but there can be no doubt that he is in some need of discipline as a writer. This

is all the more apparent because of his notable gifts. He is readable, lively and up to a point has an excellent grasp of character. These are virtues which have to be set against a most painful facetiousness, little grasp of construction and a tendency to allow the convincing figures he creates to tail off into mere vehicles for expressing certain points of view.

Powell concluded: 'The death of a cadet by drowning is well done (Mr Lodwick should not be afraid of being serious)', adding, perhaps with tongue in cheek, 'the novel is one from which sailors should certainly profit'. The *New York Times* reviewer Burke Wilkinson saw it in a kindlier light: 'My own inclination is to call the whole thing a half-merry, half-mocking ride on a streetcar called nostalgia.'

Richard Usborne (1910–2006) was one of several reviewers to cast an eye over Lodwick's major wartime autobiography *Bid the Soldiers Shoot*. Whether his views should resonate more than others is hard to say, but he and Lodwick had much in common. He was yet another of the myriad Children of the Raj (born in Simla, where his father worked in the Indian Civil Service), found himself in World War II serving briefly in SOE and later the Political Warfare Executive, worked in advertising, and wrote a definitive biography of P.G. Wodehouse. Writing in the *Observer* in April 1958, Usborne found Lodwick 'gay, sardonic, irreverent, sometimes frightened, probably always brave, a soloist, a bit of a poet, a *débrouillard* [i.e. a smart cookie]… with a sense of history and humour as sharp as pins'.

A soldier's view of the book came from one of Lodwick's readers. C.P.J. Brighty, an officer captured at Dunkirk and force-marched to a prison camp in Poland, wrote to Lodwick to say how much he had enjoyed the book. In his reply Lodwick told him that

One of the reasons I live out of England is to escape the awful literary atmosphere of knives in the back and that sort of thing, but of course this does make one rather isolated and a bit of a lone wolf.

His isolation made letters of praise all the more welcome, and it was good to be 'complimented by a man who had a war such as yours'. We shall quote from Lodwick's reply again later, in a different context.

Lodwick borrowed and embroidered generously from *Somewhere a Voice is Calling*, and thus his own life, when he published *Stamp Me Mortal* (a quote from Samuel Taylor Coleridge) in 1950. An English expatriate hero whose alcoholic wife and their child have died tragically in a French seaside town; a French lover in the background. But he was an author to be reckoned with, and *The Times Literary Supplement* called on Anthony Powell again. He thought Lodwick had 'good points as a novelist… but is not altogether happy in his blend of romance and reality'.

'In general,' the patrician Powell wrote, 'the book contains stray good ideas rather than carefully worked out studies in the way that eccentric persons behave – for it is in the eccentric that Mr Lodwick seems most interested.'

Commenting on the same book in the *Observer*, the author, editor and journalist Francis Wyndham thought the love story 'very real and at times moving'. But he did not care for the way in which Lodwick punctuated the narrative with his own form of humour: 'At its best it is bitter and stimulating, at its worst it is vulgar and facetious.' In the end, though, he put his thumb on the positive side of the scales. 'Mr Lodwick's individual manner is at the same time aggressive and sensitive; his book has vitality and reflects an original mind.'

Reviewing *Contagion to this World* in 1956, John Metcalf told readers of the *Sunday Times* that Lodwick

continues to be one of the most exciting, quite the most exasperating of English writers. For years now I have come to his latest evening of fireworks with a thumping heart. Each has started with exhilarating brilliance; green, shrieking rockets of invective, subtly shifting fire-rivers of character, fizzing crackers of wit, Roman candles of metaphor soaring and swinging. And each time as the moon has risen, so the evening has died in a casual splutter of carelessness. The bad-tempered impresario has lost interest and left his guests for another party… Mr Lodwick is still a talented novelist. One day (and I'll still go to all his parties, hoping) he'll write a whole book and it will be a very good book indeed.

To borrow from a nineteenth-century 'Punch' cartoon, 'You pays your money and you takes your choice', as there was usually a contrary opinion, sometimes on the same day, often in the same week. Commenting in the *Observer* on *Brother Death*,

Maurice Richardson thought that 'the standard is very uneven and much of it reads as if it was written in a tearing hurry'. Angela Milne closed the same book sighing with exasperation that Lodwick was 'a clever writer who goes all out to be tough. It should gratify him that this reviewer thinks *Brother Death* is a perfectly horrid book, for he can hardly have meant anything else.' The *Illustrated London News* opined that 'attractive is the last word one could use about *Brother Death*, which is tough and hideous all through'. Unconsciously evoking *The Cenci*, which the young Lodwick had been keen to present on the stage to shock the burghers of Dublin, its anonymous reviewer thought the book's 'extreme wickedness, that bitter gusto in evil-doing' was rather like 'what one might find in a minor playwright of the Great Age'.

In contrast, when Marghanita Laski[8] pitched in with a review, she thought that, 'Although fashion-bound in manner and setting', it was

> rather a good book… with much feeling and invention… and as it ambles along with a spot of archaeology and a spot of murder, a foul villain and a good angel, one reads with appreciative interest and is pleasantly uncertain what will happen next. This is the most adult and intelligent of the week's books.

The Waugh comparison suggested by Anthony Burgess was also made by John Betjeman[9] in a comment in the long defunct *Daily Herald*, the date of which we cannot now trace; he also praised Lodwick's 'richness of invention [and] debunking wit'. Placing Lodwick's novels at the same level as Waugh's might be a stretch, but there are many flashes of his mordant wit, such as the sketch of Major Chipstead, or the characterisation of Mr Mendoza, that can really delight.

We have made – probably laboured – the point that since the reviewers did not know the personal background, we cannot expect them to have realised how much of himself Lodwick mixed into the cocktail of his narratives. One exception, with deep-etched World War II memories of Crete, the Special Boat Service and SOE, was Christopher 'Monty' Woodhouse, one of the trio of senior SOE officers parachuted into Greece whose reports we cited earlier. *The Times Literary Supplement* sent him *Bid the Soldiers Shoot* to review in tandem with the autobiography of the author Geoffrey Household, who, until he found fame and fortune with *Rogue Male*, had been a banker in Romania, a banana salesman in Spain, a hack writer in New York and Los Angeles, an SOE saboteur manqué in Romania and a field security officer in World War II Cairo. Woodhouse had a sharp pen:

> Mr Household and Mr Lodwick are both characters whom many novelists would have been proud to invent… Indeed, if Mr Household had invented Mr Lodwick and Mr Lodwick had invented Mr Household, each of them might have written a masterpiece. As it is, they have each written a highly entertaining if not very profound account of picaresque experiences.

Woodhouse's conclusion: Lodwick's book 'is written in a style of tough, disarming flippancy, which makes good, if exhausting, reading. But it is not to be compared for serious self-portraiture, with Mr Household's more mature and sophisticated work.'

We can't trace how often Lodwick fired back, but one example in his papers is a copy of his undated riposte to the high-end quarterly journal *Courier*, which had commissioned a review of one of his novels. From the copy letter we have it is not clear which one, nor whether in writing to 'Mr Kark' Lodwick was addressing Norman Kark, listed on the masthead as the magazine's proprietor, or the latter's son Austen, who joined the business after a spell at Dartmouth and service at sea as a midshipman in 1944. The review, which might be dated to the late 1940s, had described Lodwick's book as 'improbably sordid' and took issue with his 'eternal hunt for the unusual'.

'Well,' Lodwick snaps back,

> the book you are writing about is substantially true, more than substantially true, and the plot of the one before that was so far removed from fiction that a number of British and American expatriates on the Côte d'Azur would have liked to take libel actions against me had they dared to face the subsequent ridicule. I take my stories as I find them, from life… But never mind! Thank you very much for the review, and for the sight of your excellent magazine.

Here the Roundabout stops again, leaves Grub Street and takes us back from Lodwick the author to Lodwick the man, beginning with a part of his life he must have felt he had left safely behind.

22

Death in the Morning

How odd it must have been after so many years, his roots firmly – at least as firmly as his ever could be – in Spain, a new wife and two young children, for Lodwick to find on his desk a letter from his first wife, Dorothy Collins. Her father had died on 3 October 1954 and she must have written to Lodwick soon after the funeral, for which 'half Ireland' turned out, since his reply is dated 6 November.[1] We don't have her letter. Our copy of his reply, passed on by a family member, is signed 'John' and though it was typed, and letters of condolence tend to be rather stereotyped, one gets the sense of a welling up of sympathy and even a tug of nostalgia when he writes that 'I am terribly sorry to hear your news. Your handwriting is quite changed with the upset of it. I do feel for you very deeply.'

'I admired and liked your father very much and wish that I had seen more of him in recent years, though of course this would have been difficult, I suppose,' Lodwick wrote.

He remembered John Collins for being 'almost the first person I met who taught me about good literature, and it was fascinating to listen to him'. He also recalled the de Quincey edition her father had given him.

It would be surprising if the exchange didn't also revive a memory not just of Sheila, but of her world of the surreal, and an essay first published by the movement's creator André Breton back in 1939 and later reprinted in the short-lived Surrealist journal *le Ciel*. Breton, dressed all in green, had opened the London exhibition at which Sheila had a starring role. Whether he believed de Quincey himself was an ur-Surrealist, Breton certainly agreed with him that murder should be treated 'aesthetically and appreciated in terms of its qualities as one would appreciate a work of art or a medical case study';[2] words which surely resonated with Lodwick as a writer. We will never know what Lodwick

told Sheila about the Dublin marriage but, in giving him the *Essays*, John Collins'
intuition about the dark side of Lodwick's mind may have been keener than we
might have expected.

There is another more distant Breton link with Lodwick's and Sheila's past; so
distant that we are 'running on empty' as far as evidence goes, except that given
Sheila's passion for Surrealism it would be surprising if she had not read Breton's
1928 novel *Nadja*, one of the movement's key books. The storyline is too gruesome
and convoluted to recast here, and the book rates a mention only because Nadja is
an alternative spelling of Nadia, the girl whom Sheila knew before World War II
and who helped Lodwick when he was on the run in Paris and found herself in a
concentration camp. Some of Breton's turn of phrase – for instance children 'with
their mania for taking out their dolls' eyes to see <u>what's there</u> behind them' (the
underlining is Breton's), or Nadja's cry that 'I am the soul in limbo' – are rather in
the Lodwick style.

Going back now to a comment of Dorothy's about her father, Lodwick writes
to her:

> I am not surprised that he kept my letters, but why did you burn all except three?
> I don't suppose there was anything very controversial in them.
>
> How sad the world is I think perhaps people only realise when they reach
> your age or mine, for it is then that we see people we have known all our lives,
> and considered as permanent, suddenly lopped off and gone forever.

That she burned 'all except three' of his letters to her father suggests on the one hand
a rather regular correspondence over the years and on the other that the letters she
destroyed may have touched on the long-ago marriage and its consequences; always,
one imagines, a painful and powerful drag on the memory of everyone involved,
however guiltless they may have convinced themselves they were.

Lodwick was 43. Even at his blackest, which could be black indeed, he cannot
have contemplated that he would soon be 'lopped off' himself, and that – to borrow
a phrase first used as an epigraph by the ubiquitous Maugham in retelling an Iraqi
folk fable, then borrowed by the American writer John O'Hara for his successful
first novel – his own *Appointment in Samarra* lay not far away. But he would keep
it closer to home.

The headline of the report in the *La Vanguardia Española* newspaper of 12 March 1959 translates as 'Tragic road accident on the outskirts of Villafranca del Panadés'. Nowadays, mandatory Catalan has imperceptibly rejigged it as 'Vilafranca del Penedès'. It makes no difference to the grim photograph of the wreckage of the Alfa Romeo saloon, number M-193674, which looks as though it has been rolled over by an avalanche.

Lodwick was one of five men in the car, looking forward to something they all enjoyed: one of the many Catalan folk festivals. This one was in Valls, some 60 miles from Barcelona, a *calsotada* (*calçotada* in Catalan), a cheerful blend of eating *calsots* (large shallots roasted over a charcoal grill), drinking the local *cava* sparkling wine or the potent red known locally as *vi negre*, the noisy election of a festival 'queen' and processions in medieval costumes that Maugham's favourite Spanish painter Zurbarán would have recognised. The climax is a centuries-old tournament in which, as a drum beats out a traditional rhythm, teams compete to build the highest human tower or *castell*, scrambling skyward on a base which looks like several rugby scrums combined, until a lightweight youngster known as the *anxeta* wobbles nervously but triumphantly at the top; the record is said to be a *castell* nine grunting, sweaty layers high.

The irony, sadness – call it what you will – of this is less that Lodwick never got to see the spectacle but that if he had, he might have travelled back in time to memories of his Grandpapa. Before the trip, which he had been invited to join at the last minute, he had been up all night writing, presumably crafting those early pages of his unfinished autobiography, which opens with his Grandpapa and the handyman digging up the lawn to create an asparagus trench. Had he seen the *calsots* sizzling on the charcoal, someone would have told him proudly that in the 1800s a local farmer had worked out how to grow them with a firm and appetising white stem. The secret was to plant them in trenches 'similar to the method of growing white asparagus', a bewildering backflip from Catalonia to Cheltenham.

Now the publisher Janés was dead, along with his son Angel – who had called at Lodwick's flat that morning to urge him to come along – his nephew Carlos Puig and Miguel Zafra, his printer – a man of importance to publishers in those pre-computer days, and who the press reported had been behind the wheel. They had been just a couple of miles from Valls, chatting unsuspectingly about nothing in particular, when the car skidded on a bend to avoid a cart and smashed into a clump of pine trees. The others died on the spot but Lodwick survived the crash and was rushed to the Comarcal Hospital in Vilafranca, where the doctors found he had multiple major fractures and concussion (a distant echo of the diagnosis invented by the friendly Mixed Medical Commission to allow him to leave France).

Understandably, the Barcelona press gave most prominence to the death of Janés, the news of which, as a friend wrote, had hit Barcelona like a thunderclap. Only a few days before Janés had told the same friend: 'Things are going fine. I am back on an even keel. I may start work on a new book of poems, maybe a memoir too. I am full of ideas.'

Early press reports on Lodwick claimed that blood transfusions had significantly improved his condition. They hadn't. Despite the desperate work of two surgeons from Barcelona and their local nursing team, he died three days later. His two children, who had heard the news report of the accident as they listened, all unknowing, to the kitchen radio, were thought too young to visit him, even though they were adolescents. To this day his eldest son wonders with puzzled nostalgia whether his father had some premonition of what lay ahead. He had told the boy he could not come with him, the car was already crowded, and added that while he was away he must remember 'that you are the man of the house'. Lodwick had actually sent him a postcard in 1957 addressed to 'El Jefe de Casa' ('The Head of the Household').

Not for the first or last time we may wonder about the genes of superstition in Lodwick's bloodstream. When one day the same lad saw his father trimming his nails, he noticed that Lodwick carefully scooped up the clippings and dropped them into a small box. He muttered something about luck. Might he have been reflecting the folk adage in Ireland and elsewhere, even some old Essex peasant memory from centuries past, that it was unlucky to cut your nails on a Friday or Sunday, and that the clippings had to be burned or buried? If not, the old wives warned, misfortune lay ahead.

We remember, as mentioned earlier, that in one of his novels a Spanish secret policeman asks the Lodwickian central figure, 'Are you a Catholic?'

'I was born a Catholic.'

'Then you will die a Catholic.'

Lodwick did. After a Mass in the chapel of the Comarcal Hospital, and as the noonday bell pealed, the interment rites were performed by the Reverend Don

José Colomé. Like the terrible phrase 'he had a good war', we can say that Lodwick had 'a good turnout'. The British Consulate, the British Institute, 'El British', publishers, civic figures, family, a contingent from the hospital who had tried so hard to save him, friends from the British community and many locals who wanted to pay their last respects.

The reference to 'family' was initially a puzzle, since it listed the chief mourner as a 'Mr Simón Lodwick, brother of the deceased.' One can excuse the Spanish reporter hovering on the fringe of such a personal and distressing event for not grasping the nuances of English names and relationships. In fact it was Simon Ruck, John's half-brother by his mother's remarriage, a globetrotting teacher who happened to be in Spain when the scythe swung. Only God knows – literally – what Lodwick thought of the last farewell, the religious Passing Out Parade. Lodwick himself thought Spain and Franco far too heavily overborne by the Church. And in his sad paragraphs about 'Gloria'/Sheila the agonised 'Thornton' rounds on the local priest who is doing his best to give him comfort. 'You poor bloody black crow, you *capelan*' he yells, using the Catalan word for a chaplain which from the context must have had a distinctly pejorative meaning. 'You want to persuade me in my hour of weakness that God comes – even to the sinner in his last moments. Talk to me when you have some personal experience in the matter. Will you?' In the same passage he puts into Thornton's head what must have been his own thoughts about the final moments. 'And since there is no return from the last breath, so like a lover's sigh, then the hypotheses which men advance in explanation of what follows death must surely in themselves be dubious and most suspect.'

Though family members have been generous with their time and recollections of the man, readers were reminded when we started out that this narrative has deliberately not dug further into Lodwick's two marriages after Sheila's passing. (In one of his more bitter novels Kingsley Amis, who had marital upsets of his own, wrote: 'Stopping being married to someone is an incredibly violent thing to happen to you, not easy to take in, ever.'[3]

The first did not work. She is the Frenchwoman who is sketched into the canvas of *Somewhere a Voice is Calling*. She left him, in a swirl of white dresses and costumes, to work briefly as a fashion model in Barcelona before going back to France, closing and bolting the door on her memories. That and taking his two children by Sheila to see their first bullfight is at least how one of the children remembers it.

It is a selective snapshot memory of a long-gone childhood, breathed into life by a ticket stub from the Plaza de Toros de Cadiz, dated 9 June 1955; the seats were in the 'sun' section of the ring rather than the more expensive 'shade' or 'sun and shade'. The door remains bolted even today.

We have already mentioned Lodwick's subsequent marriage, to an unquenchable lady from Extremadura, which lasted until his death. She first came into his life as a housekeeper/governess/housemother, a Hispanic Mary Poppins, in answer to a newspaper advertisement. He chose her for the job from a throng of applicants because, he told her, she shared the birthplace of so many of the conquistadores who had built the Spanish Empire. He also dedicated *Equator* to the region itself, as 'The Land in which Truth Took Refuge'. Though it may have been the Spanish sense of propriety that led them to marriage, surviving correspondence suggests a real, tender and loving relationship. Without her support, and the care and worry of Lodwick's mother Kitty, the family would surely have fallen apart.

Kitty 'was a saint to me', her eldest grandson sighed; a slew of letters show how she looked after her grandchildren in the UK after Lodwick's death, first trying to get them to learn English, coping with bad behaviour and later fretting about their prospects. Her husband Charles had retired but went back to his dental practice to help support the family, and although remembered by one grandchild as 'tall and slightly distant' never showed any hint of resentment at putting his shoulder back to the wheel for step-grandchildren, even playing beach cricket with the boys.

We won't probe further into all this, or try to chart the lives of his children, because it would have meant invading living space and memories to which only those involved have a right. This is compounded by a personal reason for reticence, though arguably a biographer should not be swayed by these sensitivities. But the fatal accident which slams closed the covers of the Lodwick storybook is a scar-ripping personal reminder of what happens to a family when an unknown car crunches up the drive and, rat-tat-tat on the door, bluntly delivered news of a fatal accident guts its centre of gravity. Disbelief, denial, rage at the person responsible, the world spinning out of control, the home sold, the well-meant but potentially conflicting advice and initiatives of friends and relatives, for whom young children are inevitably less real people than problems for which a speedy solution must be found: in Lodwick's case infant children who had been brought up as Spanish speakers and who if they were to be schooled in England would need first to learn the language. Children who, if this author's memory is any guide, will have slipped in those first bewildering few days into a troubled semi-sleep, convinced that when they wake up the grim news will turn out to have been a nasty dream. There is the legal stuff, in his case a World War II will, the inquest and the money.

But within our self-imposed limitations about not stretching this story into family life, what can we say about Lodwick as a father? What does being 'a good father' mean anyway to his wives or his children, either as school-kids or burdened by the pangs and distractions of adolescence? We know he was strict about intrusions on his work, with guests and friends he could be irritable in the extreme, and we know that like many other parents he was fond of red wine. He was also fond of music of the 1930s, 40s and 50s, jazz as played by King Oliver and Louis Armstrong, and greatly enjoyed *Singin' in the Rain*. The marriage to Dorothy is a puzzle. But if we look back to Sheila, the *mésalliance* with his French wife and his move to Barcelona, we can see a man who could have, but did not, run away from the burdens of single parenthood and sorrow, the never-to-be resolved Dublin episode apart. Sheila gave him two children, and more would follow. He fretted about schools, how they were doing, whether they should be sent to England to learn what was literally their 'mother tongue'; remembering his eldest son's football game, taking the kids to basketball and sending postcards when he was travelling. From the fragments we have seen he could be a jovial dad. Ahead of a trip to Madrid, he wrote to Mervyn Jones:

> We are just off with monkey, baby and cats. There will be panic in the hotel in which we have to spend the day in Madrid tomorrow. I intend to smuggle the monkey into the Prado too and to let it run on its chain among the largest crowd of officially conducted American tourists.

There are echoes here of the ur-Surrealist Edward James. When he passed through Mexico City with additions to the menagerie he was building in the hinterland, he often stretched the tolerance of the hotel's owner by bringing in cages of exotic pets, including a small monkey and, on one memorable visit, a pair of boa constrictors.

In another whimsical postcard Lodwick wrote home from the Canary Islands, where he was researching *The Forbidden Coast*, he thanks God and his parachute training that he was able to roll out of the way of a bus which almost ran him down, escaping with minor cuts and a rather dusty suit. One of the nicer echoes of those days is a story he wrote for the London *Evening Standard*, based on a real-life attempt by his first son to run away. It is charming in style, and shows a considerable if slightly exasperated fondness for the boy. In contrast to the negative comments we and others have made about the authoritarian Spanish state, it shows that at a local level at least the '*policias*' still upheld the Spanish traditions of care for a wandering stranger. They took the lad in, listened patiently to his tale that his father was Governor of Gibraltar and looked after him in the Chief of Police's house, where the ladies smothered him with matronly love, breakfast, lunch and comics until Lodwick turned up.

But, as in his books, he could also be grim: when a cat needed to be neutered, he asked the same son to take it to the vet and to hand over a sealed note which told him that his son had to watch the actual procedure. Though like many fathers he might at times have been seen by his children as inaccessible, distracted, even cruel, he had much to be distracted about, and, all said and done, he loved his children. He was also kind to Sheila's son by her first and unfortunate marriage.

These comments allow a brief backtrack to Dorothy. As we know she had a son, whom some of Lodwick's children met in later years and who helped in finding a job for Lodwick and Sheila's boy. Lodwick never mentions him, even in those of his letters to Dorothy we have seen, and according to one direct statement never sought him out, an indication perhaps that he did not see him as 'part of the family'. But no more than an indication since the memory may just have been too uncomfortable to revive, let alone convert into another relationship, another responsibility.

We quoted earlier from Lodwick's reply to a reader's letter praising *Bid the Soldiers Shoot*. He expresses two wishes which would escape anyone unaware of the background. First, Lodwick hopes that if the writer, C.P.J. Brighty, ever finds himself in Spain, 'you will come to see me – and that goes for your son too, to whom by the way, I wish every success'. Since the son later became a senior diplomat and, at the apex of his career, Britain's ambassador in Madrid, by coincidence at least one of the wishes came true.

In the same letter, Lodwick wrote about his plans to send his own restless first son to a Swiss hotel school when he turned 15.

That is not so awful as it sounds. They start in the kitchen and then work through the whole building from the wine cellars to the Managerial offices. In the process they pick up four or five languages, a very extensive knowledge of life in general and people in particular, and a thorough contempt for class distinctions of any kind whatever. And if later they want to pull out of it, they are at least equipped to do a number of other things!

Had Lodwick lived to see this happen, he might have relished John le Carré's 1993 novel *The Night Manager*. But he did not. The skidding car on a Spanish hillside turned hopes and dreams to mangled metal, white-gowned surgeons and a hovering priest.

23

After the Ball

Lodwick's good friend (Harold) Denis Lisney of Cadaqués organised a 'Memorial Fund' appeal to friends and family, which generated actual or promised contributions from, among others, Lodwick's worried and supportive mother, Gregory Ratoff and George St George, Somerset Maugham and, intriguingly, Francis Stuart. It would be too complex to convert the French francs and sterling in which the contributions were made back into 1959 pesetas and then guess at the modern equivalent, but at a rough guess Kitty and the two Hollywood mini-moguls barons sent cheques for what in today's values would be $5,000 each. But though the responses were generous, the money was not enough to keep the family afloat without a breadwinner in the long or even medium term. Lodwick would have been deeply grateful to Lisney, who took the eldest son to his Leicestershire estate until Grandmother Kitty could find a school place for him. Equally deserving of his gratitude were Kitty herself and his Spanish wife, who had to get the children sorted out, find a foothold in remarriage and begin a new life in a foreign country.

For the reasons given earlier I have not named her, nor laid out on the page all the many difficulties she and the children had to overcome and which were bravely shared by Lodwick's mother, who also had to care for an ageing husband. They were considerable.

Janés would be delighted to know that his firm continues as an important Spanish-language imprint, coincidentally within the same major international publishing group to which what remains of Heinemann now belongs.

What Lodwick would have made of his obituary in *The Times* on 19 March 1959, we cannot guess. Most likely he would have just shrugged. As his eldest son ruminated, if his father had known someone was going to write his biography, 'he would have wondered what all the fuss was about'.

Capturing Lodwick and his life in 242 words, the anonymous author, who we can perhaps surmise was one of the reviewers we have quoted along the way, had this to say about his output:

> At the time of his death he had published some dozen books, many reflecting his uninhibited romantic personality, marked with a distinctive swagger and ingenuity. Some were good – like *Somewhere a Voice is Calling* and *The Starless Night* – but he never perhaps fulfilled the promise that some saw in his earlier writing. A prodigal, undisciplined writer, he had undoubtedly a feel for language and a deep concern for human suffering.

Writing in the left-wing journal *Tribune* a short while later, Lodwick's friend Mervyn Jones snapped about these comments that 'I am still angry at the fatuous obituary which an editor with pretentions to literary taste[1] allowed his paper to give Lodwick,' although read through an objective lens, unclouded by loyalty, the obituary may be short but is not 'fatuous'.

Casting a jaundiced eye over *The Moon Through a Dusty Window* for readers of *The Times Literary Supplement* a year or so after Lodwick's death, the writer and drama critic Irving Wardle conceded that his earlier books had been 'praised for their ruthless wit, their zest and inventiveness'. There was, however, a major 'but'. Wardle thought – quite rightly, as it happens – that Lodwick

> sounds the sort of man not to be overawed by the opinions of literary journalists; all the same they seem to have left their mark on his last novel. Self-conscious almost to the point of unreadability, [*The Moon*] carries the laboured air of a man striving to live up to his own reputation… a diffused and monotonously unvaried tone of arrogant cosmopolitan one-upmanship.

An anonymous review of the same book in *The Times* thought Lodwick

> had an enormous zest for living – a quality he sometimes communicated in his novels; 'sometimes' because he was the most uneven of writers, at his best brilliant and capable of living through experiences which rival anything he described in his fiction.

'But' is a qualification of which Lodwick's reviewers were quite fond. In this case the writer goes on to comment that 'the restless element in Lodwick's nature which prevented him from ever writing an entirely satisfactory book is once again at work here'.

An observer with India in his blood, though in his case through World War II military service and amoebic dysentery rather than imperial history, was Paul Scott,[2] who, after many early struggles as a writer, published *The Raj Quartet*, later much praised as the television series *The Jewel in the Crown*. Scott's life has been well chronicled. He shared with Lodwick and countless others a fondness for drink and a tendency to be disagreeable in his cups. His Indian depictions are sensitive, fascinating, complicated and dwell heavily on class and racial distinctions. This is vividly expressed through the contempt of the sadistic, racist, grammar-school-educated policeman Ronald Merrick for the British officials and officers with whom he had to deal, many of whom shared what to him was the unappealing caste mark of schooling at 'Chillingborough'. It is not unrealistic to translate that into Cheltenham.

He and Lodwick may well have met when Scott was working as a literary agent. Though what he wrote as a quasi-obituary for *The Times Literary Supplement* was framed as a review of *The Asparagus Trench*, he has some personal post-mortem notes which help our understanding; the phrase 'restless energy' is a curious echo of the 'restless element' highlighted by the anonymous reviewer we have just quoted.

> Straightforward accident though it was, it struck most of those who knew him as a typical Lodwickian gesture. He had a restless energy which dominated his life; it certainly dominated his letters. Well before the end of a novel there were to be seen, not infrequently, signs that he was already scorched by the heat of the one he would write next. He drove himself fast from book to book; but his courage was high and he deserved the stroke of luck that would have taken on to the straight, foolproof road and across the finishing line of lasting achievement.

Scott takes the view that Lodwick's creative talent was always overshadowed by memories of his Grandpapa: 'an obsessional, larger-than-life figure which relentlessly pursued him until it was brought to an abrupt and permanent halt on a Spanish roadside.'

He may be right, but in his wartime autobiography Lodwick self-deprecatingly casts the net a little wider and further back.

> We all have our private wars. While I waited for mine I was fortunate in one respect; I never believed for a moment I would be as brave as my father or his own Grandpapa, an East India Company General, but I trusted I would be adequately brave; and in the first year this hope was realised, but later rather less than realised and at the last not realised at all. I began my war as a young fire-eater of conventional rather than Homeric proportions. I finished it, six years later… as a coward sustained only by straggles of pride.

Read against the background of what we know from the record, he is being unfair to himself, though there is perhaps a hint of those gnawing internal demons glimpsed by Merwin and fictionalised by Pelorson, for all the faults and mischaracterisations in the latter's novel.

Who are we to judge? As to the writer, it is clear that had Lodwick lived we would have known his full life story, at least as he wished it to be told, and that, based on the charm of *The Asparagus Trench*, he might well have mellowed his style, burned off the anger as the years ticked by, and told us a great deal more. But, like Gaudí's *Sagrada Familia* in Barcelona, his work remains unfinished.

Lodwick would still find Spain a complicated territory, or group of sometimes fractious territories. Forty years on, Franco and his regime are still not welcome topics of public debate or dinner table chitchat. A survey recently quoted in the *Financial Times* found that six out of ten Spaniards believed Francoism had 'both good sides and bad sides', an equivocal answer which could just as readily be given by Russian old-age pensioners harking back to the Stalin era or some scarred, guilt-ridden veteran of the Waffen SS. And like Russia, Spanish feelings buried so deeply in so many opposing hearts can only be addressed delicately, and at what seems, to outsiders, glacial speed. Even in 2016 suggestions of replacing the names of Franco-era soldiers and officials carried by some of Madrid's key streets have sparked vehement debate. Meanwhile, the government continues to foot the bill for the massive basilica complex in the Guadarrama Mountains, resting place for

33,000 victims of the Civil War and for Franco himself, the man who began and outlasted it, confounding the dictum of Jacques Mallet du Pan that 'the revolution devours its own children'.

Had he 'made his century', unlike Grandpapa, Lodwick would have seen Ireland shaking itself loose, or looser, from the power of the Catholic Church, Dublin despoiled, Ireland the Celtic Tiger, gralloched but now miraculously stitching its insides back together. Barcelona has been heavily rebuilt. Earls Court would be an unfamiliar and still unappealing maze; perhaps only in Cheltenham might he still be able to navigate by memory with any success, dodging between tourists and the off-duty cryptographers of GCHQ, eyes down and intense.

Stretching to accentuate the positive, we might say about John Lodwick that he was at least spared the creeping agues and anxieties of ageing. But all that is cold comfort. There would have been good parts. Grandchildren, sports days, school prizes and first loves, new books, professional recognition, a nudging up towards the Pantheon, reprints, even awards. Who knows? Not all writers' trajectories go ever upwards. Far from it. We last spotted Angus Wilson taking a jaundiced view of Lodwick's *The Butterfly Net*. Had Lodwick lived he would have found it ironic, or more likely sad, since at heart he was sympathetic, to read D.J. Taylor's obituary of Wilson in 2013, which pointed out that his later years were spent 'in a dementia-cushioned twilight, with his books tumbling out of print and his finances in ruin'.

But the bottom line, to descend to banker-speak, is that by any test Lodwick went too soon, in the words of one of his family 'sadly missed by many and beautifully remembered by others'. Years earlier, Lodwick, as a thinly disguised Dormant, had asked the fictional ghost of the long-dead Lord Drawbridge, 'What is death like?' The apparition told him: 'It depends on the case… it is the death of a man whose life has been cut short which is the most painful.'

On that note, as in *La Ronde* the narrator swaps his cloak and top hat for a mundane greatcoat and vanishes into the night in a puff of cigarette smoke, while the handsome, hung-over but still impeccably uniformed Count strolls into the unknown with his elegant greyhound, Haras. Time to go.

It was tempting to give the last words to the fictional Gloria, words undoubtedly uttered by the real Sheila. 'Darling…' she said, 'I do wish for your sake that the war had never finished.'

We could also crowd the final pages with nuggets of poetry on life and early death. Given the Irish tinge to our tale, we can take as one example W.B. Yeats' sombre view that:

> Never to have lived is best, ancient writers say;
> Never to have drawn the breath of life, never to have looked into the eye of day;
> The second best's a gay goodnight and quickly turn away.

But perhaps the best summing up is a line borrowed from the Quaker poet John Greenleaf Whittier:

> For of all sad words of tongue or pen,
> The saddest are these: 'It might have been!'[3]

NOTES

INTRODUCTION

1   Principal pen-name of John Burgess Wilson, 1917–93, teacher, writer, composer, critic; see A. Burgess, *The Novel Now*, London, Faber & Faber, 1967.

2   J. St. John, *William Heinemann: A Century of Publishing, 1890–1990*, London, Heinemann, 1998.

3   D.J. Taylor, *After the War*, London, Chatto & Windus, 1993; idem, *The Prose Factory: Literary Life in England Since 1918*, London, Chatto & Windus, 2016.

4   Arthur James Balfour, 1st Earl of Balfour KG, OM, PC, DL, 1848–1930.

5   *Oxford English Dictionary.*

6   See e.g. A.J. Cruz, *Approaches to Teaching Lazarillo de Tormes and the Picaresque Tradition*, New York, Modern Language Association of America, 2008.

1. THE BLOOD OF INDIA

1   R. Kipling, 'The Exiles' Line', available at http://www.kiplingsociety.co.uk/poems_exiles_line. htm (accessed 9 December 2012).

2   E. Buettner, *Empire Families: Britons and Late Imperial India*, Oxford, Oxford University Press, 2004.

3   Jeremy Brooks, 1926–94, novelist, dramatist; adapted several classic plays for the Royal Shakespeare Company.

4   S. Bradley, *The Railways*, London, Profile Books, 2016.

5   W.H. Thornton., *Reminiscences and Reflections of an Old Country Clergyman*, London 1897 and 1899, reprint edited by D. Hart-Davies, Ludlow, Excellent Press, 2011. See also *Devon and Cornwall Notes*, Vol. IX, n.p., 1917; and C. Moore, 'A Reverend Rough and Ready for Anything', *Daily Telegraph*, 7 March 2011.

6   R.W. Lodwick, *John Bolt, Indian Civil Servant: A Tale of Old Haileybury and India*, London, British Library Historical Print Editions, n.d. [Digby & Long, 1891].

2. CAPTAIN COURAGEOUS

1   Sir Henry Ashbrooke Crump, KCIE, CSI, 1863–1941.

2   R. Kipling, 'The Exiles' Line', available at http://www.kiplingsociety.co.uk/rg_exiles1.htm (accessed 21 December 2012).

3   Buettner, *Empire Families.*

4   Valentiner published his memoirs in 1934, re-emerged in World War II as one of the German Navy's U-boat advisors, and died in 1949.

5   The distinction between officers and men extended beyond birth and schooling to uniforms, not just as a matter of whether officers wore barathea and 'the men' serge, but including the actual cut. As Jane Tynan has found, instructions for military tailors in World War I conceded that 'The British Officer is not of such an erect or square shoulder build as members of the rank and file, the drill he puts in is less exacting, and the labour he has to perform is less heavy, so that he does not develop the muscles of his shoulders or produce so much prominence of chest as these who are under him.' J. Tynan, 'Military Dress and Men's Outdoor Leisurewear: Burberry's Trench Coat in First World War Britain', *Journal of Design History*, Vol. 24, No. 2, 2011. The differences even extended to footwear. Officers were issued with brown ankle boots in soft leather. The rank and file wore boots of a heavier, coarsely pebbled black leather, the soles loaded with metal studs.

3. SCHOOLDAYS WITH GRANDPAPA

1   'Leighway', 'Some Corner of a Foreign Field', *Journal of the Leigh Society*, Issue 13, p. 2, 2004, available at http://www.leighsociety.com/pdf/13%20Leighway%20Winter%202004.pdf (accessed 9 December 2016).

2   Among the many books on his shelves was an 1811 English translation of *Don Quixote*; a copy stamped 'R.W. Lodwick' on the inside cover passed through the auction rooms some years ago for $350 and prompted the Cervantes quotation with which this story opens.

3   Barbara Stoney, *Enid Blyton: The Biography*, Stroud, The History Press, 1974.

4   Film-maker and theatre director, 1923–94.

4. CARRY ON, SAILOR

1   Alan George Heywood Melly, jazz singer, author and critic, 1926–2007.

2   Until the early twentieth century English landed society's fixed but unwritten rules dictated that the eldest son inherited the estate, daughters were to be married off to wealthy men, clever sons joined the army or the navy, and 'the fool of the family' went into the Church. Quite where that might have left an army dentist is a nice puzzle.

3   [H.D. Ziman], *Instructions for British Servicemen in France*, London, the Foreign Office, 1944.

4   The present author still has a Bible presented to him at his preparatory school as 'The Divinity Prize'.

5   G. Orwell, 'Such, Such Were the Joys', *Partisan Review*, London, 1952.

5. DUBLIN'S FAIR CITY

1   J. Jordan, 'Ewart Milne: For His 80th Birthday', *Poetry Ireland Review*, No. 8, Dublin, 1983, available at www.poetryireland.ie/publications/poetry-ireland-review/online-archive/view/ewart-milne-for-his-80th-birthday (accessed 9 December 2016).

2   Sean O'Casey, 1890–1964; Sean O'Casey Papers, National Library of Ireland, List 75.

3   All three, references to whom will be found in the bibliography, appear as fuller characters at several key points in our narrative.

4   G. Elborn, *Francis Stuart: A Life*, Dublin, Raven Arts Press, 1990; J.H. Natterstad, *Francis Stuart*, New Jersey and London, Associated University Presses, 1974; K. Kiely, *Francis Stuart: Artist and Outcast*, Dublin, Liffey Press, 2007; and 'Francis Stuart', *Writing Ulster*, No. 4, 1996.

5   William Butler Yeats, 1865–1939, formidable poet and formidably unrepentant mystic.

6   J. Royer (trans. D. Sloate), *Interviews to Literature*, Montreal, Guernica, 1996, accessed via Google Books.

7   G.M. Trevelyan, *British History in the Nineteenth Century and After*, London, Longmans, Green & Co., 1944.

6. FACES IN THE RAIN

1   Enid Starkie, CBE, LittD, 1897–1970.

2   Comments made by one 'KRJ', 'for many years a colleague and a warm admirer' of Starkie in Spain, in a letter in response to his newspaper obituary.

3   Borrow is usually pigeonholed as 'the man who wrote about Gypsies', but he was also a skilled translator, sent to St Petersburg in 1833 by the British and Foreign Bible Society to oversee the printing of a Manchu version of the New Testament.

4   J. Hurtley, *Walter Starkie: An Odyssey*, Dublin, Four Courts Press, 2013.

5   P.J. Dempsey, 'Collins, J', *Dictionary of Irish Biography*, Cambridge, Cambridge University Press, accessed via the London Library, 2014.

6   George Orwell (Eric Arthur Blair), 1903–50, a writing genius, was also a 'child of India', born in Motihari, the son of yet another Englishman sent out to administer the Raj, in his case in the 'Opium Department' of the Civil Service.

7   M. Wildemeersch, *George Orwell's Commander in Spain: The Engima of Georges Kopp*, London, Thames River Press, 2013.

7. 'A MARRIAGE HAS BEEN ARRANGED'

1   Thomas Penson de Quincey, English essayist, 1785–1859.

2   J.P. Donleavy, *The Ginger Man*, Paris, The Traveller's Companion, 1955.

8. THE LEG AND THE LEGIONNAIRE

1   S. Levy, *Sheila Legge: Phantom of Surrealism*, Rhos on Sea, Dark Windows Press, 2014. (See also *Le Blog de Albert Callis*, April 2014, available at http://albert.callis.over-blog.com/article-2014-avril-123396586.html (in French, accessed 9 December 2016).)

2   We mentioned earlier the manual on the Hotchkiss machine gun. Its back cover has a brief blurb for *Military Sketching and Map Reading for Non Coms and Men*. Its author was Major R.F. Legge of the Leinster Regiment.

3   David Gascoyne, 1916–2001, British-born poet and authoritative commentator on Surrealism.

4   Man Ray, born Emmanuel Radnitzky, visual artist and photographer, 1890–1976.

5   A. Bennett, *Writing Home*, London, Faber & Faber, 1994.

6   Edward William Frank James, poet and patron of the arts, 1907–84.

7   R. Graves and A. Hodge, *The Long Weekend*, London, Macmillan, 1940.

8   G. Melly, *Rum, Bum and Concertina*, London, Weidenfeld & Nicolson, 1977.

9   G. Melly, *Don't Tell Sybil*, augmented edition, London, Atlas Press, 2013.

10   Roger Edmund Heude Roughton, 1916–41. R. Roughton (ed.), *Contemporary Poetry and Prose: May 1936–Autumn 1937*, London, Frank Cass, 1968.

11   D. Porch, *The French Foreign Legion*, New York, HarperCollins, 1991.

12   S. Spanier, A. Defazio and R.W. Trogdon (eds), *The Letters of Ernest Hemingway 1923–1925*, Vol. II, Cambridge, Cambridge University Press, 2013.

10. ORANGE BLOSSOMS

1   M.R.D. Foot, *SOE In France: An Account of the Work of the British Special Operations*, London, HMSO, 1966.

2   Major (later Lt Col.) Lewis Evelyn Gielgud, MBE, 1894–1953.

3   Nancy Grace Augusta Wake, AC, GM, 1912–2011.

4   A cherished SOE principle 'more honoured in the breach than the observance' by many of its people – Lodwick was fond of *Hamlet* quotations.

5   W. Mackenzie, *The Secret History of SOE: The Special Operations Executive 1940–45*, London, TimeWarner/St Ermin's Press, 2000.

6   Foot, *SOE in France*.

11. BEATING THE BOOKMAKER

1   D. Steury, 'The OSS and Project SAFEHAVEN: Tracking Nazi "Gold"', *Studies in Intelligence*, Washington DC, Center for the Study of Intelligence, 2007, available at https://www.cia.gov/library/center-for-the-study-of-intelligence/csi-publications/csi-studies/studies/summer00/art04.html (accessed 9 December 2016).

2   J. Whiston, 'Walter Starkie' in *Oxford Dictionary of National Biography*, Oxford, Oxford University Press, accessed September 2014.

3   (Harold) Julian Amery, Baron Amery of Lustleigh, 1919–96. J. Amery, *Approach March*, London, Hutchinson, 1973. His elder brother John Amery (1912–45) was a Fascist sympathiser who, along with Francis Stuart, wrote some of the early scripts for the propaganda broadcasts of William Joyce.

4   J. Burns, *Papa Spy: Love, Faith and Betrayal in Wartime Spain*, London, Bloomsbury, 2009.

5   E. Sparrow, *Secret Service: British Agents in France,1792–1815*, Woodbridge, Boydell Press, 1992.

6   E. Meyer, *The Factual List of Nazis Protected by Spain*, available at https://archive.org/details/

THEFACTUALLISTOFNAZISPROTECTEDBYSPAIN (accessed 9 December 2016); also Steury, 'The OSS and Project SAFEHAVEN'.

7   The officer who wrote that file note was Helenus 'Buster' Milmo (1908–88), the Irish-born barrister who singularly failed to make a dent in the armour-plated carapace of the KGB penetration agent Kim Philby when he interrogated him after Philby first came under suspicion as the 'Third Man'. Philby, whose first steps on a long and successful road of spying were as a *Times* correspondent in the Spanish Civil War was, incidentally, yet another Child of the Raj.

8   There is more in the same vein, but of more interest in the context of Lodwick as an author is the comment in the same memorandum that 'in the early part of the war he completed a novel which has been successfully sold… winning a large money prize. It has undoubtedly gone to his head and by virtue of its financial advantages increased his already natural sense of independence and given him a selfish motive for anything he does as being a possible "experience" about which he can write.' The book, *Running to Paradise*, already mentioned, was first published in New York in 1943, by Dodd Mead, who gave it their 'Best War Novel Prize' of $1,000. The firm has long since been swallowed up and what remains of its archive gives no clue as to how the book came their way, who judged the prize, and above all why it was awarded, since the US reviewers who took notice of it were disenchanted with the style, the editing and even the 'slovenly' proofreading. John Chamberlain, in the august *New York Times*, gave it the kudos of several analytical column inches of space but concluded that it left him 'bored'. The *New Yorker* too griped about major and minor flaws. Neither gave him credit for a first novel by a young man written under pressure of events, and of timing; when it was written, where and how, all remain puzzles. A parallel edition in London by Methuen seems to have sunk without trace, though their advertisement cited praise from the *Manchester Guardian*.

9   Sir Robert Edward Laycock, 1907–68, KCMG CB DSO; served with the Commandos, initially as commander of 'Layforce' in North Africa, Crete, Sicily and Italy, promoted to Chief of Combined Operations 1943, later Governor of Malta.

10   First published in 1934.

11   G. Elborn, *Francis Stuart: A Life*, Dublin, Raven Arts Press, 1990.

12. HIGHLANDS AND ISLANDS

1   B. Richards, *Secret Flotillas*, Vol. 2, London and Barnsley, Whitehall History Publishing/ Frank Cass/Pen and Sword, 2013.

2   S.H. Allen, *Classical Spies: American Archaeologists with the OSS in World War 2 Greece*, Ann Arbor, University of Michigan Press, 2013.

3   L. Almonds-Windmill, *A British Achilles*, Barnsley, Pen and Sword, 2005.

4   E. Sparrow, *Secret Service: British Agents in France,1792–1815*, Woodbridge, Boydell Press, 1992.

5   Sir (Archibald) David Stirling, 1915–90. The Germans eventually captured him in the Tunisian desert and locked him away in Colditz Castle with other 'prominent' POWs. Some of his postwar roles in support of causes that were seen as right-wing and 'union-bashing'

might suggest a certain lack of political sensitivity but his World War II achievements could never be gainsaid.

6   Anders Frederik Emil Victor Schau Lassen, VC, MC and Two Bars, 1920–45.

7   Colonel David Sutherland, CBE, MC (bar) 1920–2006. Hero.

8   In 1945 his countrymen, who had once cheered him to the echo, shot him and his mistress and hung their bodies by the heels from the canopy of an Esso filling station.

13. KILLING THEM LOUDLY

1   (Sir) J.M. Stevens, KCMG, DSO, OBE 1913–87, postwar central and international banker of distinction; D.J. Wallace, 1914–44 (in action in Greece), Eton, first in Greats at Oxford, scholar of ancient Greek castles and fluent in modern Greek; Christopher Montague Woodhouse (5th Baron Terrington), 1917–2001, DSO, OBE, Winchester and double first in Greats at Oxford.

2   L. Baerentzen (ed.), *British Reports on Greece, 1943–44*, Copenhagen, Museum Tusculanum Press, 1982.

3   Kurt Arthur Benno Student, who became the youngest Colonel General in the Luftwaffe, 1890–1978.

4   D. Brewer, *Greece: The Decade of War*, London, I.B.Tauris, 2016.

5   A. Beevor, *Crete: The Battle and the Resistance*, London, John Murray, 1991.

14. JAILHOUSE BLUES

1   The Commando Order issued by Hitler is said to have been his foam-flecked response to an SBS raid on the Channel Island of Sark led by the ruthless Anders Lassen in which, in the German version, Wehrmacht prisoners were shot after their hands were bound and their mouths were stuffed with grass.

15. GUERRILLA WAR

1   P.N. Hehn, *The German Struggle Against Yugoslav Guerillas in World War II*, Boulder, CO, East European Quarterly, distributed by Columbia University Press, 1979; M. Mazower, *Hitler's Empire*, London, Allen Lane, 2008.

2   The applause of the first-night audience brought Shaw onto the stage. But one man booed, prompting Shaw to remark, 'My dear fellow, I quite agree with you. But what are we two against so many?'

3   A. Allport, *Demobbed: Coming Home after the Second World War*, New Haven, Yale University Press, 2009.

4   M. Wildemeersch, *George Orwell's Commander in Spain*.

5   Eileen Maud O'Shaugnessy, 1905–45; the story of Kopp and Eileen, who may have had a brief affair when they were both in Spain during the Civil War, is an unnecessary diversion for us. Though some commentators have suggested that she influenced Orwell's

major works, *Nineteen Eighty-Four* is the novel most often mentioned in that context. An added twist is that Marc Wildemeersch's biography of Kopp suggests that in physical terms the complex Belgian might have been the model for Orwell's description of the cruel and duplicitous O'Brien in the novel (Wildemeersch, *George Orwell's Commander in Spain*).

6   *Manchester Guardian*, 11 July 1946.

7   Available at http://www.worldcourts.com/imt/eng/decisions/1946.05.10_United_Kingdom_v_Student.pdf (accessed 8 December 2016).

8   Imperial War Museum Oral Histories Catalogue Number 9331.

9   Interview with Selwyn Jepson in the Imperial War Museum Oral History Archive, available at http://www.iwm.org.uk/collections/item/object/80009120 (accessed 19 January 2017).

16. SOUTH OF THE BORDER

1   J. St John, *William Heinemann: A Century of Publishing, 1890–1990*, London, Heinemann, 1998.

17. RIVIERA GLIMPSES

1   W.S. Merwin, *Summer Doorways: A Memoir*, Emeryville CA, Shoemaker & Hoard, 2006.

2   In another unlikely twist, *Le Chagrin et la Pitié* was directed by Marcel Ophuls, the son of *La Ronde* director Max Ophuls.

3   V. Giroud, 'Transition to Vichy: The Case of Georges Pelorson', *Modernism and Modernity*, Vol. 7, No. 2, pp. 221–48, 2000, accessed via the MUSE Project of Johns Hopkins University Press, available at https://muse.jhu.edu/article/23324 (accessed 9 December 2016).

4   Y. Limore, 'Les Èquipes Nationales 1942–1944', *Guerres mondiales et conflits contemporains*, No. 184, Paris, 1996 (accessed via JSTOR).

5   Giroud, 'Transition to Vichy'; J. Jackson, *France: The Dark Years 1940–41*, Oxford, Oxford University Press, 2001; R.O. Paxton, *Vichy France: Old Guard and New Order 1940–1944*, London, Barrie and Jenkins, 1972.

6   F. Hutton-Williams, 'Pulverizing the Pretty Charlock: Review of *The Letters of Samuel Beckett*', *Oxonian Review*, Vol 17, No. 3, 2011.

7   P. France (ed.), *The New Oxford Companion to Literature in French*, Oxford, Clarendon Press, 1995.

8   Gaston Bonheur in *Les Nouvelles Littéraires*, Paris, Éditions Julliard, 1965, commenting on Belmont's novel *Chris*.

9   G. Belmont, *Souvenirs d'outre-monde*, Paris, Calman-Levy, 2001.

10 Merwin, *Summer Doorways*.

11 R. Fanning, *Eamon de Valera: A Will to Power*, Boston, Harvard University Press, 2016.

12 Liam O'Flaherty, 1896–1964, a major figure in the Irish literary renaissance.

13 Peter de Polnay, 1906–84, Hungarian-born author with a taste for 'cafe society'.

14   Mervyn Jones, 1922–2010, biographer, novelist and, above all, journalist. He was the son of Ernest Jones, close colleague and biographer of Sigmund Freud.

18. ON THE ROAD AGAIN

1   A. Cazorla Sánchez, *Fear and Progress: Ordinary Lives in Franco's Spain 1939–1975*, London, Wiley Blackwell, 2009.
2   M. Bousquets, *This Too Shall Pass*, London, Hogarth Press, 2016.
3   Sir Victor Sawdon Pritchett, CH CBE, 1900–97.
4   Mavis Leslie de Trafford Gallant, 1922–2014, prolific and perceptive author, mainly of short stories, 116 of which were first published in the *New Yorker*.
5   C. Tóibín, *The South*, London, Serpent's Tail, 1990.

19. READER AND WRITER

1   William Sansom, 1912–76, successful author, several of whose themes – romance, comedy and murder among them – would have struck a chord with Lodwick; Percy Howard Newby, 1919–97, novelist, Managing Director of BBC Radio and first winner of the Booker Prize.
2   Though he wrote in German, Franz Kafka, 1883–1924, was born in Prague. Jakob Wassermann, 1873–1934, born in Fürth, was a poet, novelist and short-story writer of distinction. Both were of Jewish descent.
3   André Malraux, 1901–76, novelist, art theorist and Minister of Cultural Affairs under de Gaulle; Henri Bosco, 1888–1976, Avignon-born novelist whose main themes dealt with Provençal life.
4   Benito Pérez Galdós, 1843–1920, a prominent literary figure in nineteenth-century Spain. One of his novels was adapted and filmed as *Viridiana* by Luis Buñuel.
5   Budd Schulberg, 1914–2009, screenwriter, novelist and self-styled 'Hollywood Prince'. Among the many fine books translated into French by Belmont was Schulberg's *On the Waterfront*; he told Lodwick it was 'a terribly good novel, close to being a great one'.
6   Shelby Foote, 1916–2005, American novelist and historian, remembered in particular for his *The Civil War: A Narrative*.
7   T. Norman (ed.), R. Pryde (intr.) *Walter Fitzwilliam Starkie (1894–1976), A True Friend of Spain*, Madrid, British Council.
8   Stephen Hemsley Longrigg, CMG, OBE, 1923–2007.
9   *Journal of the Royal Institute of International Affairs*, Vol. 34, No. 4, October 1958.
10   *Harvard Business History Review*, No. 33, October 1961.
11   J. Lodwick, *Raiders from the Sea: The Story of the Special Boat Service in WWII*, with a new foreword by Lord Jellicoe, London, Greenhill, 1990.
12   Dame Cicely Isabel Fairfield (professionally known as Rebecca West), DBE, 1892–1983, author, journalist and critic.
13   Brendan Francis Behan, 1923–64, Irish writer of poems, plays, novels and short stories.
14   A. Lycett, *Dylan Thomas: A New Life*, London, Penguin, 2004.

15   Ratoff was born around 1897 – the records are confusing – in Samara, on the Volga's eastern bank, and known as Kuibyshev in the former USSR; he died in Switzerland in 1960.

16   In 1971 Jill St John did get to star in a Bond movie, as Tiffany Case against Sean Connery's 007 in *Diamonds are Forever*.

17   J. Duns, '*Casino Royale*: 60 Years Old', *Daily Telegraph*, 13 April 2013.

18   Ben Hecht, 1894–1964, one of the most notable and successful screenwriters of the twentieth century.

19   E. Waugh, *Ninety-two Days: British Guyana and the Brazilian Savannah*, London, Duckworth, 1934.

20. PUBLISH AND BE DAMNED

1   J. St John, *William Heinemann: A Century of Publishing, 1890–1990*, London, Heinemann, 1998.

2   Michie, who became a notable man of letters as well as a publisher, was an Oxford friend and poetic sparring partner of Kingsley Amis. In his Heinemann role, Amis remembered acidly after an expensive lunch, he was 'feared all over London as the fellow who gets the other fellow to pay'.

3   J. St John, 'Frere, Alexander Stuart', in *Oxford Dictionary of National Biography*. Frere was a publisher of great talent, with the ability to make close friends among his disparate authors, though his background would not have excited the editors of *Debrett's*.

4   J.H. Natterstad, *Francis Stuart*, New Jersey and London, Associated University Presses, 1974.

5   Taylor, *The Prose Factory*.

6   (Sir) Angus Frank Johnstone Wilson, KBE, 1913–91, novelist and short story writer; D.J. Taylor, 'Angus Wilson, Obituary', *Guardian*, 23 August 2013.

21. SCORECARD

1   I am indebted to John Lewis of the *Bookseller* for this background.

2   J. Kelly, 'The Operation of the Censorship of Publications Board: The Notebooks of C.J. O'Reilly', *Analecta Hibernia*, No. 28, 2004, Dublin, Irish Manuscript Commission.

3   Ibid.

4   A. Burgess, *The Novel Now: A Student's Guide to Contemporary Fiction*, London, Faber & Faber, 1967.

5   (Baron) Charles Percy Snow, CBE, 1905–80, writer, civil servant, and, briefly, a junior minister in Harold Wilson's Labour administration. Snow was yet another of the Dublin Censors' targets.

6   A highbrow BBC weekly, which ceased publication in 1991.

7   Anthony Dymoke Powell, CH, CBE, 1905–2000, English novelist best known for his twelve-volume work *A Dance to the Music of Time*.

8   Marghanita Laski, 1915–88, journalist, biographer, novelist and tireless contributor to the *Oxford English Dictionary*.

9   (Sir) John Betjeman, CBE, 1906–84, poet, writer, staunch advocate of Victorian architecture, and an English legend.

22. DEATH IN THE MORNING

1   The funeral Mass, at the Church of Our Lady Queen of Peace, was indeed well attended, with the Irish President represented by his ADC, along with members of the Dáil and high-ranking civil servants. Dorothy is recorded among the family mourners as 'Mrs Dorothy Lodwick'.

2   J.P. Eburne, *Surrealism and the Art of Crime*, Ithaca, Cornell University Press, 2008.

3   K. Amis, *Stanley and the Women*, London, Hutchinson, 1984.

23. AFTER THE BALL

1   (Sir) William John Haley, KCMG, 1901–87.

2   Paul Mark Scott, 1920–78, literary agent, author and Booker Prize winner.

3   John Greenleaf Whittier, 1807–92, American Quaker poet and abolitionist. From his poem 'Maud Muller' (1854).

BIBLIOGRAPHY

Allen, N., 'Gonne, Iseult', *Dictionary of Irish Biography*, Cambridge, Cambridge University Press, accessed via the London Library, 2014.

Allen, S.H., *Classical Spies: American Archaeologists with the OSS in World War 2 Greece*, Ann Arbor, University of Michigan Press, 2013.

Allport, A., *Demobbed: Coming Home after the Second World War*, New Haven, Yale University Press, 2009.

Almonds-Windmill, L., *A British Achilles*, Barnsley, Pen and Sword, 2005.

Amery, J., *Approach March*, London, Hutchinson, 1973.

Amis, K., *Stanley and the Women*, London, Hutchinson, 1984.

Anon., 'William Butler Yeats', *Poetry Foundation*, n.d., available at https://www.poetryfoundation.org/poems-and-poets/poets/detail/william-butler-yeats (accessed 9 December 2016).

Anon., *A True Friend of Spain, Professor Walter Starkie and the early years of the British Council in Spain*, Madrid, British Council, 2010.

Apostolou, A., 'The Betrayal of Salonika's Jews', *Jewish Ideas Daily*, 18 April 2013, available at http://www.jewishideasdaily.com/6341/features/the-betrayal-of-salonikas-jews/(accessed 9 December 2016).

Baerentzen, L. (ed.) *British Reports on Greece, 1943–44*, Copenhagen, Museum Tusculanum Press, 1982.

Barrington, B. (ed.), *The Wartime Broadcasts of Francis Stuart*, Dublin, Lilliput, 2000.

Bassett, R., *The Last Imperialist: A Portrait of Julian Amery*, Settrington, Stone Trough Books, 2016.

Beevor, A., *Crete: The Battle and the Resistance*, London, John Murray, 1991.

—— *The Battle for Spain*, London, Penguin, 2006.

Belmont, G., *Un homme au crépuscule*, Paris, Juillard, 1966.

—— *Souvenirs d'outre-monde*, Paris, Calman-Levy, 2001.

Bennett, A., *Writing Home*, London, Faber & Faber, 1994.

Berdah, J-F., 'La Propagande Culturelle Britannique En Espagne Pendant La Seconde Guerre Mondiale: ambition et action du British Council (1939–1946)', *Guerres mondiales et conflits contemporains*, No. 189, March 1998, pp. 95–107, Presses Universitaires de France (accessed via www.jstor.org).

Bousquets, M., *This Too Shall Pass*, London, Hogarth Press, 2016.

Bradley, S., *The Railways*, London, Profile Books, 2016.

Brewer, D., *Greece: The Decade of War*, London, I.B.Tauris, 2016.

Buettner, E., *Empire Families: Britons and Late Imperial India*, Oxford, Oxford University Press, 2004.

Burgess, A., *The Novel Now: A Student's Guide to Contemporary Fiction*, London, Faber & Faber, 1967.

Burns, J., *Papa Spy: Love, Faith and Betrayal in Wartime Spain*, London, Bloomsbury, 2009.

Cazorla Sánchez, A., *Fear and Progress: Ordinary Lives in Franco's Spain 1939–1975*, London, Wiley Blackwell, 2009.

Cruz, A.J., *Approaches to Teaching Lazarillo de Tormes and the Picaresque Tradition*, New York, Modern Language Association of America, 2008.

Curtis, M., *Verdict on Vichy*, London, Weidenfeld & Nicolson, 2002.

Davie, M. (ed.), *The Diaries of Evelyn Waugh*, London, Weidenfeld & Nicolson, 1975.

Davis, W., *The Ariadne Objective*, London, Bantam Books, 2014.

Davison P. (ed.), *Orwell's England*, London, Penguin, 2001.

Dempsey, P. J., 'Collins, J', *Dictionary of Irish Biography*, Cambridge, Cambridge University Press, accessed via the London Library, 2014.

De Polnay, P., *My Road*, London, W.H. Allen, 1978.

Doherty, M.A., *Nazi Wireless Propaganda*, Edinburgh, Edinburgh University Press, 2000.

Donleavy, J.P., *The Ginger Man*, Paris, The Traveller's Companion, 1955.

Duns, J., 'Casino Royale: 60 Years Old', *Daily Telegraph*, 13 April 2013.

Elborn, G., *Francis Stuart: A Life*, Dublin, Raven Arts Press, 1990.

Eburne, J.P., *Surrealism and the Art of Crime*, Ithaca, Cornell University Press, 2008.

Fanning, R., *Eamon de Valera: A Will to Power*, Boston, Harvard University Press, 2016.

Foot, M.R.D., *SOE In France: An Account of the Work of the British Special Operations*, London, HMSO, 1966.

Foster, R.F., *Modern Ireland*, London, Allen Lane, 1988.

France, P. (ed.), *The New Oxford Companion to Literature in French*, Oxford, Clarendon Press, 1995.

Giroud, V., 'Transition to Vichy: The Case of Georges Pelorson', *Modernism and Modernity*, Vol. 7, No. 2, pp. 221–48, 2000, accessed via the MUSE Project of Johns Hopkins University Press, available at https://muse.jhu.edu/article/23324 (accessed 9 December 2016).

Graves, R. and Hodge, A., *The Long Weekend*, London, Macmillan, 1940.

Hastings, S., *The Secret Lives of Somerset Maugham*, London, John Murray, 1989.

Hehn, P.N., *The German Struggle Against Yugoslav Guerrillas in World War II*, Boulder, CO, East European Quarterly, distributed by Columbia University Press, 1979.

Hortet, Eusebio Ferrer, *Pemán, 84 Años en España*, Madrid, Palabra, 1993.

Hull, M., *Irish Secrets: German Espionage in Ireland, 1939–1945*, Dublin, Irish Academic Press, 2003.

Hurtley, J. *Walter Starkie: An Odyssey*, Dublin, Four Courts Press, 2013.

Hutton-Williams, F., 'Pulverizing the Pretty Charlock: Review of *The Letters of Samuel Beckett*', *Oxonian Review*, Vol 17, No. 3, 2011.

'Instructor, An', *Complete Guide to the Hotchkiss Machine Gun* (reprinted), Uckfield, Naval and Military Press, 2009.

Jackson, J., *France: The Dark Years 1940–41*, Oxford, Oxford University Press, 2001.

Jellicoe, G., 'Introduction', in Lodwick, J., *Raiders from the Sea*, London, Greenhill Books, 1990.

Jordan, J., 'Ewart Milne: For His 80th Birthday', *Poetry Ireland Review*, No. 8, Dublin, 1983, available at www.poetryireland.ie/publications/poetry-ireland-review/online-archive/view/ewart-milne-for-his-80th-birthday (accessed 9 December 2016).

Kaplan, A., *The Collaborator: The Trial and Execution of Robert Brasillach*, Chicago, University of Chicago Press, 2000.

Kelly, J., 'The Operation of the Censorship of Publications Board: The Notebooks of C.J. O'Reilly', *Analecta Hibernia*, No. 28, 2004, Dublin, Irish Manuscript Commission.

Kiely, K., *Francis Stuart: Artist and Outcast*, Dublin, Liffey Press, 2007.

King, J., *Roland Penrose: The Life of a Surrealist*, Edinburgh, Edinburgh University Press, 2016.

Kipling, R., 'The Exiles' Line', available at http://www.kiplingsociety.co.uk/poems_exiles_line.htm (accessed 9 December 2012).

'Leighway', 'Some Corner of a Foreign Field', *Journal of the Leigh Society*, Issue 13, p. 2, 2004, available at http://www.leighsociety.com/pdf/13%20Leighway%20Winter%202004.pdf (accessed 9 December 2016).

Levy, S., *Sheila Legge: Phantom of Surrealism*, Rhos on Sea, Dark Windows Press, 2014. (See also *Le Blog de Albert Callis*, April 2014, available at http://albert.callis.over-blog.com/article-2014-avril-123396586.html (in French, accessed 9 December 2016).)

Limore, Y., 'Les Èquipes Nationales 1942–1944', *Guerres mondiales et conflits contemporains*, No. 184, Paris, 1996 (accessed via JSTOR).

Lodwick, R.W., *John Bolt, Indian Civil Servant: A Tale of Old Haileybury and India*, London, British Library Historical Print Editions, n.d. [Digby & Long, 1891].

Lycett, A., *Dylan Thomas: A New Life*, London, Penguin, 2004.

Mackenzie, W., *The Secret History of SOE: The Special Operations Executive 1940–45*, London, TimeWarner/St Ermin's Press, 2000.

Matthews, K. 'Life in General Franco's Spain', broadcast reprinted in *The Listener*, 26 July 1951, London.

Mazower, M., *Hitler's Empire*, London, Allen Lane, 2008.

Melly, G., *Rum, Bum and Concertina*, London, Weidenfeld & Nicolson, 1977.

—— *Don't Tell Sybil*, augmented edition, London, Atlas Press, 2013.

Merwin, W.S., *Summer Doorways: A Memoir*, Emeryville CA, Shoemaker & Hoard, 2006.

Meyer, E., *The Factual List of Nazis Protected by Spain*, available at https://archive.org/details/THEFACTUALLISTOFNAZISPROTECTEDBYSPAIN (accessed 9 December 2016).

Moore C., 'A Reverend Rough and Ready for Anything', Daily Telegraph, 7 March 2011.

Natterstad, J.H., *Francis Stuart*, New Jersey and London, Associated University Presses, 1974.

[O'Casey, S.] Sean O'Casey Papers, National Library of Ireland, List 75.

O'Halpin, E. (ed. and intr.), *MI5 and Ireland, 1939-1945: The Official History*, Dublin and Portland, Irish Academic Press, 2003.

Orwell, G., *Homage to Catalonia*, London, Secker and Warburg, 1938.

—— 'Such, Such Were the Joys', *Partisan Review*, London, 1952.

Osborne, H. and Winstanley, M., 'Rural and Urban Poaching in Victorian England', *Rural History*, No. 17, Cambridge, Cambridge University Press, 2006.

Parcerisas, P., *Duchamp en España*, Madrid, Edition Siruels, 2009.

Paxton, R.O., *Vichy France: Old Guard and New Order 1940–1944*, London, Barrie and Jenkins, 1972.

Porch, D., *The French Foreign Legion*, New York, HarperCollins, 1991.

Richards, (Sir) B., *Secret Flotillas*, Vol. 2, London and Barnsley, Whitehall History Publishing/ Frank Cass/Pen and Sword, 2013.

Roth, A., 'Francis Stuart's Broadcasts from Germany, 1942–4: Some New Evidence', *Irish Historical Studies*, Vol. 32, No. 127 (May 2001), pp. 408–22.

Roughton, R., (ed.), *Contemporary Poetry and Prose: May 1936–Autumn 1937*, London, Frank Cass, 1968.

Royer, J. (trans. Sloate, D.), *Interviews to Literature*, Montreal, Guernica, 1996, accessed via Google Books.

Sagarra, E., 'Walter Starkie', in *Dictionary of Irish Biography*, Dublin, Royal Irish Academy, accessed September 2014.

St John, J., *William Heinemann: A Century of Publishing, 1890–1990*, London, Heinemann, 1998.

St John, J., 'Alexander Stuart Frere', in *Oxford Dictionary of National Biography*, Oxford, Oxford University Press, accessed January 2017.

Spanier, S., Defazio, A. and Trogdon, R.W. (eds), *The Letters of Ernest Hemingway 1923–1925*, Vol. II, Cambridge, Cambridge University Press, 2013.

Sparrow, E., *Secret Service: British Agents in France,1792–1815*, Woodbridge, Boydell Press, 1992.

Stannard, M., *Evelyn Waugh: No Abiding City, 1939–1946*, London, Dent, 1992.

Steury, D., 'The OSS and Project SAFEHAVEN: Tracking Nazi "Gold"', *Studies in Intelligence*, Washington DC, Center for the Study of Intelligence, 2007, available at https://www.cia.gov/ library/center-for-the-study-of-intelligence/csi-publications/csi-studies/studies/summer00/ art04.html (accessed 9 December 2016).

Stuart, F., *Black List, Section H* (with a foreword by Colm Tóibín), New York, Lilliput, 2014.

[Stuart, F.] 'Francis Stuart', *Writing Ulster*, No. 4, 1996.

Taylor, D.J., *After the War*, London, Chatto & Windus, 1993.

—— 'Angus Wilson, Obituary', *Guardian*, 23 August 2013.

—— *The Prose Factory: Literary Life in England Since 1918*, London, Chatto & Windus, 2016.

Thornton, W.H., *Reminiscences and Reflections of an Old Country Clergyman*, London 1897 and 1899, reprint edited by Hart-Davies, D., Ludlow, Excellent Press, 2011. See also *Devon and Cornwall Notes*, Vol. IX, n.p., 1917.

Tóibín, C., 'Francis Stuart', in *Dictionary of Irish Biography*, Cambridge: Cambridge University Press, accessed via the London Library.

Tóibín, C., *The South*, London, Serpent's Tail, 1990.

Trevelyan, G.M., *British History in the Nineteenth Century and After*, London, Longmans, Green & Co., 1944.

Tynan, J., 'Military Dress and Men's Outdoor Leisurewear: Burberry's Trench Coat in First World War Britain', *Journal of Design History*, Vol. 24, No. 2, Oxford, Oxford University Press, 2011.

Vinen, R., *The Unfree French: Life Under the Occupation*, London, Allen Lane, 2006.

Waugh, E., *Ninety-two Days: British Guyana and the Brazilian Savannah*, London, Duckworth, 1934.

Warner, M., 'Rebecca West, the Art of Fiction' (interview), *Paris Review*, No. 79, 1981.

Whiston, J., 'Walter Starkie', in *Oxford Dictionary of National Biography*, Oxford, Oxford University Press, accessed September 2014.

Wildemeersch, M., *George Orwell's Commander in Spain: The Engima of Georges Kopp*, London, Thames River Press, 2013.

[Ziman, H.D.], *Instructions for British Servicemen in France*, London, the Foreign Office, 1944.

JOHN LODWICK'S BOOKS

Running to Paradise 1943

Myrmyda 1946

Peal of Ordnance 1947

Raiders from the Sea 1947 (reissued 1990 as *The Filibusters*)

Twenty East of Greenwich 1947

Brother Death 1948

Something in the Heart 1948

Just a Song at Twilight 1949

First Steps Inside the Zoo 1950

Stamp Me Mortal 1950

The Cradle of Neptune 1951

Love Bade Me Welcome 1952

Somewhere a Voice is Calling 1953

The Butterfly Net 1954

The Starless Night 1955

Contagion to this World 1956

The Forbidden Coast 1956

Equator 1957

Gulbenkian (with D.H. Young) 1958

Bid the Soldiers Shoot 1958

POST MORTEM

The Asparagus Trench 1960

The Moon Through a Dusty Window 1960

INDEX

References to notes are indicated by n.

Abbey Theatre (Dublin) 52, 55, 56, 59
Amery, John 197, 198, 228n.3
Amery, Julian 108, 140–1
Anderson, Lindsay 178
anti-Semitism 100
Arms and the Man (Shaw) 140
Asparagus Trench, The (Lodwick) 2, 10,
    17, 23–4, 39–40
  and critics 221–2
  and grandfather 19, 20

Balfour, Arthur 4, 5
Barcelona 179–80, 223
Basket of Fruit, The (Lodwick) 53
Beckett, Samuel 56, 57, 158, 173–4, 201
Behan, Brendan 6, 188–9
Belmont, Georges 5, 65–6, 156–62,
    163–4, 170; *see also* Pelorson,
    Georges
Betjeman, John 206
Bickley Park 37
Bid the Soldiers Shoot (Lodwick) 71, 75,
    79–80, 186, 200
  and critics 204, 207
  and Heinemann 193
Birds of Britain, The (Fisher) 200
Black List, Section H (Stuart) 170, 171
Blanchin, Titin 80
Blyton, Enid 37
BOOKMAKER operation 92, 93, 96,
    97–8, 99, 101–7

Bosco, Henri 181
Brandram, Richard 37
Breton, André 209–10
Brighty, C.P.J. 204, 216
British Empire 16–17, 24–5, 44
British Raj 1, 13, 14, 19, 21
Brooks, Jeremy 17
Brother Death (Lodwick) 2, 3, 5, 71,
    72–3
  and critics 205–6
  and religion 14, 39
Buckmaster, Maurice 86, 92–3, 95–6,
    118
Bulgaria 133–4
Burgess, Anthony 3, 202, 206
Butterfly Net, The (Lodwick) 21, 194,
    195–7, 201

Cadaqués 176
Cakes and Ale (Maugham) 184
Casino Royale (film) 190–1
Catholicism 14–15, 35, 39, 49, 212–13
  and illegitimacy 64–5
  and Ireland 53, 57–8
  and Opus Dei 173
  and Spain 177
  and Spanish Civil War 61
Cenci, The (Shelley) 53, 206
Censorship Board 53, 57, 59, 200–1
Cheltenham 16–17, 33–4, 223
Cheltenham College 3, 23, 37–8, 39–41

Chetniks 137–40
Chetwynd-Inglis, James 72
Churchill, Winston 85, 122, 123, 145
Clockwork Orange, A (Burgess) 202
Collins, John 54, 58, 60, 68–9, 209, 210
  and Lodwick marriage 63, 66, 67
Contagion to this World (Lodwick) 115,
  205
Cradle of Neptune, The (Lodwick) 43, 48,
  77, 115, 201, 203–4
Crump, Sir Henry Ashbrooke (grand-
  father) 24, 52, 78–9

Dalí, Salvador 75, 176
Dartmouth Naval College 3, 43–4, 45–50
De Graaf, Johannes 109–10
De Polnay, Peter 172, 173, 174, 183,
  231n.13
De Quincey, Thomas 63, 81
De Valera, Eamon 60, 169
Doctor Faustus (Mann) 162–3, 164
Don Fernando (Maugham) 183
Dostoevsky, Fyodor 182
Douglas-Scott-Montagu, John 28
Dublin 51, 52–4, 55–7, 59

Earls Court (London) 38–9, 223
East India Company 16, 17–19, 21
English People, The (Orwell) 199
espionage 8–9, 107–10
Essex 31–3
Exiles (Joyce) 53

Fields, Gracie 56
Filibusters, The (Lodwick) 187
First Steps Inside the Zoo (Lodwick)
  203
Fitzgerald, F. Scott 181
Flaubert, Gustave 182
Foot, Michael 98, 99, 101, 117
Foote, Shelby 181–2, 232n.6
Forbidden Coast, The (Lodwick) 191

Foreign Legion
  see French Foreign Legion
France 48, 58, 80, 147–9, 155–6
  and World War II 156–8
Franco, Gen Francisco 61, 107, 109,
  172–3, 175, 222–3
  and rule 178, 179
French Foreign Legion 3, 78–9, 80, 81,
  83–9
Frere, Alexander 6, 184, 186, 193–4, 195,
  197

Galdós, Benito Pérez 181, 232n.4
Gallant, Mavis 179
Gant, Roland 193
Gascoyne, David 73, 74–5
Gibb, George S. 185
Gielgud, Maj Lewis 93–4
Görtz, Hermann 165–7, 169
Greece 119–21, 123, 125–9, 131–3, 134,
  144–5
Greene, Graham 2, 48
Gulbenkian (Lodwick) 184–6

Haileybury 18–19
Hamelot, Nadia 103–5
Handful of Dust, A (Waugh) 48–9, 115
Heimann, Oscar 99–100, 101, 102,
  117–18
Heinemann 3, 184, 191, 192, 193–8
Hemingway, Ernest 80–1
Hill, Anne 193
Hinton, Norman 99, 101, 102, 117
Hitler, Adolf 84, 86, 122, 230n.1
Hollywood 189–91
Homage to Catalonia (Orwell) 177
Homme au crépuscule, Un (Belmont)
  65–6, 73, 158–60
Household, Geoffrey 206–7
*Humorous Sketches of the World We Live
  In* (Lodwick, R.W.) 21
Hurst, Brian Desmond 56

If... (film) 40–1, 178
India 13–14, 15–16, 17–19, 21, 35–6, 148
   and father 24
   and Scott 221
Indian Army 24–5
Innisfail (magazine) 56
Instruction Manual on the Hotchkiss
   Machine Gun (anon) 28–9
IRA 62, 165, 166, 167, 169
   and Behan 188, 189
Ireland 39, 51–2, 55–6, 57–8, 223
   and Spanish Civil War 61–2
   and World War II 165–9
   see also Censorship Board; Dublin
Irish Academy of Letters 55–6

James, Edward 75, 76, 215
Janés, Josep 6, 174, 183, 184, 186, 219
   and death 211, 212
Jellicoe, George 6, 121, 134–5, 141,
   187–8
Jepson, Selwyn 8, 94, 97, 113, 145
John Bolt (Lodwick, R.W.) 21
Jones, Mervyn 177–8, 185, 220, 232n.14
Joyce, James 53
Joyce, William 168, 197, 198
Just a Song at Twilight (Lodwick) 65, 71,
   202, 203

Kafka, Franz 181, 232n.2
Kent 36–7
Kerr, Ida Evelyn 72
Kierkegaard, Søren 77
Klugmann, James 138
Kopp, Georges 6, 60–1, 88–9, 142–3,
   230n.5

Laski, Marghanita 206
Lassen, Anders 121, 230n.1
Laycock, Lt Col Robert 113, 114
Le Kid (Beckett) 56–7
Legge, Rupert Maximilian Faris 73

Legge, Sheila (2nd wife) 6, 69, 71–5,
   76–8
   and death 149–53
   and France 91
   and SOE 96–7, 103
   and Spain 176
   and Surrealism 209, 210
Lisney, (Harold) Denis 219
Lisney, Hugh 176
Lodwick, Dorothy (1st wife) 63–4, 65,
   66–7, 68, 69, 209, 210
   and son 216
Lodwick, Eliza Frost 32–3
Lodwick, Florence (grandmother) 20–1
Lodwick, John 1–4, 5–11, 35–6, 37–40
   and Belmont 159–61, 162, 163–4
   and Chetniks 137, 138–40
   and critics 200, 201–7, 220–2
   and Dartmouth 45–6, 47–8, 49–50
   and death 210–13, 219–20
   and Dublin 52–4
   and family 15–16, 23–4, 31–2, 214–17
   and first marriage 63–4, 65–9
   and Foreign Legion 78–9, 80, 81, 83–4,
   85–6, 87–9, 90
   and France 147–9
   and grandfather 19, 21, 33, 34
   and Gulbenkian 184–7
   and Hollywood 190–1
   and Kopp 142–3
   and Legge 91
   and literature 181–2
   and marriage 213–14
   and Merwin 164–5
   and publishers 191–2, 193–7
   and religion 14
   and SBS 118–19, 121–2, 123–4, 125–9,
   131–5, 143–4
   and SOE 92–7, 100–7, 111–14, 141–2,
   145–6
   and Spain 172, 173, 174, 175–6, 177–8
   and Stuart 169–72

Lodwick, Capt John Thornton (father)
17, 23–4, 25–6, 28–9
Lodwick, Kathleen ('Kitty') (mother) 24,
25, 34, 35, 36–7, 145
and grandchildren 214, 219
and navy 43, 44, 45
Lodwick, Peter (great-grandfather) 21
Lodwick, R.W. (grandfather) 16, 17, 18,
19–21, 29, 33–4
and John 37–8, 211
Lodwick, Sheila
see Legge, Sheila
Longrigg, S.H. 184–5
Love Bade Me Welcome (Lodwick)
201
Lowry, Malcolm 182

McCormack, John 202
Magritte, René 76
Mahabaleshwar 15–16
Malraux, André 181, 232n.3
Man Ray 73, 74, 176
Mann, Thomas 162–3
Maugham, Somerset 6, 183–4, 185–6,
188, 219
Meissner, Gertrude 165, 168, 170, 172
Melly, George 6, 44, 71, 75–6
Men Crowd Me Round (Stuart) 56
Merwin, W.S. 6, 155, 156, 162–5
Mesens, E.L.T. 76
Metcalf, John 205
Methuen 169, 191, 192
MI5 3, 6, 77, 97, 110
Michie, James 193, 233n.2
Mihailović, Draža 137
Mill, John Stuart 60, 67
Milmo, Helenus 'Buster' 229n.7
Milne, Angela 206
Moon Through a Dusty Window, The
(Lodwick) 174, 193, 220
Mussolini, Benito 122

Nadja (Breton) 210
Neuve Chapelle, battle of 24–5, 72
Newby, P.H. 181
Nineteen Eighty-Four (Orwell) 230n.5
Nixon, Bombardier 123, 128, 131, 132–3,
138, 139–40

O'Casey, Sean 52–3
O'Duffy, Eoin 61
O'Flaherty, Liam 169, 231n.12
O'Reilly, C.J. 201
Orwell, George 49, 60, 88, 142–3, 227n.6
and Kopp 230n.5
and Spain 177
O'Shaugnessy, Eileen Maud 230n.5

patriotism 44–5
Paul, David 203
Peacock Theatre (Dublin) 52, 56–7
Pelorson, Georges 54, 56–7, 58;
see also Belmont, Georges
Pemán, José María 172–3
Penrose, Roland 74
Persia, SS 25–8
Philby, Kim 141, 229n.7
Powell, Anthony 203–4, 205
Price, Jonathan 194–5
Pritchett, V.S. 178
publishing 199–200;
see also Heinemann; Methuen
Puig, Carlos 211

Ratoff, Gregory 6, 189–90, 191, 219
Ravensbrück (concentration camp)
104–5
Richardson, Maurice 206
Riders to the Sea (Synge) 56
Roughton, Roger 77
Royal Navy 43–5
Ruck, Maj Charles (stepfather) 35, 36–7,
214
Ruck, Simon (half-brother) 213

Running to Paradise (Lodwick) 56, 79, 202, 229n.8
Russia 19

St George, George 190–1, 219
'Sailing to Byzantium' (Yeats) 57
Sansom, William 181, 232n.1
SBS
    see Special Boat Service
Schulberg, Budd 181, 232n.5
Scotland 118–19, 142–3
Scott, Paul 221–2
Security Service
    see MI5
Shaw, George Bernard 53, 55, 140
Short Survey of Surrealism, A (Gascoyne) 73
Snow, C.P. 203
SOE
    see Special Operations Executive
Somewhere a Voice is Calling (Lodwick) 5, 71, 149–52, 171, 197–8, 202
   and censorship 201
Spain 106, 107–9, 147, 148, 172–3, 175–80
   and car crash 210–12
   and Franco 222–3
   and Maugham 183–4
   and Starkie 182–3
Spanish Civil War 60, 61–2
Special Boat Service (SBS) 3, 9, 119–24, 125–9, 131–5, 143–4
   and *The Filibusters* 187
   and Sark raid 230n.1
Special Operations Executive (SOE) 3, 6, 8–9, 141–2, 145–6
   and Heimann 117–18
   and Legge 71, 72, 77–8
   and Lodwick 92–7, 118–19
   and operations 97–8, 99, 100–7, 111–14
spies
    see espionage

Stage Society 52–3
Stamp Me Mortal (Lodwick) 205
Starkie, Walter 6, 54, 55, 59–60
   and Spain 182–3, 189
   and World War II 107–9, 110
Stendhal 182
Stirling, Sir (Archibald) David 120, 229n.5
Strong, L.A.G. 169
Stuart, Francis 5, 54–6, 189, 219
   and Lodwick 169–72, 182
   and World War II 165–6, 168–9
Stuart, Iseult 165–6, 167, 172
Student, Gen 144–5
Surrealism 73, 74–8, 209–10
Sword of Honour (Waugh) 113, 114–15

Taylor, D.J. 3, 195, 223
theatre 52–4, 56–7
This Hot Hereafter (Lodwick) 53
Thomas, Dylan 74, 77, 189
Thornton, Eleanor Velasco 28
Thornton, Rev William Henry 20, 21
Tóibín, Colm 171, 179
Twenty East of Greenwich (Lodwick) 140

U 97 (Forester) 53
Usborne, Richard 204

Valentiner, Max 25, 26–7
Victor Gollancz 199

Wake, Nancy 94
Wardle, Irving 220
Wassermann, Jakob 181
Waugh, Evelyn 2, 6, 9, 48–9, 191, 195
   and Lodwick 206
   and World War II 113–15
Wellington, Sir Arthur Wellesley, Duke of 15, 16
West, Rebecca 6, 188, 197, 198
Whittier, John Greenleaf 224

Wilde, Oscar 53
Wilson, Angus 196–7, 223
Winslow Boy, The (Rattigan) 48
Within the Gates (O'Casey) 52–3
Woodhouse, Christopher 'Monty' 206, 207
World War I 17, 24–5, 26–8, 44–5, 229n.5
World War II 9, 54, 108–10, 137–40, 165–9
 and France 156–8
 and SBS 119–24, 125–9, 131–5
 and SOE 100–8, 111–14, 141–2
 see also French Foreign Legion
Wyndham, Francis 205

Yeats, W.B. 55, 56, 57, 115, 165, 224
Yugoslavia 137–8

Zafra, Miguel 211